MY THIRTY-THIRD YEAR

MY THIRTY-THIRD YEAR

A Priest's Experience in a Russian Work Camp

GERHARD A. FITTKAU

CLUNY

Providence, Rhode Island

Cluny Media edition, 2021

This Cluny edition is a republication of *My Thirty-Third Year*, originally published in 1958 by Farar, Straus and Cudahy.

For more information regarding this title
or any other Cluny Media publication,
please write to info@clunymedia.com, or to
Cluny Media, P.O. Box 1664, Providence, RI 02901

§   VISIT US ONLINE AT WWW.CLUNYMEDIA.COM   §

ISBN: 978-1952826948

NIHIL OBSTAT:
JOHN A. GOODWINE, *censor librorum*

IMPRIMATUR: FRANCIS CARDINAL SPELLMAN, *Archbishop of New York*

Cover design by Clarke *&* Clarke
Cover image: Jacek Malczewski, *Christ in Emmaus*,
1897, oil on canvas
Courtesy of Wikimedia Commons

CONTENTS

To my parishioners, *scattered over the earth from Canada to Siberia.*

To all the uprooted people of the world,
*and to those who help them send down new roots
in order to find a peace the world cannot give.*

ACKNOWLEDGMENTS

FULFILLING A REQUEST OF THE LATE CARDINAL KONRAD Graf von Preysing, Bishop of Berlin, after his return from a visit to the United States, *My Thirty-Third Year* was first drafted with the energetic and patient assistance of my English tutors, Ralph Wiltgen, SVD, and Joseph Connors, SVD, of St. Mary's Seminary, Techny, Illinois.

The title was suggested by Arthur and Elizabeth Sheehan of New York. I am grateful for the encouragement and help of Dr. Anna Selig, Geraldine Carrigan, Robert McDonald, Alma Savage, Margaret Schimanski, Dorothy Dohen, Maria Theresia Strake, Dr. Elisabeth Vitzthum, and John Peck. The book would not have reached its final form without the help of the talented pen of James G. Shaw.

To these and many other helpers, and especially to the generous and openhearted American audiences at my lectures, I am deeply indebted.

PROLOGUE : *Pastor of Suessenberg*

ON TOP OF THE HILL I ASKED THE DRIVER TO STOP THE carriage. The steeple of the church of Suessenberg, "Sweet Mountain," rose over the trees on the crest of the next rise. I wanted to savor this moment of looking at it. I wanted to take possession of it with my eyes. This was my first parish.

I felt like a king being introduced to his kingdom, like a man meeting the fulfillment of a childhood dream. As I looked, I could hear my grandmother's voice speaking to a ten-year-old boy from her deathbed: "What a joy it would be for me, Gerhard, if some day from heaven I could look down and see you a priest, and maybe even parish priest of Suessenberg!"

And here I was—the new pastor of Suessenberg coming to be installed on the one throne he desired, on the parish feast day, the Nativity of Our Lady, September 8, 1944.

As the carriage jolted uphill on the rough country road I thought of the longer road, often just as uphill and just as rough as this one, that lay between my grandmother's wish and its fulfillment.

Ill health struck early in my studies and developed into tuberculosis. My superiors sent me home with little hope that I ever could be admitted to holy orders. But I knew there was only one vocation for me and I kept on trying. These efforts took me out of Germany in 1930. With intervals of illness, I studied philosophy and theology in Austria, Rome, and Switzerland, where I spent two

years in a sanitarium and had a lung collapsed. I completed my
theology in our own diocese of Ermland and was ordained in our
cathedral of Frauenburg, a classic example of the early red brick
Gothic churches of East Germany. Declared a "public menace" by
the commissioner of public health, I was kept from regular pastoral
work and from teaching. Our bishop, Maximilian Kaller, took me
into his house as his personal secretary until, after some clashes
with the Gestapo following the outbreak of World War II, he sent
me to do postgraduate work at the University of Breslau.

And now, with two finished manuscripts on the sacramental
theology of St. John Chrysostom in my luggage, I was finally being
carried to my first parish. The long-restrained desire to apply what I
had learned during the first seven rather meager years of my priesthood was to be realized.

It was an eminently satisfying feeling, restful yet exciting. I was
reaching an end which was a beginning. For me, Suessenberg was
an ideal place.

Ideal, yes, but not idyllic. I had found out some things about
Suessenberg my grandmother had not told me. For all its sweet
name, there was bitterness in its history and in its reputation. Its
horse traders were better known for their shrewdness than for their
honesty. The farms were small and hard to cultivate. The hilly
country with its limey soil did not easily produce good crops and
the farms often changed hands. And the rectory changed hands
almost as often as the poorer farms. My colleagues had thought it
no great ambition on my part to want to be pastor of Suessenberg.

This was Ermland, a land of Catholic tradition planted and
grown in seven centuries of benign rule by its bishops who, until
the time of King Frederick II of Prussia, were also the sovereign
princes. The storms of the Reformation had beaten against it on
all sides and fallen back, leaving it a Catholic island in the heart of
Protestant Prussia. The Ermland triangle points at the Baltic Sea.
It is about eighty-five miles long and its width grows from about

fifteen miles at the seaboard to about fifty miles at the forests of the Masurian lakes. By its different Catholic tradition it was so clearly marked off that Ermlanders speak of their neighbors living in the rest of East Prussia as "foreigners." It is a land of wayside shrines and calvaries, of daily living centered around the Church's liturgical year and made bright by its outward signs and symbols.

I had had to hurry to get there in time for the parish feast, my inauguration day. But the parishioners had things well in hand. On the morning of the feast, an outdoor altar stood against one wall of the six-hundred-year-old church. Above it, a picture of the Blessed Virgin, patroness of the parish, was circled with flowers. I stood at the front door, vested in surplice, cope, and biretta, with the holy water sprinkler in my hand ready to bless the processions that would arrive from the neighboring parishes.

The villages closest to Suessenberg were Stolzhagen, three miles south, Wernegitten, two miles north, and Reichenberg, two miles west. The roads the people came along that early morning to celebrate our feast were not named after the villages. They were known by the names of the patrons of the neighboring churches, the St. Lawrence Road, the St. Margaret Road, the St. Roch Road.

One after another, the three processions arrived in good time for Mass. Each was led by a boy carrying a crucifix on a long pole and flanked by other boys with banners. Behind them marched the parish band playing hymn after hymn with the solemn devotion to duty only a German band can show.

Following the band, but clearly separated from it as befitting their dignity, came the church trustees, each carrying a big votive candle symbolic of his festival offering. Then came the children, the few youths not yet drafted, the girls gaily dressed in blouses and elaborately embroidered skirts, what was left of the menfolk, and the women outnumbering all other groups. At the end of each parish procession walked the pastor, drooping somewhat under the weight of his dignity and of his ceremonial cloak.

As they passed the front door of my church I sprinkled them with holy water and blessed them. The arriving pastor was greeted with the Pax Christi embrace and offered the parish reliquary to kiss. Then we joined the procession as it passed once around the outside of the church and entered, all singing the Salve Regina.

Inside the church the people were glad to rest their feet as we priests heard the confessions which were as customary at those feasts as at Easter.

Outside again for the open-air Mass, the people of all four parishes stood and knelt in the meadow or among the maple trees that lined it. Old Father Teschner, who had been thirty-five years pastor at Wernegitten, preached the sermon. In the closing procession around and into the church it was my privilege to carry the Blessed Sacrament and bestow the final blessing.

Then we four priests retired to the rectory for the festival meal of doves. With an air of challenge that indicated that Suessenberg could do just as well as, and perhaps a little better than, the neighboring towns, the senior spinster of our first family, Bertha Poschmann, brought the birds and saw to it that nothing was lacking for the occasion.

There was a fair amount of the usual gruff, good-natured bantering of the baby pastor by the veterans. In normal times my lack of any previous parish assignment, my obvious intention of turning the rectory into a study centered around my painfully gathered collection of Chrysostom's Greek writings, my novice enthusiasm for my new appointment, all would have made me fair game for these men, the youngest of whom had been living his vocation of tending souls when I was a boy in grammar school.

But these were not normal times. The joking was a bit forced and the apparently casual atmosphere was strained and unreal. It was somewhat like a frontline officers' mess when conversation skips over a thin surface everyone knows may give way at any moment. These priests had been through years of harassment by the Nazi Party and the Gestapo. Now, just as there were hopes that this might end, they knew that only a thin edge of time and circumstance separated them from a Soviet domination which they realized would be merciless.

It had become commonplace for them to awake in the morning to the news that some one of their fellow priests had been taken away by the Gestapo for ministering to Polish or other prisoner-laborers, or that another had disappeared under accusation of having "abused the pulpit." They knew that the pastor of the nearby church of Freudenberg had been taken to Bartenstein Prison for having persisted in teaching catechism classes. My predecessor was still expecting his trial in the same jail.

They were average priests, and any one of them would have laughed at words like "heroism" applied to himself. Yet almost to the last man the three hundred and fifty priests of my diocese who survived the Nazi regime refused to flee before the Russian troops. And no fewer than one hundred and twenty-five of those paid for their fidelity with their lives.

Looking back on that day over the years, I see my inauguration in the parish of Suessenberg in a dreamlike air of unreality. It seems impossible to believe that we were sustaining the fiction, "It can't happen here," even while "it" was happening all around. We were not dreamers. We were practical men and realists. Yet we moved along in the pattern of seven centuries of Ermland tradition as though that alone were real and the actual things that were happening were the nightmares we would awake to find gone.

Our realism, our awareness of the unmentioned danger, kept breaking through in the very conversation in which we were being so elaborately casual. As I showed off my cherished volumes of Chrysostom, one of the old priests riffled through the pages as though greatly impressed and offered the comment, "I hope the Russians haven't forgotten their Greek." The bulkiness of my manuscript drew the remark, "They tell me paper is scarce in Siberia."

I showed them my unfinished bookshelves and explained that I had to turn carpenter myself because in the middle of the job old Hans heard a rumor of Russians coming and decided he would be safer among the bombs in his native Berlin from where he had been evacuated. All the sympathy that I got was, "Those Berliners were always smarter than Ermlanders." One visitor looked balefully at my typewriter and remarked, "I hope this isn't another enemy of the state."

This last remark was a reminder that these veteran priests had previously known me as the bishop's secretary. I had held the job just when our bishop was counteracting the crippling measures of the anti-religious campaign, spearheaded by a callous speech of Goebbels in Königsberg. My work had included the preparation and distribution of the papal and episcopal directives and exhortations Bishop Kaller continued to issue to his churches in spite of the penal laws against them. After stenciling the messages I would distribute them to trusted laymen posted throughout an intricate five-hundred-mile "route." The priest himself would not know of the pastoral to be read on a given Sunday until the paper was delivered to him just before Mass. This activity had involved me in several brushes with the Gestapo. One of these had been a surprise raid of the bishop's house in his absence, well designed to instill fear and a feeling of helplessness. It was followed a few days later by a grueling three-hour interrogation and ended with a written warning to me and the confiscation of my typewriter—which they had proved to be the one that had made the stencils—as an "enemy of the state."

But before the meal was over we were just four neighboring priests talking together on a traditional feast day. In this autumn of 1944 Hitler and Himmler and Goebbels had other things to think about. The Soviet Union had been on our borders for so many years that we had become used to it. The three older priests were sure they would live out their lives attending to their parishes. My own mind was centered on getting settled down among the people and the books I loved.

Just once, as my three guests were leaving for home, was a somber note sounded. Father Teschner looked over at the outdoor altar and the deserted meadow in front of it. Normally it would have been a lively scene this afternoon—excited children chasing each other noisily, young girls with flushed faces pretending not to notice that they were being noticed and dreaming of the evening's dancing, young men being ostentatiously unostentatious, women chattering endlessly as they set out their home cooking, old men having a pipe beneath the trees and talking of other feast days. But today they had all melted back to their homes when the services were over. Father Teschner looked at the empty field and spoke the words the rest of us were refusing to let into our minds: "I wonder if we will see another parish feast day."

The following weeks brought harvest time. Our people were too busy with their work, as I was with mine, to let rumors, and reports that were more than rumors, disturb them. What did it really matter that the Russians had crossed into East Prussia in October? Life had to go on in its timeless pattern. If the fields were not harvested the cattle, horses, and pigs would starve in the winter. There would be no potatoes, no grain in the storehouse. This was inexorable, permanent. This was the necessary flow of living. The presence or the absence of strangers was an accident like blight or bad weather. You took it as it came and survived it.

Then the remnants of the village manpower, old men and boys, were called to service in the Home Guard, the Volkssturm, and taken away to dig tank traps in the surrounding woods. The ambitious gauleiter of East Prussia, Erich Koch, was trying to out-Hitler Hitler and make a name for himself. When the men persisted in slipping back to their fields, he imported young diehard Nazis to hold them to their posts at gun point.

The farm labor was being carried on by the women and by

a mixture of prisoner-laborers, refugees, and evacuees of bombed cities. There were Frenchmen, Poles, Italians, White Russians, Lithuanians, and Ukrainians among them. Most of them had settled into the farms to which they had been assigned like members of the family. But there were also cases where some were treated with the harshness of mean masters toward helpless servants. Sunday after Sunday during those months I went to the pulpit and spoke to my people of fraternal charity toward the strangers living under their roofs.

Advent came, the beginning of the liturgical year, and the liturgy gave me my texts. On the first Sunday we prayed in the Mass, "That from the threatening dangers of our sins we may be rescued by Thy protection." The Epistle of the second Sunday was from St. Paul to the Romans: "May then the God of patience and of comfort grant you to be of one mind toward one another according to Jesus Christ... Wherefore receive you one another even as Christ has received you."

We celebrated Christmas with a joy that held back our fears that this Advent had been preparation for another kind of coming. It was a happy holiday season for me, a family Christmastide. My sister Irmgard had come to keep house for me in November. She was recuperating from a siege of illness that kept her away from her work as a social worker. One of the conditions on which she came was that she could bring Renata, a homeless child she had been caring for in Königsberg. She also demanded that she have several days each month to return to Königsberg and look after several other bombed-out children for whom she had found a temporary home.

Then my mother came for a visit. She enjoyed sitting for hours in my study gazing her fill on the kind of room she had always dreamed I would one day have. It had taken her six years to make the fine rug that covered the study floor. She had patterned it after an old Persian tapestry hanging in the Kaiser Friedrich Museum in Berlin. The chairs and the corner bench were covered with my sister's embroidery and weaving. In a niche between the crowded bookshelves of natural wood I had built a little altar. On it rested a Christmas crib. Irmgard had carved it from beeswax. Behind the crib stood a wooden plate my soldier cousin Gerhard Philipp had carved to symbolize the mysteries of the life of Christ. Over the altar hung a reproduction of Dürer's "The Apostles," and on either side of it stood two giant cactuses, prize products of a hobby my brother Hans had developed through reading Karl May's American Indian stories.

There was a good reproduction of Rembrandt's "St. Paul in Prison" on one wall and a portrait of Cardinal Newman on another. But my most precious artwork was an old crucifix in the Bavarian baroque manner.

One afternoon my mother pointed toward the two large rooms that stood empty in the attic. "Maybe it's only a silly dream of mine," she said, "but I think I'd like nothing better, after a few years, than to come to you and live up there. That nice view over the garden! And right beside the church! All my life I've had to walk at least three miles to get to church." Then she sighed and added, "But I don't think I'll live through another year."

Just then Renata burst in on us holding out a little knapsack packed with all it could hold. "See what the *Christkind* brought me for Christmas!"

She opened it up and proudly displayed its cargo of underwear, stockings, and cans of food. We looked at it with the usual exclamations of wonder and tried not to worry about what it meant.

Irmgard had made several knapsacks like this out of old curtains and stocked them with supplies for flight in the event the Russians came.

When the child had gone we talked over our plans against a Soviet invasion of Ermland. We had already sent packages to some in-laws deeper in Germany so that they could provide for us if we had to flee. But my mother thought flight was now out of the question. My father was about to be drafted from his teaching job and taken, in spite of his sixty years, into the Volkssturm. My sister Birgitta was expecting her first child in a few weeks. My mother did not see how they could get away and she was not going without them.

Flight before the Russians was not a new experience for my mother. She still remembered 1914. Just ten days after giving birth to her third child, two days after my father had been drafted into the army, and when I, her oldest son, was just two and a half years old, she had to gather us up and flee before another advancing Russian army. For four days and five nights we lived in a boxcar with eleven other families and one goat. At the end of that frightful journey, my mother's hair was suddenly gray. The baby, my brother Hugo, was so weakened by the trip that he had to have special care for years afterward. He survived that flight in the First World War only to die in the second.

But neither the memory of those things nor the thought that they might be upon us again spoiled our visit. We went over to the old farmhouse my grandmother had loved so much. My Uncle Franz, Aunt Elizabeth, and Aunt Anna, all in their seventies, exchanged news with my mother and talked over old times.

ANOTHER joy of that Christmas had been closer contact with the prisoners and refugees among us.

A company of army veterinarians had arrived in the village with some four hundred broken-down horses. Since my two big barns housed only four Plymouth Rock hens, the army commandeered them to stable forty-five horses. This was more of a blessing than an inconvenience. It gave me lots of fertilizer for my garden. The hens enjoyed it too. Their combs became redder and I knew they were laying more eggs—though I never saw a single one of them.

The German veterinarians had as assistants a detachment of

"Badoglios." These were soldiers from the surrendered Italian army who had chosen to cooperate with the German forces rather than to stay in prison camps. They were wretchedly clothed and poorly fed. They were delighted to learn I had picked up Italian during my student days in Rome, and I got along well with them.

Now I was determined to do all I could for these Italians in my parish and to have my parishioners do the same. I got permission from the army to hold a special service for them the day after Christmas. On the Sunday before I asked for donations of cakes and sweets for our special guests. At the parish midnight Mass our people turned out in full strength, but I was still doubtful as to how they would respond to the being welcomed in their challenge I was offering them. In my sermon I reminded them that the feast of the Christ Child is not merely a feast of beautiful sentiments. It is a feast of faith and of all that the faith means. If they could kneel at the communion rail with the Italians and the Poles, they should also sit at their own tables with them and have them share their Christmas dinners.

Next day the Italians were acting like little boys let out of school as their German sergeants rounded them up from their various billets. It was the gayest congregation I had had since coming to Suessenberg. But they became very attentive in church and showed their pleasure at being welcomed in their mother tongue.

Before starting Mass I knelt in front of the altar, then turned and spoke quietly to the men. I called up a picture of their wives and families back home and suggested that they might have been praying for years that their men would have just such an opportunity to make their peace with God. I told them I knew how they hated war and asked them to rid themselves of the cause of war, which is sin.

All sixty-five of them came to confession.

This was a great consolation to me. But it didn't do anything to warm Irmgard and our organist, Ursula Werr, who had to wait in the freezing choir loft for over an hour before the confessions were completed.

After the long interval, the old organ responded valiantly to Ursula's huge rough hands. I had the distracting hope that the Italians would receive the special grace granted Suessenberg parishioners to put up with Ursula's playing, which was a little on the squeaky side and more loud than correct. Ursula had good excuse for her rough hands. She did the hardest of men's work on the family farm. Her father, my best parishioner, had lost his right arm in the First World War and her brother had been killed in the Second.

Our congregation had the Italian love of singing and they were in the mood for it that morning. They sang from their hearts, each apparently following his own melody and paying little attention to what Ursula was doing. When I turned for the Dominus Vobiscum I could see the radiance in their faces. Carried away by the enthusiasm, one man seized the only three silent moments in the Mass, climbed up on a pew just before the Consecration and sent his tenor voice soaring in a solo "Ave Maria."

After Mass we distributed the good things our people had brought, including a large Silesian cake the size of a small table, donated by one of our poorest farmers. I made sure that the soloist received an extra-large slice.

ON the eve of the Epiphany my mother left for our home village thirty-five miles away. In spite of my determination to believe that the things we feared would not happen, I could not help thinking that I might not see her again.

CHAPTER I : *The Eleventh Hour*

THE BEGINNING OF JANUARY 1945 BROUGHT A MOUNTING sense of fear, even of panic, to the village of Suessenberg. Up till now the people had retained their stolid peasant acceptance of the inevitable. They had long become inured to living under arbitrary regulations that filtered down to them from some mysterious authority which, being authority, was beyond question. They had learned to live with a war that swallowed up their husbands and sons on some distant battlefield and sent in return prisoners or evacuees to work their farms. They had even become familiar with, without ceasing to be frightened by, the sight of a captured Russian parachutist being brought into the village at the end of a steeplejack's broomstick. But this was different. The Bolsheviks were coming!

The very word Bolshevik was enough to make the blood of these people run cold. From the days of the Russian Revolution they had filled their minds with horrible pictures of Bolshevik atrocities. The Bolsheviks were atheists. They had no human decency, no respect for human lives. They had let millions of their own people starve for cold-blooded political reasons; they had slaughtered thousands of others and sent millions more to die in the slave camps of Siberia. Their soldiers robbed and raped and slaughtered everywhere they went. The thought of falling into the hands of the Bolsheviks was worse, much worse, than death.

And now the fear, the certainty, that the Bolsheviks would soon be hammering down our doors was strengthened by the increasing flow of refugees from towns closer to the Russian lines. These refugees knew what Soviet occupation was like. They had been engulfed in the first Russian advance and liberated when the German army pushed them back, and they did not intend to be caught again. The villagers' fear was increased when the remaining men were ordered out to dig trenches and build tank obstacles in the surrounding woods and countryside.

In this atmosphere I tried to settle into my normal parochial duties. But these very duties were colored with the threat of invasion at every step. The Volkssturm, for instance, had to go out to the woods on Sundays as on other days. Their leader came to ask me if they could have a Mass at four o'clock in the morning before their day's digging. I was gratified when not one of them missed the opportunity for the sacraments.

I announced the date of the regular First Communion class and revived an old parish custom in order to round up all the children. After the feast of the Epiphany, January 6, the pastor, accompanied by three boys dressed as the three kings, goes from home to home in the parish. He blesses every house, every barn, and all the other buildings. Then he watches the father of each family place the initials of the three wise men, Caspar, Melchior, and Balthasar along with three crosses and the current year on the lintel of the door, in this form, 19 C—M—B 45. Then the whole household gathers for a prayer, all sing the Magnificat and the pastor leads the singing procession through the house blessing each room and sprinkling it with holy water. The house-to-house visitation served several purposes in addition to finding what children were ready for First Communion. During the fourteen days it occupied, I met all my people in their own homes; consequently, when the Russians came I was familiar with the location of each farm. I also found out about any non-Catholic evacuees or prisoners people had been hiding from me for fear I would discover how poorly they were being provided for.

Some of my good Catholics made last-minute efforts to prevent me from seeing the embarrassing quarters of their guests. "Don't bless this room, Father; there are Protestants in it!" But they did not stop me from seeing all the rooms when I replied, smiling, "Then I'm sure you think they need three times as much holy water as I use on you!"

The texts we needed most to meditate in those days were again put into our mouths by the liturgical cycle of the Church year. On the third Sunday after the Epiphany the Epistle of the Mass was St. Paul's message to the Romans: "If it be possible, as far as in you lies, be at peace with all men...if thy enemy is hungry, give him food; if he is thirsty, give him drink... Be not overcome by evil, but overcome evil with good."

The Gospel of the same Mass was the story of the good centurion with Christ's warning words: "Amen, I say to you, I have not found so great a faith in Israel. And I tell you that many will come from the east and from the west, and will feast with Abraham and Isaac and Jacob in the kingdom of heaven, but the children of the kingdom will be put forth into the darkness outside; there will be weeping and the gnashing of teeth."

In the middle of my sermon I saw the church door slowly open. A group of men shuffled awkwardly in with more than the ordinary self-consciousness of latecomers interrupting a sermon. Their appearance was ominous. They were Volkssturm, the last dregs of our manpower who had been rounded up and sent off to the northern front just a week before.

After Mass everyone gathered around them, welcoming their own and learning the reason for their unexpected reappearance. The whole northern front had been routed. The German army was in disorderly retreat. The Russians were pushing swiftly west toward Königsberg. These old men had found themselves with only rusty Italian rifles and five rounds of ammunition to oppose heavily armored Russian tanks. They had run for their lives back to their homes where they might still be of some protection to their families.

This first-hand evidence outweighed all the propaganda from the German radio and public authorities. It shook us out of believing the voices that had told us there was no immediate danger, that a new German push was being prepared and that new secret weapons were ready to destroy all threat of Soviet invasion.

This word carried by our own men from the north also brought dull certainty that similar reports we had heard from the south were equally true. The German front had broken down there too and the Russians were heading for Allenstein, Elbing, and Danzig. Our little village was caught in the huge pincers of a twin Soviet drive for the Baltic coast. The pincers were closing. It was no longer a matter of "if the Russians come." It was only a question of when.

Our first reactions were almost automatic. We would flee as deep into the Reich as possible, wait till all this was over, and then come back. My own mind was busy over a double responsibility: my parish, my family. My sister Irmgard, so recently ill, and the child she was caring for were still in the house. I decided they should leave immediately for my parents' home. Irmgard went quietly to work packing our knapsacks.

I left for Heilsberg, our county seat and railroad center, to see what I could do about arranging transportation. Just outside the town groups of Volkssturm men were sawing down trees to make tank blocks. Farther on long lines of army trucks were unloading crowds of refugees from Allenstein and other places in neighboring Masuria. These people had hoped to be brought as far as Elbing on their way to the Reich. They were being dumped here because Elbing was already besieged by the Russians. Bombardments had paralyzed the railways, and communications with the Reich had been cut off.

There was no such thing as arranging for rail transportation. Irmgard would have to attempt the thirty-five miles by road. I made my way to a store owned by a friend of mine who generously gave me his last sled. It was small enough for my sister to load and pull by hand over the snow.

Dragging the little sled behind me, I plodded over to the church to find what plans our dean, the pastor of Heilsberg, was making. The thought of talking to him warmed me a little and brought a relief from tension.

A very tall man with a heavy-set body, the dean had a disproportionately small head. He always wore imposing hats to compensate for this. He had been sergeant of a Prussian regiment in World War I and a militarily zealous and efficient administrator ever since. But he was as naive as he was ambitious and forceful. There was a large innocence about his way of trying to impress the bishop and win ecclesiastical position. He made no bones about the fact that he expected to be moved up from dean to canon.

He took a lot of joshing from disrespectful assistants and younger colleagues about the relentless march of his triumphal progress. But nothing could change him. Even when playing cards he had to win. When he did win, he was expansive and generous, but he took his defeats very hard. He was a bit of a problem accompanying the bishop on the annual visitation of parishes in his district. He would barge in with orders of his own and upset the already nervous country pastors. Then we hit on the idea of giving him charge of the bishop's crozier. This gave him proper satisfaction.

I smiled as I knocked on his door and made a little bet with myself about what his answer would be when I asked what he intended to do when the Russians came.

I won my bet. He drew himself to his full impressive height and made a brave speech about captains not leaving their sinking ships until all others were safely off.

I won my bet, but I need not have smiled. There was more than bombast to the words. Our dean never became canon. He died with some of his parishioners as a brick worker in a Siberian slave camp.

On the road back to Suessenberg I saw a sleigh coming toward me out of the village. The driver was our good parishioner, Mr. Poschmann. Bundled up in his sleigh were Irmgard and Renata. There was no time to waste on delayed farewells. I tied the little sled to the back of the sleigh, made the sign of the cross with my thumb on the foreheads of both girls and urged them to hurry on toward home as fast as they could.

All next day I was much too busy to give thought to the reports and rumors that were flying around. It seemed certain that the road to my parents' home had been cut off and barricaded by the Russians. I had no time to worry about Irmgard. I could only work on, pray and hope.

I had to prepare the children for First Communion. There were visits to outlying farms all the rest of the day, to comfort the sick and the aged and to offer everyone whatever encouragement I could. When I got back to the rectory I crawled into bed and fell dead asleep.

I awoke struggling to get out of the depths of sleep. I could sense rather than hear a voice outside calling wildly to me. I dragged myself out of bed. As my bare feet hit the cold floor, the voice became a woman's screaming. The Russians had come! Some woman was being attacked and she had run here for help! Then I could make out some words. "Pack! Pack everything! Pack!" I ran across the room and struggled with my second-floor window. It was frozen tight and wouldn't budge. I smashed the glass with my fist. The action and the cold wind ripping through my nightshirt brought me completely to my senses.

When I looked out I saw that the woman was Bertha, the domineering sister of our old burgomaster, and nobody else was near her. One of the facts I had learned about my parish was that the old man lived under the orders of four women—a wife and three sisters—but Bertha was chief of staff. It was a sufficiently official notification when Bertha called up at me, "We must all go down and report at Raunau. The whole village has to be evacuated tonight."

I pulled out a big suitcase and started packing. In went Bible, breviary, and missal. Then the precious Chrysostom manuscripts that represented five years of study and note-taking. I couldn't possibly leave *them*. The chalice that was a gift for my First Mass I wrapped in heavy underwear, socks, and a blanket. When I added the food Irmgard had prepared for just this moment I found I could still squeeze in a dozen books and close the suitcase by sitting on it and using a strap instead of the snaps that would not hold.

Then I started to put on as much of all my clothing as I could: two sets of underwear, two pairs of pants, three shirts, two pairs of socks, my heaviest boots, one overcoat and then another, and a fur coat on top of all.

I hauled the suitcase outside and strapped it on the rack over the back wheel of my bicycle.

At the door of the church I found Bertha with three other women. The sight of these three was enough by itself to make the night memorable. They had been feuding and not talking to each other since long before I came to the parish. Now they were chatting away as if they had been bosom friends all their lives.

I distributed Holy Communion to the four women—not without pausing to think what an unliturgical figure I made, stuffed in all that clothing under a great fur coat.

The remaining hosts I placed in the pyx used for sick calls and stowed it away next to my heart. In anticipation of a time such as this I had been careful to leave only a few consecrated hosts in the tabernacle at any time. I had also hidden away the sacred vessels except for one ciborium. If some article was not left in sight any despoilers of the church would be certain to use force on some of the parishioners to find out where the sacred vessels were hidden.

I looked around the church in farewell, knelt for a final prayer and then prepared to go to the assembly point. This lay at the foot of a steep hill covered with a foot of newly fallen snow. I put another half dozen books in a bag and balanced them on the right handlebar, my typewriter on the left. Between those at the front and the suitcase at the back, I had no easy time steering the bicycle through the snow.

All went well for about five minutes, except that I was dripping with perspiration from my swaddling of clothes. Then, near the foot of the hill, the overloaded rear rack gave way, the suitcase slipped and I plunged into the ditch.

I sat there for a moment in the snow—bicycle, suitcase, books, and typewriter scattered around me, and suddenly saw what a picture I made. I thought ruefully of the courageous sermon I had given only a couple of days ago.

That was the end of my running away from the Russians. I rose from the ditch and walked away leaving everything right where it was. I felt immeasurably free. As I approached the gathering of villagers I was grateful that darkness had prevented the parishioners from seeing their pastor's undignified fall. I could join them feeling I still had some authority left.

The greatest panic and the loudest grief was evident among the evacuee and refugee families. They were certain that the Suessenberg people would look after their own and leave them to the mercy of the Russians. One woman cried out, "Why can't some planes come over and kill us all right here? That would be a lot easier than being left to the Bolsheviks!"

It seemed impossible to comfort them. But the minute Bertha Poschmann appeared on the scene, everything changed. She proved to be the Valiant Woman and all took new courage from her. She turned to the refugees and spoke to them in very definite and reassuring words: "Not one of our families will leave this village without taking along one of your families. Get your baggage ready—only what you absolutely need. We have three hay wagons coming and there will be enough food put on them to last us on the four-hundred-mile trip to Berlin. We're having trouble getting horses for the wagons, so if they don't come right away we'll just have to wait until they do. If we can't all leave together none of us will leave."

All the other women agreed. Some of them did not want to leave anyhow without their menfolk who were being held to their digging in the woods at revolver point by a fanatic young sergeant. The decision to stay was made for us when a couple of sleighs arrived back along the road they had taken in advance of the rest, just an hour earlier. They had reached the main road which was our avenue of retreat and found it blocked and littered with dead horses. "We're going back home," they told us. "It's better to die there than out in a snowdrift."

It was then five o'clock so I suggested to the people that they take their things back home and come to the church for a Mass at six.

The church was filled. Since it was the feast of St. Polycarp I sang the High Mass in the red vestments symbolizing martyrdom. Normally there is no sermon at a weekday Mass, but as I sang the Gospel the words put me to shame and I felt I had to speak. There was no need to add much to the words of St. Matthew:

"Do not be afraid of those who kill the body but cannot kill the soul. But rather be afraid of him who is able to destroy both soul and body in hell. Are not two sparrows sold for a farthing? And yet not one of them will fall to the ground without your Father's leave. But as for you, the very hairs of your head are all numbered. Therefore do not be afraid; you are of more value than many sparrows."

At the end of the Mass I made two announcements: there would be a High Mass and a sermon every day that was left to us; the children's First Communion, scheduled for April, would be moved up to next Sunday, just two days away.

Our people had little leisure to brood over their own predicament. Their homes were filling up with refugees from other villages who could not go any farther because of the blocked roads. Fortunately the party officials of our area had thought of their own skins first and had vanished. Our farmers could slaughter their animals without bothering about an official license and thus keep their increased households fed.

I tramped from farm to farm to bring the sacraments, perhaps for the last time, to the aged and sick. On my way to the home of Grandpa Schenk, oldest man in the village, I overtook two girls, Tatjana, a Russian, and Marusja, a Pole. The fourteen-year-old Tatjana was shivering in her rags as we plodded through the snow. She had already seen enough suffering for a lifetime. She had come to the village with her mother, grandfather, and sisters. Two years previously they had been driven by SS troops from their homestead near Leningrad. They were sent to a large camp in Masuria and now they were in flight again, this time from the Russians.

When the girls learned I was carrying the Blessed Sacrament, it was a heartbreaking moment for all of us. Tatjana had been brought up a devout Russian Orthodox and she missed the consolations of her Church. It was she who turned to Marusja and said, "Let's both go with Father and pray for the old man." It was she who urged Marusja to take the opportunity of going to confession. When I gave Holy Communion to the old man and the young Polish girl, Tatjana, who had greater desire for the sacrament than either of them, knelt with bowed head, torn between the certainty that God was present in the Eucharist and loyalty to her own tradition. Never had I felt the effects of schism so bitterly.

On the way back to the village I invited the girls to come and get the clothes my sister had left behind. Tatjana taught me some Russian phrases that would come in handy when the Red Army came.

Night fell like a robe of peace on the countryside. I decided to hike the three miles over to my neighbor pastor at Wernegitten and put my own soul in order. Father Teschner was always glad to see me. The only time his housekeeper used real coffee beans was when a brother priest came.

The streets around Father Teschner's rectory were milling with German soldiers seeking quarters. A shipment of new equipment had just arrived and they all seemed very happy about it.

The pastor was not in his office. Instead, a group of officers were gathered around maps plotting their next movements. They were so intent and the room was so dark and thick with smoke that they did not notice me. I found Father Teschner in the dining room. Neither the Russians nor the army seemed to be worrying him in the least. "Who's going to bother about an old donkey like me?" he said. "I've been in this place thirty-five years and I'm not leaving now when it's time to die. And anyhow, with these varicose veins I couldn't run if I wanted to." I learned that he had been in touch with other pastors of the area and they were all staying. But on the question of what was going to happen next he had only the same answer we were all giving, "Your guess is as good as mine." As he was giving me his blessing after confession a lieutenant burst into the room and asked, "What's the best road to Suessenberg?"

I told him who I was and offered to trade directions for a ride. In the Volkswagen, the talk was all of the three huge Hummel weapons, monstrous mobile guns just off the assembly line, that would be mounted in our village that very night. Along with the guns we would get their fifty artillerymen and, I did not have to go very far to learn, some other people too. One of the others was sitting in the back seat with a young captain. She was supposed to be a refugee from the frontier. At the burgomaster's, Bertha assigned billets for the carload of soldiers. I had the honor of providing lodging for the captain, the lieutenant, and the "refugee woman."

I began to regret this right after supper—which I had prepared and served myself. The young lady decided she would rather sit smoking and joking with the officers than do the dishes. To put an end to it, I announced it was bedtime and showed them upstairs. I assigned the woman to one room, the officers to another, with my own room between the two. My lady guest was not pleased with this arrangement but she had to put up with it.

Next morning the officers called in their personal cook, told him to round up four fat pigs and slaughter them for future supplies and ordered ten hamburgers each for breakfast. When I got back from High Mass a master sergeant was sprawled out with his dirty boots on the couch my sister had covered so painstakingly with her delicate needlework. He had been drinking and was shouting wildly.

"The whole damn mess is finished. They don't let us drill these kids the way we used to. They've got no more guts. Should blow up that damn bunker...Berchtesgaden...finish the whole stinking thing...have it done."

He was about thirty years old.

The captain, a ripe twenty-three, came in fresh from a hot bath and tackled the hamburgers swimming in grease. He bolstered his courage with a bottle of schnapps.

The "refugee woman" was enjoying it immensely. She told me she'd love to stay a while in our wonderful village and do a little skiing.

That was all I could take. "Whoever that woman is, she's in the wrong place here," I told the captain. "If you don't get her out of this village in an hour I'll call your chief of staff."

The threat of authority was enough. He ordered a sleigh to come and take her to Heilsberg.

Half an hour later a soldier old enough to be the officer's father came in and announced the arrival of the sleigh. Without as much as looking at the man, the lieutenant yelled, "Get out!" I went out too, and caught another glimpse of the state of the German army in the older man's muttering: "We got that kind marked down—on some bullets we're saving just for them."

SEPTUAGESIMA Sunday was First Communion day. Catholics are always deeply moved at the sight of their white-veiled children going to the altar rail for the first time; solicitude for what the future will bring these souls in their care, nostalgia for their own far-off innocence. A pastor always knows that hearts hardened by time are vulnerable on that day, and his sermon is more for the parents than it is for the children.

I could not possibly have written a better sermon for the occasion at that time and place than the Mass itself provided with the Gospel parable of the workers at the vineyard.

It was not difficult in the presence of those First Communicants to point out to my people the Gospel parable's message of mercy. I did not even have to make the obvious comparison about the "eleventh hour." "Surrounded by the groans of death" (Introit) we prayed intensely for the "deliverance from the just afflictions caused by our sins" (Collect).

CHAPTER II : *"In the Dust of Death"*

IN A WAR OF MOVEMENT THE LITTLE PEOPLE WHO occupy the ground being moved over are among the last to learn in which direction the bloody tide is flowing, just as they are the first to feel its grim effects. On the Monday after Septuagesima we in Suessenberg had a choice of reading two sets of signs pointing in opposite directions.

We could see a glimmer of hope in a new wave of refugees who came upon us that morning. In the district they came from the Russians had been pushed back twenty miles. The artillerymen quartered upon us tried to make us believe we were safe. They were elated at the news of the German advance. They had just received twenty gallons of gasoline to move the big Hummels into position. The snowstorm was giving them time to prepare. They would certainly hold off the Russians and beat them back. We had nothing to fear.

But other signs dominated and made all this talk sound like whistling in the dark. There were reports of Communists, prisoners who had escaped from the army in the confusion, hiding in our woods and in the barns of outlying farms ready to spring out upon us at the first approach of their comrades. German troops were appearing in the village, weary, hopeless old men, travesties of the military. Some of them had been tramping for ten days from their behind-the-lines jobs of guarding munition dumps and airfields.

Now they were ordered to report at Freudenberg, some seven miles to the southeast. The frontline troops ahead of them, their heavy armament immobilized for lack of gasoline and oil, were as good as gone. Now these old men were to be the front line against the inevitable break-through. Freudenberg was to be the last stand in defense of this particular battlefront, our battlefront. They were to hold their positions there "at any cost."

The mounting fear brought thoughts of death. Men who had long refused the open door of the church now called on God and his priest and the sacraments. Everywhere I went I carried the Blessed Sacrament as on a sick call or a visit to the dying. There was no need for me to engage in speculation over how close we were to becoming a battlefield. I increasingly found our sick and our old men sharing their straw beds with soldiers who had crawled back to the village to nurse their fresh wounds.

I wanted to talk over plans with my neighbor to the south, Father Langwald, of Stolzhagen. He was an old and dear friend of mine from the days I had been the bishop's secretary. As an administrator he was just the opposite of the good dean of Heilsberg. He was always the last pastor to get his reports into the chancery and had to be repeatedly badgered to get them in at all. But he was invariably good-natured about accepting his reprimands. When I took the tack of begging him not to embarrass himself and the bishop, the approach worked. He had been my friend and most constant visitor since my arrival in Suessenberg. A poor card player at social get-togethers, he liked to read all sorts of books, preferably in Slavic languages, and was interested in theology and my Chrysostom studies.

I found him caring for a seriously ill priest, Father Ernst Hoppe. Father Hoppe's parish had been wiped out and his housekeeper had dragged him on a small sled forty miles over the snow to Father Langwald's. The three of us exchanged advice on what should be done, what could be done, what must be done. Father

Langwald and I made an agreement that if anything happened to one the other would look after both parishes. But Father Langwald was confident that he would be left alone. He was Polish in his heart and put great faith in an identification card which established his membership in a Polish nationalist organization.

It was getting dark fast and snow was falling as I took the road for home. Through the snow I could see a red haze rising in the sky from villages burning not ten miles away. The rat-a-tat of machine guns and the blast of artillery fell on my ears and built up an illusion that it was coming closer at each repetition. Sudden fear and nausea swept over me and I was engulfed in a strong black temptation to flee. What could I do anyway? My call was to the kind of service that required the "peaceful and quiet life" St. Paul speaks of in the first Epistle to Timothy. I certainly could not find that life or answer that call in this place now. Why not leave while I had the chance and fulfill my vocation where it was possible? My mind was as dull and heavy as the night around me as I plowed through the deepening snow.

I was almost on top of two soldiers slogging in the opposite direction before I noticed them. They were not young, and looked as weary and beaten as I felt. They were in Indian file, one walking ten paces behind in the path broken by the other. The collars of their dirty uniforms were turned up to protect their ears from the snow and the biting wind. They had clumsy mufflers wrapped around their necks up to their chins. Coats and mufflers were rimed with frozen breath.

Their blanket rolls and heavy rifles seemed to make loads that had deadened them past all realization.

"Is this the right road for Freudenberg?" the first one asked.

"It is," I answered, "but this is no time to be going there. Ivan will be there before you."

"We're from the 18th and the whole division has orders to report there."

The man's Rhineland accent was unmistakable. When the second came up I asked him where he was from.

"Upper Silesia."

"So you're both Catholics," I said.

Two very astonished faces looked me over from head to foot.

"What are you? A pastor of some kind?"

"I'm a priest and I happen to be carrying the Blessed Sacrament."

They were silent for a moment, looked at one another and then at me.

"I suppose," said the Rhinelander, "we'll have to go to confession."

We kept walking. The Rhinelander made his confession between the first and second tree along the road, the Upper Silesian between the second and third. Beside the third tree there was a farmer's loading platform. I pointed at it and said, "That's our communion rail."

My frozen fingers gave me trouble opening the pyx. I had to blow on them for several minutes before I could take out the hosts.

The men knelt in a snowdrift with their hands resting on the platform. Behind me was the red sky of the burning villages. In front of me I could see a house where an old farmer had this day refused to let me prepare him for the Sacraments. He had protested that it was still two months to Easter.

In this setting, in the midst of uncertainty about everything but death, the two soldiers received the Bread of Life.

It was a moving moment and the old Rhinelander would not have been true to his breed if he had kept his feelings to himself. I think we all had tears in our eyes when he scrambled to his feet and grabbed my hand in both of his.

"How could this happen, Father, after all those years—to me?"

The Upper Silesian did not say a word. He kept fishing around in his pocket. Finally he held out what he had been looking for—a little piece of a rosary.

"Did you say it so often that it wore away?"

"No, Father. Me, I didn't say it. Never. But my wife and my six children, they did. Every day."

All three of us stood silent for a moment looking at the little fragment of a broken rosary. We all knew what the inarticulate man was trying to say by holding it out. He was confessing his faith that the prayers of his family had brought two old soldiers this strange last-minute opportunity of making their peace with God.

I watched them out of sight as they turned and marched on toward Freudenberg. It was dark, but they were silhouetted against the red glow in the sky.

Freudenberg was taken by the Russians that night.

I still don't know who received the greater blessing from that meeting, the old soldiers or the priest. Before they came along, I had been wrestling with my lowest point of discouragement. I had been frightened and ready to give up. Now my anguish had disappeared. I felt such a surge of happiness that I could not help myself from chanting out loud there in the road the "Gloria in excelsis Deo."

Inside and out I felt like a new man. I knew clearly and irrevocably that, come what may, I would stay. Nothing was too much to pay for what God had wanted to do with my words and my hands for these two men. And even if the priestly work of preaching the Word and distributing the Sacraments should be taken away completely, there would still be something left for me to "do"—to suffer with my flock.

Arriving home late for evening devotions, I walked into the church down the center aisle dressed as I was from the road and told the congregation about the two men. We prayed the Sorrowful Mysteries, remembering our loved ones and all others caught in this moment of approaching death and asked that all might receive and accept their own opportunities for reconciliation with the God of Love.

The snow stopped falling that night and there was not a cloud in the sky the next morning. That meant the end of the lull, of the chance the storm had given to set up defenses. My military guests reacted with more promptitude than they had yet shown. The pampered captain even forgot to take his hot bath. The lieutenant left eight of his ten hamburgers on his plate. They sent soldiers scurrying to pack their belongings, to make a pyre of all the equipment they could not take with them, to set dynamite charges inside the brand-new big guns. They transferred into their own vehicles the gasoline meant to move the Hummels. They set fire to the piled equipment, dynamited the Hummels and drove away with some girls they had picked up. Their legacy to us was the broken windows shattered in the concussion from the shiny new weapons brought in to protect the village.

Our road became a stream of retreating soldiers and civilians. Sleighs and trucks and farm wagons and decrepit cars churned along in an uneven procession. But the deep slushy snow made walking the fastest locomotion.

Russian planes strafed the slow-moving line of defeat. The people huddled miserably for shelter wherever they could. There were not nearly enough beds for the wounded, the exhausted, the sick, and the frostbitten. The refugees were mostly women and children. Their suffering was a terrible thing to watch. "Woe to those who are with child, or have infants at the breast in those days! But pray that your flight may not be in the winter" (Mt. 24:19–20).

Moving among them I learned of scenes that had put the terror in their eyes. Just five miles down the road the sleighs of two fleeing families had been hit by the planes. The survivors told how four of their number had been killed outright. Another woman, from a village just three miles away, had removed the covering from the sled on which she had packed her three children. She had wanted to feed them. But she found all three frozen to death. She had to bury them quickly in the snow by the roadside because another sled with the rest of the family was already a hundred yards ahead of her and she had to catch up with it. Another sleigh was carrying the

body of an aged grandfather who had frozen to death. The corpse
had been rolled in a carpet and tied beneath the box. They stopped
for the night and the next morning the bundle had disappeared.
Some desperate thief had imagined it to contain something freshly
slaughtered and just handy for a meager table.

My own house was able to shelter about fifty people. A dozen
exhausted soldiers lay snoring on the kitchen floor. At dinner that
evening a government military administration officer spoke to me
with great seriousness and urgency. The pincers movement was
closing in on us and would definitely swallow us up. It was imper-
ative, he said, that I leave at once. It was useless, even suicidal, for
a priest to stay. Others would have a chance for survival, but not
a priest. If I stayed there was no doubt that I would either be shot
or transported to Siberia. He named six priests of the region who
had already been killed. He had a good sleigh and a span of strong
horses. He could make room for me on it.

I asked if he could also make room for our old people and children. He replied that he could not even find space to carry back his
own wounded.

I wrote a letter to my parents and gave it to him. He promised
to get it to them if he succeeded in escaping the trap. Signing that
letter and watching the officer ride off with my last hope of escape,
I should have had some feeling of making a big decision. I did not.
The struggle for decision had passed with the two old soldiers on
the road. My only feeling while writing the letter was desire to comfort my family. I reminded them that this was the feast of my special
patron, St. John Chrysostom, who had himself been transported to
the East back in the year 407. It was not likely that I would have to
suffer any more than he had. Even if this did look like the darkness
of Calvary on Good Friday, that merely meant that the brightness
of Easter was not far away. I ended with Chrysostom's last words,
"God be praised for all."

Our little village had become such a confused crossroad of

needs and anxiety that its pastor had no time for either brooding or heroic thoughts. I headed for the church and bumped right into a frail but energetic and fearless woman I had not seen for years. She was Sister Imelda of the Gray Sisters of St. Elizabeth. She had left the burning town of Nossberg with a busload of aged women. Her destination had been Heilsberg but the roads were blocked and the battle had now reached the town itself. I told her she was welcome to use my house and she was soon bustling around finding space and food for everyone in it.

This master manager was just setting one of my favorite meals in front of me when I had another surprise guest. A knock at the door took me away from the steaming *klunkermus* and *flinsen* and I peered out at a figure in the dark vestibule. I could just make out the shape of a one-armed man and I did not recognize the voice which said, "Pastor, you have to help me out. I can't make it any farther. This is where I'll have to die."

I flung the door open in welcome but the voice went right on. "Do you have any oats? Just let me feed my horses and then the Russians can come and kill me if they want."

"I've plenty of oats. But before you die you might as well come into the kitchen and get warm."

When the candlelight fell on his face, I discovered that the man was my Uncle Keichel. He had not known of my appointment to Suessenberg and I had imagined him safe at his farm and brick factory.

He stared at me in surprise, hugged me with his one arm and said, "Now I know for sure that I'm not going to leave here."

Warmed up by my last three shots of solid Silesian kümmel, he went out to feed his horses. At ease again, he sat down to the milk soup and the potato pancakes with bacon and forgot all his troubles. Sister Imelda helped me get him to bed in my study.

I brought the Blessed Sacrament over from the church to the cellar, and also hid the most important parish records, the precious

Bavarian crucifix, and some valuable books and manuscripts. It was two o'clock when I got to bed.

The bed was not yet warm, my mind still racing with the happenings of the day, when a burst of shells landed on our hill and shattered the windows. I leaped from bed and ran in my pajamas to the cellar. In a matter of minutes the whole motley household was crowded down there waiting apprehensively for the next shell burst. But one face was missing, old Uncle Keichel's.

Sister Imelda ran upstairs to see what had happened to him. She came back with a reassuring smile. She had found him snoring on the couch, blissfully unaware of all the noise and confusion.

When a couple of soldiers insisted on waking him and bringing him downstairs, the old man was grumbling at having been disturbed. "My life is finished anyway. The Lord will be taking me any time. What difference does it make?" How much real concern his gruff words were hiding came out in his next words to me. "I would like to make my last confession, a general confession of my whole life." He was completely without fear and even seemed happy as I gave him Holy Communion with the others in the cellar.

No more shells landed so close, but it was clear we were in the direct line of gunfire. I decided to move my headquarters to the farmhouse at the western end of the village, the house in which my grandmother had been born. Old Uncle Keichel insisted on staying behind to look after church and rectory.

Other relatives had come to share the old house with my Uncle Franz and my Aunts Elizabeth and Anna. One of them was a cousin, Josef, who carried news that decided my next duty. He himself was one of a number of older family fathers who stole away that night like robbers into their own homes to see their wives and children once again before returning for a last hopeless stand. His news was that our band of Volkssturm men had managed to lock their young supervisor in an outhouse and commandeer two sleighs to bring them out of the woods back to the village. Josef received the Sacraments there in the farmhouse, begged me to look after his wife and two small children and then went back to his unit.

I knew I had to seek out the men who had returned. The farm of Mr. Poschmann, chairman of our parish trustees, would be a likely rendezvous for many families. It lay about two miles away, across what was now obviously a no man's land. I packed my Mass things and started out for it in the hope of saying Mass there that night. Theresia, a thirty-year-old refugee, volunteered to accompany me. It was uncomfortably weird walking through the strangely silent village.

In the kitchen of the farmhouse the mothers of four families were preparing supper over the one stove. The floors of the three other rooms were covered with mattresses. The parlor was filled with baggage. Some seventy people were being fed and sheltered in that one farmhouse.

Mr. Poschmann was making identification placards out of cardboard for his children, who ranged in age from three to the teens. The placards would be hung around the neck by a string and worn under the clothes. He had also prepared seven linen bags. In each bag there was a letter, a few prayer leaflets, and a family picture so that they wouldn't forget their parents.

From the windows we could see the city of Heilsberg burning five miles away. From Wernegitten, only two miles away, the Russians were sending up green and red rockets that were being answered from Reichenberg, four miles off. As we watched there were intermittent bursts of flame along the surrounding hills. Our situation was only too clear.

The men had come back from the Volkssturm. But for the families who had waited for them it was now too late to flee.

February 1 is the feast of St. Ignatius of Antioch, bishop and martyr. The Mass I celebrated that night in Mr. Poschmann's living room contained an Epistle that can scarcely have had more meaning for any congregation since it was first addressed to the Romans:

"Brethren, who shall separate us from the love of Christ? Shall tribulation or distress, or persecution, or hunger, or nakedness, or danger, or the sword? Even as it is written, 'For Thy sake we are put to death all the day long. We are regarded as sheep for the slaughter.' But in all these things we overcome because of Him Who has loved us. For I am sure that neither death, nor life, nor angels, nor principalities, nor things present, nor things to come, nor powers, nor height, nor depth, nor any other creature will be able to separate us from the love of God, which is in Christ Jesus our Lord" (Rom. 8:35–39).

When I got back to my uncle's farmhouse I found that the front line had moved right in with us. A German soldier stood on the porch staring out at the horizon of fire. "Ivan will be here tomorrow," he said, "but he has his hands full tonight. You can get one more night's sleep."

The living room floor was littered with sleeping soldiers. Three officers sat around a smoking kerosene lamp on a tiny table. Two were studying maps and making notes. The third, a captain, was trying to read a little book in the flickering light.

I passed through to the kitchen just in time to see Aunt Anna stalking out of the pantry with an angry sergeant yelling at her. "What difference does it make?" he was shouting. "If we leave anything, the Russians'll take it tomorrow. And if you try shouting at them they'll eat more than the food. They'll devour you too."

But he made no impression on Aunt Anna. She tossed her head and yelled back just as loudly, "If you're going to take all our food then you're just as bad as the Russians."

A noise drew me to Uncle Franz's bedroom. He had been feverishly ill and bedridden for several days. A couple of tired soldiers were making him get up so they could have the bed themselves. Uncle Franz was protesting as I walked in. I tried reasoning with the sergeant. "I know you're exhausted and under pressure. But can't you have a little consideration for old people?"

My quiet words sent the sergeant into a tirade. At this the captain came in. He was a tall blond man wearing spectacles. His fine features and his controlled manner spoke of a well-disciplined character. When the sergeant and I had told our stories he lifted the heavy feather-stuffed comforter and pointed to the sweat-drenched sheets. "This is a sick man," he told the sergeant. "He must be left in his bed." So Uncle Franz climbed back into bed and the soldiers sprawled on the floor.

Few of us slept much that night and none of us wanted to talk. The captain, however, did exchange a few words with me.

"Are you the Catholic pastor here?"

"I am. I'm Pastor Fittkau."

"Do you intend to stay behind?"

"Yes. I think I should be with my people."

"I understand. May God watch over you."

I was close enough to see that the book he kept reading was a small Bible. As the men prepared to drive off just before dawn one of the last soldiers to leave turned to me and said, "That's a fine captain we have. He is a Protestant minister."

The soldiers were scarcely out of the house when Aunt Anna was swishing her homemade willow broom over the floor sweeping out the straw they had slept on. She kept up a constant mumbling and grumbling as she tried to fix up the mess they had made. When she saw the pantry she rushed back to the front door and started waving and yelling after the soldiers going down the road.

Uncle Franz spoke up very calmly from his bed.

"You *would* yell at them! They got even with you. They passed everything out through the little pantry window. If you had behaved yourself they might have left us at least one shelf."

It was February 2, the first Friday of the month and the feast of the Purification. We sent word out to the three nearest farmhouses that there would be Mass here. Aunt Elizabeth had been so crippled with arthritis that she had not been able to get to church for ten years. Now she could attend Mass again, and in her own home; a Mass said by her own priest-nephew using the very chalice she and the rest of the family had given him on ordination. She sat up in her chair dressed in the velvet and lace of her Sunday best, waiting for the Mass to begin.

For all the forty people present that Mass was a solemn and moving experience. We knew that day would bring the Russians, and we did not know how or when we would be together again, if at all. At the Offertory I offered up, in expiation for our own sins and for the many crimes that would be committed, all that my people might have to suffer. Everyone present received Holy Communion.

After Mass I hid my chalice under a pile of peat in a corner of the woodshed. We spent the rest of the day waiting from hour to hour for the Russians and taking whatever measures we could think of against their inevitable arrival.

The reports of violations of women had been too constant, too factual, for anyone to disregard them, and this dread was the most nerve-racking element in our waiting. There were those in the house who had first-hand knowledge of what to expect. Lydia was one. She was a White Russian housemaid who had been a faithful friend and helper to poor old Aunt Elizabeth for several years. She had been caught in eastern Poland when Stalin took that region over after the Moscow treaty of 1939. She had already chosen a hiding place in the hayloft and taken herself off to it with a small supply of milk and bread two days previously. She would come out for Mass only when we had convinced her that the Russians had not yet arrived. As soon as Mass was over she rushed out of the parlor and back to her hayloft.

We decided that the potato cellar was the best place for Sister Imelda, Theresia, and three young women from neighboring farms. It was directly under the kitchen and could be entered only through a trapdoor in the floor. We leveled out the potatoes and covered them with mattresses and blankets. The women went down and we lowered them some filled knapsacks, a little baggage, and a candle. Then those of us who remained upstairs just sat around and waited for something to happen.

CHAPTER III : *The Russians Arrive*

WE WAITED ALL THAT DAY. SHELLS WERE BURSTING, gunfire crackling very close to us in several directions. We could not read the sounds well enough to tell which way the action was moving or what was happening to the small band of soldiers defending the entrance to the village. We just waited, expecting from minute to minute that the Soviet troops would be upon us.

As darkness fell, the artillery fire died down. The farm was a clearing in a wooded valley. In the dusk we could occasionally see small groups of soldiers scurrying across the back fields. At midnight a few of them, soaking wet from the thawing snow, came cautiously to the door and asked for food. They told us that Russian machine guns were on the hill not a hundred yards away from us. Their objective was the last German position, on a neighboring hill close enough to be within their range.

We all went down to the cellar after the soldiers left. Whenever I came up to take a look, all I could see were fleeing German soldiers. It would be any moment now.

Just at daybreak we got our first news of Russian troops in the village. Two girls came running over the hill from the neighboring Funk farm. They were breathless, pale, and frightened. The Funks had been kneeling around their little family altar saying the rosary when the first Soviet soldiers burst in on them during the previous night. They had shouted rough questions. But the Funks, not understanding

Russian, had kept their eyes fixed on the altar, clutched their beads with terror-frozen fingers and gone on praying. "Holy Mary, Mother of God, pray for us sinners now and at the hour of..."

Angry at being ignored, the soldiers strode over to the oldest man present, the eighty-four-year-old grandfather. They grabbed his shoulder, swung him around and yelled into his face. When they got no answer they pounded him till he keeled over and sank to the floor. Then they turned to the father, a man over sixty. They were beating him bloody when a Russian army officer banged into the house and started outroaring them all. His entrance terrified the Funks still more until it dawned on them that he was yelling at the soldiers, not at them. He grabbed each of the other soldiers by the arm and practically threw them all out of the house.

He turned and nodded smilingly toward the family as though to assure them that they need not worry. Then he found a common language to express himself. He stood in front of a picture of the Holy Family, made a triple sign of the cross in the Eastern fashion and pointed to the figures in the picture, saying, "Jesus, Maria, Josef." Then he took from his pocket the small metal cross Eastern Christians receive at baptism and held it out for them to see. He smiled and nodded again, wheeled out of the door and was gone.

The girls had spent the rest of the night in the hayloft until it was light enough to make their way to us. They seemed to have complete confidence that I would be able to protect them from the Russian soldiers.

This first report of Russian troops in our village was not what we had expected. Even the girls in their terrified state realized that not every Russian soldier was a brute.

I put on the impressive fur-lined cassock and my fur cap. Across my breast I put a small cross made from the wood of the Garden of Gethsemane, which I had received on entering the seminary. I talked with Vladimir, the White Russian who would act as our interpreter. Vladimir was the man who had driven me to Suessenberg on the day of my arrival. He was devoted to my Uncle Franz and the old aunts, but exceedingly fearful of what might happen to him when the Red Army came.

Uncle Franz was still burning with fever, but he was a farmer and one of his cows was expecting a calf. Russians or no Russians, fever or no fever, he insisted on going out to the barn to look after it. He only got halfway when he turned sharply and came running back. He had seen about a dozen soldiers in strange brown uniforms creeping slowly along the gorge straight toward the farmhouse.

I fixed my crucifix in place, called on our guardian angels for help and stepped into the doorway to meet them. One of them, well in advance of the rest, bent over in a half crouch with a submachine gun at the ready, was stepping as guardedly as a frightened cat along the side of the house. When he saw me he made one huge leap and stood pointing his gun at me in the doorway.

He was a stout, stony-faced sergeant. His eyes were dilated with a mixture of fear and greed. His men, a long way behind him, were frozen in similar attitudes.

Seeing them so fearful took away much of my own fear. My strange costume seemed to immobilize the leader. But not for long. He jerked his gun up and down imperatively and barked out a group of words we were to hear so often that they became like a leitmotif running through some grotesque opera: "Uhrr! Schnapps! Deutscher soldat!"

This first wave of troops obviously had the assignment of cleaning out any remaining German soldiers and then moving on. But they also had first pickings at the loot. Since they had little time and they knew what they wanted, they got right down to brass tacks. The order in which they placed their demands showed what was uppermost in their minds. First watches, then liquor, and then whatever German soldiers might still be around.

I gave him the Longines watch I had received from friends in Switzerland, saying, "Swiss uhrr—charosh uhrr." As he put it to his ear and listened his hard features softened into a parody of child-ishness. He stuck his gun into its sling, pushed it aside, embraced me with both arms and gave me a resounding kiss.

"Russki soldat, kultur soldat!" he exclaimed. That was another tune we were to hear played over and over.

He obviously believed the words. He had been told that the Russian soldier was the most civilized and progressive soldier in the world. They were fighting to avenge barbarian attacks on their people. They were bringing freedom and culture to the world.

He found on my person a few other things he considered becoming to a *kultur soldat*: a fountain pen, a penknife, and a tiny Kienzle alarm clock. He was especially delighted with a small piece of chocolate he found in a corner of one of my pockets. The amiable looting left me lighter in spirit as well as in possessions. I invited the sergeant to come inside. His men looked crestfallen when he forbade them the opportunity of proving that they too were *kultur soldaten*. He ordered them to wait outside.

Arthritic Aunt Elizabeth could not rise from her chair, but she bowed graciously and welcomed the visitor with her Sunday smile. His answer was to step forward and kiss her very tenderly twice. As though to prove that the kiss was not prompted only by the bright eyes and the gentle face that still showed signs of the beauty it had held in youth, the sergeant went over and bestowed another hearty kiss on Aunt Anna, who had a stubbly chin and a grinning mouth that showed one lone long tooth. Even Uncle Franz, his gray beard uncleaned for a week and now green with snuff, got a hearty buss from the genial Russian.

Vladimir told him there were no German soldiers in the house and that we were all poor, plain, honest people, neither capitalists nor Nazis. The sergeant said he would have to search the house and find out for himself. In the kitchen the first thing that caught his eye was the trapdoor. We had to open it. Sister Imelda came up first, her face as pale as her white nun's veil, but quietly welcoming the

Russian with a friendly: "Sdrasdongtje" (Good day). The dumb-founded Ivan stepped back and made a reverent bow. As the other women followed the Russian kept repeating in a tone obviously intended to be reassuring, "Russki soldat, kultur soldat! Russki soldat, kultur soldat!"

He waved all the women into the parlor, satisfied himself there were no soldiers in the other rooms and then signaled his comrades to come in. They almost provided a cross section of the peoples that make up the Soviet Union. There was a Leningrad Jew, two Mongolians, three other Siberians, a Kalmuck, and a couple of Great Russians. They wore roughly made long heavy overcoats and each carried a submachine gun.

Aunt Anna promised some food and disappeared into the kitchen. The sergeant took over as host and waved his soldiers and our womenfolk to alternate places around the table. Some of the soldiers were left standing, but soon moved within arm's length of the table.

Perhaps because of the tender kiss, Aunt Anna was much pleasanter than she had been with the German soldiers who were our last guests. She went straight to the oven and brought out a large slab of ham she had just been roasting as a basic ration against emergencies. The grease was crackling in the pan as she carried it to the table.

No sooner was the pan on the table than the men had their bayonets out and were hacking off generous portions. They would stab a piece with the bayonet tip, swab it in the grease and lift the whole dripping mess to their mouths. Tracks of grease ran like spokes on a wheel across the table to each man and up on his uniform.

Like the father of a large family, the sergeant sat beaming at the head of the table. When he had had his fill, he pulled back his coat and proudly displayed a row of five or six "Medals of the Red Banner." Then he reached into his inner pocket and pulled out a dirty paper billfold. He picked through the contents and selected a "while-you-wait" snapshot from a Moscow department store. He passed it around for us all to see his fat wife in a Communist uniform with her three children by her side.

The other soldiers became very excited at sight of the photograph. With the help of Vladimir we learned what had set them talking so eagerly about this family group. They had been cut off from all contact with their own family for so long that they had swallowed entirely the current Soviet propaganda that Hitler had destroyed all their homes and slaughtered their wives and children. They were now marching on Germany to seek revenge. They would make Hitler *kaputt*. They straightened up dramatically, put their thumbs under their chins and pushed back their heads to show us how they would hang Hitler when they caught him.

I took the opportunity to suggest it was still a long way to Berlin and they had better hurry if they wanted to catch up with Hitler. One of the soldiers brought me a notebook taken from a dead German soldier and opened it to a map of Germany. I pointed out the line from where we were to Berlin. There were more than four hundred miles to go, so they decided, for all the world as though getting to Berlin were the responsibility of this little patrol alone, to get moving right away.

Their stay had lasted only half an hour. It ended with hearty thanks for our hospitality and promises that they would come back soon and see us again.

We were still stunned at this first meeting with the Soviet soldiers and the unexpected turn it had taken. Aunt Elizabeth broke the tension. She spoke meditatively, as though trying to recall something, but with a mischievous twinkle in her bright old eyes. "It must be about forty-five years since the last, Anna. Eh? Since Robert?" But Aunt Anna refused to take the bait about the sergeant's hearty kiss beyond thumping the dishes she was already clearing away and mumbling uncomplimentary remarks about her unsuccessful suitor of long ago.

THIS first Soviet wave hit us gradually, but it mounted relentlessly to a peak of horror. The occupation troops were granted one hundred hours of license to loot and ravage at will. These unbridled hours let loose lusts that tear the mask of military glamor from the hideous face of war.

Our younger women were back in the potato cellar and they stayed there, uncomfortable but undiscovered, for eighteen hours. All through the long sunny afternoon groups of Soviet soldiers passed across the slushy fields. Many of them stopped at the farmhouse but Vladimir's explanation of my cassock and crucifix disarmed most of them and they passed on. Only once, after the groups had begun to include "partisans" who had joined themselves to the regular soldiers, were we faced with real danger.

Two young fellows burst through the door, shouldered Vladimir aside and pointed their rifles at my breast.

"Schnapps!" they ordered. "We want schnapps right away. Get it!"

Their only uniform was an army jacket over civilian clothes. They had probably been freed from a German farm or from a labor camp and tagged along with the army. They were totally irresponsible and might pull the trigger wantonly at any second.

Vladimir stepped up and spoke rapidly and soothingly to them, the routine that had kept others off. But they waved him aside and continued to point their rifles. Vladimir talked more urgently. He changed to asking them questions and found that they had come from White Russia like himself. His talk softened the boys and calmed them down. They turned around abruptly and walked out.

I found out later how many had been killed by just such drink-crazed boys. One was our most scholarly and famous canon of Frauenburg, Professor Switalski, a priest of Polish descent. He had been shot down by a passing group of drunken youths as he stood by a shed in his garden.

Twilight came and we began to breathe a little easier. The women became impatient of their long stay in the potato cellar.

Theresia pushed up the trapdoor and asked in a whisper, "How much longer do we have to stay down here?"

She got her answer without any words from us. Traute Braun, fourteen-year-old curly haired daughter of the watchmaker, rushed into the house sobbing uncontrollably, and threw herself at my cassock. Not until we had her down in the cellar being comforted by her cousins Margaret and Rosa could she tell her story. It was the story we had all been waiting for and dreading. The first of many.

In the presence of her mother and her sisters she had been raped successively by twelve soldiers who stood in line. Finished with her, they had reached for her twelve-year-old sister. The mother had thrown herself desperately in front of the soldiers. In the struggle, Traute had jumped out the window. The soldiers strapped the mother to the floor and all twelve of them treated her as they had her daughter. Traute had raced across the fields to us.

Our fear that the trapdoor would again be discovered was sharpened. We hit upon the idea of spreading Aunt Elizabeth's mattress over it and putting her to bed on it. About ten inches of the trapdoor still showed. So I spread out my cassock and stretched out over the visible part which was just inside the kitchen door. The only trouble was that the wooden trapdoor was raised about an inch higher than the cement floor. The padding of my cassock made my resting place tolerable. It didn't really matter that it wasn't quite comfortable enough for sleep. We were expecting company.

The hours dragged. Waiting. Waiting. That paralysis of normal thought and normal reaction which is far worse than focused fear. The three septuagenarians and I were trying to pretend we could sleep, and the younger women huddled in their refuge under the trapdoor.

Around eleven o'clock there were voices and footsteps outside. It was almost a relief. I rose and went to the door. A light flashed in my eyes.

They were apparently surprised to come across a young man in this village of children and the old. They jumped to an obvious conclusion I was to face many times.

"German officer?"

"No," I answered, pointing to the cross on my breast.

"Catholic priest."

The flashlight played over me from head to foot. No other word was spoken.

An officer with two golden stars on his shoulders stepped forward and I led him into the parlor. He was no more than five feet tall, but very energetic, erect, and well-disciplined. Dark sparkling eyes gave his face an appearance both businesslike and military. Other soldiers followed him.

He lit the kerosene lamp and unfolded a map on the bureau which had served as an altar just the day before. He beckoned and asked me to point out our position. It was the most detailed map I had ever seen, all in colors. Even our little farmhouse was clearly marked. All the village names were printed in Russian characters. When I had shown him where we were, he dismissed me with a curt, "Get out!" I went back to my place on the kitchen floor along the edge of the trapdoor.

The din outside grew louder: stamping and shuffling feet, voices, equipment being dragged around. The parlor next door sounded full of people and movement. We began to hear the clicking of a telegraph. For the rest of the night the noises kept on. Boots banged up and down the stairs to the attic; there was a continual thumping overhead.

Aunt Anna couldn't stand it anymore. Her remaining slabs of bacon were up there, all her good linen, oats, rye, the wheat flour she used only for cakes, her sewing machine. She was sure they were carting everything away, and not all our shushing could keep her from mumbling what she thought of them. She was up rattling around the stove when the kitchen got its first visitors.

They were two lady sergeants in the gray-green uniform of Soviet women soldiers. Both were beautiful and about twenty years old. One was tall and slender, the other a typical peasant, short and chubby. They had blond hair braided around their heads in a crown. Their uniforms looked tailor-made and were neat and well pressed. Slung across their breasts from their left shoulders were brand new submachine guns.

Aunt Anna grumbled about having to make way for them while they scrambled some eggs. From time to time a soldier would stick his neck in the door and the stout girl would play up to him by making fun of me. I could not understand her words but there was no mistaking the kind of laugh they brought on. Otherwise the women did not bother us and they appeared to command the respect of the rank and file soldier.

Around three in the morning two rough looking soldiers appeared in the doorway and shouted at us, "Kartoshki" (potatoes). All our potatoes were under the trapdoor we were desperately hoping to conceal and it seemed an impossible thing to say that this farmhouse had no store of potatoes. The men made an eerie picture that added to our fear. They were carrying two lighted candles pointed straight out like flashlights and the guttering light flitted queerly across their grim faces. We remained silent, pretending not to understand. Wax from the queerly held candles kept dripping over my cassock and the coat that covered Aunt Elizabeth.

Getting no answer from a third round of shouting, the soldiers stepped right over Aunt Elizabeth, chased Uncle Franz and Aunt Anna out of the kitchen and started to make a search. We held our breaths as they pushed the burning ends of the candles down to the floor, obviously looking for a trapdoor. I prayed Archangel Michael that he would guard the entrance to the cellar where the women, the girls, and the nun were hiding. Down below, the women could hear every sound in the kitchen. They would be praying their rosaries through fingers moist with perspiration.

After about ten minutes the soldiers gave up their search and stepped over Aunt Elizabeth, myself, and the mattress on their way out.

At dawn we were allowed to go outside for five minutes. The whole yard was in disorder. Most of the garden trees had been sawed down during the night. Six five-inch guns stood in position out in the fields. Horses, wagons, and sleighs were scattered about and some one hundred fifty soldiers were busy sorting out their booty.

All morning the parlor hummed with telegraph signals and field telephone calls to and from other units. About noon the tempo of the messages quickened and there was an obvious reaction of excitement. Men went running about the parlor, voices rose, and we began to hear commands being shouted outside, "Pa-yekhli! Pa-yekhli!" With surprising dispatch, wagons, gun mounts, and sleighs were in position and started moving down the road. The house began to empty and I looked out on one last sleigh that waited in front of the door. Up on top of it was the yellow suitcase I had hidden away so carefully. But more important still, beside the suitcase was the little black box that held my chalice. Their rummaging must have been thorough to uncover that from under the peat pile. The sleigh remained there and I had to stand looking on. Finally one of the women sergeants came out of the house with an officer. Both boarded the sleigh and it drove off.

It had hardly got out of the yard when the trapdoor was pushed up and we raised it to let Theresia come into the kitchen. I was very impatient with her for taking such a risk. But she would not go back down. Instead she insisted on going into the next room to see if some things she had hidden were still there.

The trapdoor was barely closed again when an angry soldier with a drawn pistol leaped through the doorway and poked a square of starched linen in my face. "Monashka," he spat out. "Where is the nun?" His face, a contortion of black rage and lust, stunned me

more than his words and action so that I could not get out a word
in answer. I shall never be able to forget that expression. He waved
the nun's headgear in front of me and let a flood of obscenity spill
from his mouth. It was only with great effort that I managed to
keep from showing the real fear that penetrated me. I just managed
to blurt out very stupidly, "Eat or drink? Some milk maybe?" He
spoke another string of filthy Russian words I was to hear day in
and day out during the coming year. Then he glanced out the window, saw his unit disappearing and ran to catch up with it. Out in
the yard, he stopped suddenly, wheeled around and stamped the
ground in diabolical madness. He had caught a glimpse of Theresia
through a side window and decided she was the nun he had been
looking for. For another dreadful second our fate was at the mercy
of a berserk man's whim. He pulled a hand grenade from his belt
and wound up to aim it at the window. Then, quite inexplicably, his
arm stopped in mid-motion and he turned round to race after the
disappearing sled.

Theresia was pale when she came back into the kitchen. I had
no trouble getting her to return to the cellar.

But we still had to restrain Aunt Anna. She had started to swing
her broom over the floor practically on the heels of the soldiers.
Her housekeeper's zeal had something to work on this time. Every
drawer in the house had been ransacked. Anything not taken had
been thrown to land where it would. Feathers from slashed pillowcases were blowing everywhere. The floors were littered with straw.

When we felt it was safe to go outside we found Lydia safe in
her hayloft hiding place but too frightened to come down. I went
looking for any hosts and wine that might have escaped the pillag-
ing. From the heap of rubbish I picked out three small medicine
bottles marked with a skull and cross-bones in which I had hidden
some wine. There were some unconsecrated hosts scattered about
the floor, and then, to my great relief, I found untouched the little flat cardboard package I had filled with small hosts. We sent a

message to our neighbor to pass word that there would be Mass after dark for any who could make their way to the farmhouse.

About forty people managed to avoid the soldiers who were still coming and going. The stories they brought made a litany of suffering.

The poor old men of the Volksstrum who had not been drafted into the regular army, who had never fired one shot even as civilian guards of their own homes, had been rounded up without exception and taken prisoner. The Russians had complete lists of their names. They had been told that they were needed to clear away debris from the streets and to put things back in order. But they knew better. Each took along food and a blanket for the long road they saw ahead. They were right. Mrs. Hoppe was to learn four years later, through another prisoner, that her husband had died from starvation in a Siberian coal mine six months after his deportation. She was one of the few ever to hear even that much about their men.

Old Mr. Fischer had been caught in his barn. The soldiers had beaten him unmercifully with gun butts, dragged him into the house, raped his wife and three daughters in his presence and killed young Hans, a disabled veteran who was in bed unable to walk because of a recent operation. Then they had gathered all the women of the vicinity and lined them up outside beside the pit where the fall crop of turnips had been buried. Without warning, one of the soldiers fired four shots at Margot, a girl of fourteen. She fell to the ground and a soldier threw a gunny sack over her. Another Russian noticed she was still moving and tramped over the bag with his heavy boots.

After a closer examination of all the women, the soldiers chose the three daughters of Mr. Fischer to go along to "peel potatoes." Their mother pleaded for them, asking that at least the eldest girl, whose husband had been killed, be allowed to stay and look after her two small children. She pushed the two children forward as proof. One of the soldiers came up, kissed each of the children and stroked their cheeks; he smiled and spoke kindly to them for a little while and then gave orders that their mother should be left behind. When the Russians left the gunny sack was still quivering slightly. Lifting it, Margot's mother found her still alive but bleeding badly from her wounds.

The Nieswandt home lay in an idyllic woodland setting. There were nine children, four of them just recovering from diphtheria. Three soldiers had stamped in making the usual demands. One had grasped the prayer book Mrs. Nieswandt held clasped to her breast and thrown it at her head. Then he grabbed for Maria, whose pretty pink cheeks had turned white with fear. She rushed to her mother and the two clung to each other tightly. The maddened soldier lifted his machine gun and shot a burst through mother and daughter, killing them both.

My good, sturdy, rough-handed Ursula had been killed resisting a soldier who had dragged her up to the attic. Her one-armed father had been shot standing quietly before his wife and daughters.

I listened to the words the torn women were repeating and my heart echoed the questions they asked me: "Why, Father, why? Why does God allow it? Why? To us?"

A china vase was the chalice. It had once held violets and now it would hold the Blood of Christ. One of Aunt Anna's best saucers was the paten, a medicine bottle the wine cruet, the water cruet a teacup. Aunt Elizabeth's bureau, the only piece of furniture left whole in the house, was used as an altar. We had one candle, shaded by a piece of cardboard. The flame was bright enough for me to read the liturgy of the day.

It was the Mass of Sexagesima Sunday with a commemoration of the virgin martyr St. Agatha. The Epistle was St. Paul's to the Corinthians, 2:11–12. I read it right through: "In many more labors, in prisons more frequently, in lashes above measure, often exposed to death..." right down to the end, "And He has said to me, 'My grace is sufficient for thee, for strength is made perfect in weakness.' Gladly therefore I will glory in my infirmities, that the strength of Christ may dwell in me."

I repeated words I had spoken to them before. Our parish was being led along its Way of the Cross to Calvary, a place that has only darkness to offer human understanding. There is no human consolation to seek; none to be found, Christ alone will give to us the answer to these days. Our way of walking now is to look up to Him and suffer in dark faith. In His grace we will learn to unite ourselves to His sufferings, to offer our pains in expiation not only for the sins of these drunken and enslaved soldiers, but also for all the sins ever committed by ourselves and our own people. All forty received Holy Communion.

It was getting light as the little congregation faded over the fields to their own farmhouses. I made ready at once to go out and seek wherever I could find the remainder of my flock. I gathered together my new Mass kit with its china chalice and its pocket edition of the daily missal. Then, not knowing when I would be stopped or what would happen to me, I took all the identification papers I could find—graduation diploma, birth and ordination certificates, and driver's license.

CHAPTER IV : *Last Days in Suessenberg*

SISTER IMELDA WAS A NURSE AND SHE INSISTED ON coming with me to give what aid she could to the sick and wounded we would surely find. "This is why I have survived," she said. So she laid aside her nun's habit, put on the ample dress and the babushka style headgear of a peasant woman and accompanied me on this grim parish visitation.

The St. Roch road leading into the village was strewn with the litter of war. Three dead horses torn open by dogs and crows lay in the middle of the road. It was lined with stalled trucks and burned automobiles, German and Russian.

The houses were menacingly empty and still. As we approached the home of Robert, our caretaker, gravedigger and bell ringer, we heard our first indications of life and movement. We pushed through the door, expecting to greet Robert and his wife, but found instead that the only living thing in the house was their big fat pig grubbing through a shambles of discarded loot. There was no sign of Robert, no sign of his wife and no sign of life from the neighboring houses.

The schoolhouse was a ruin from two direct artillery hits, one through the wall, the other through the roof.

The hill to the church was in sight when a patrol of three mounted Cossacks galloped through the silence toward us and drew rein some way ahead. Remembering my principle of showing no fear, I walked straight up to them and said I was pastor of the place on my way to my church and rectory. They were reserved but not unfriendly as they waved us on. I began to take hope. We would be able to see this thing through if only we did not lose our nerve.

But only a few steps later the chills came back into my spine. Two still figures were standing across the street staring at us. One was a Mongol gunwoman with horrible yellowish features. She was leaning motionless against a fence. Only her hands moved and they were coddling a pistol. Her face, wooden and expressionless, was much more frightening than had been the sight of three armed Cossacks riding down upon us. About five paces behind her, just as motionless and also holding a pistol, an officer leaned against the front door of a house. They were so sinister that I felt absolutely certain that either walking past them or turning away from them would bring a bullet in the back. The only course left was again the bold one. So I walked straight across toward the woman, with Sister Imelda at my heels.

Even when I stood within arm's length of her and started to speak, the woman held her pose. The face and body might have belonged to a carved figure, only the hands kept toying with the pistol. Loudly enough for the officer to hear, I repeated what I had just told the Cossacks.

There was no reply. Neither of them gave any least indication of having heard what I said. They just held to their gangster poses and cold stares. We faced them for a moment, waiting. Then we turned and began walking slowly up the road, not knowing what would happen. After fifty dreadful steps we reached the deserted and ransacked village store and stepped quickly inside.

The rectory and church lay just across the meadow in which we had held our feast day outdoor Mass. The meadow looked different now. It was filled with junk, including some things that had been our most cherished belongings only a few days ago. There was a carved cedar chest. My sister had been very proud of it and of the things that she put into it. She had used it to store her needlework piece by piece as it was completed, and the beautiful hand-woven cloth that came from her loom. Every window of the rectory had a heap of rubbish under it. The biggest pile was crowned with the broken and twisted instruments of the parish brass band.

I looked listlessly at the mess. I could not help wondering where all that rubbish had come from anyhow. With no particular feeling, I picked up a small book. It was my sister's small New Testament and I pushed it almost automatically into my pocket.

The inside of the house was something I could have cried over had I not been dry of tears. The little center of living I had started to put together so proudly such a short time ago had been given the same treatment as Robert's home and the village store. Here it was my own plans, my own dreams, my own hopes that had been pulled down to make a wreckage heap of filth and disorder. The abuse of these inanimate things gave me a dead, empty sense of the evil of wanton destruction.

Curiously enough, most of the religious pictures and even the crucifix still hung on the walls. But I found in the rubble one torn fragment of an original portrait I had prized highly. An artist friend had caught my ninety-five-year-old grandfather unaware and painted to the life his rough hands and his fine white head. The fragment I found showed part of one gnarled finger looking very much like the root of a tree. Those hands had been hard-working peasant hands, not in the least "capitalistic."

The sight of the books hurt sharply. A few that had missed the window sprawled across the floor, sprinkled with blotches of cooking fat. One of them looked like a plucked chicken. It was Nestle's New Testament in Greek and Latin and big batches of it had served as a burnt offering. The pages were just the right size and the paper a suitable consistency for rolling cigarettes.

Our visitors had apparently cooked, eaten, slept, and performed all their bodily functions wherever they had happened to be at the moment. The stench was unbearable. We went outside and gulped in some fresh air.

We passed through the gap in the hedge and were approaching the church when Sister Imelda saw it first and rushed ahead of me. It was a corpse on the ground outside the front door, arms stretched out in the form of a cross, fur jacket crumpled under the head torn by a jagged wound. It was Uncle Keichel. He had said he came to die.

I knelt down in the snow beside him, sprinkled him with holy water and began to pray. Sister Imelda interrupted me. The gunwoman and her companion were coming slowly up the hill.

We hurried into the church and down to the altar. The main aisle was scattered with shreds of my best Sunday chasuble and stole. Broken candles and candlesticks covered the sanctuary floor. The tabernacle door was open and lying before it on the split altar stone was the ciborium, smashed and twisted into a shapeless mass. Over the altar the hand-carved wooden canopy had been split into half a dozen pieces and the same ax had evidently been used to chip the entire altar surface and crack the stone of consecration in two. Near the communion rail a statue of St. Joseph that some native craftsman had carved out of wood two hundred years ago lay face down on the floor, both arms broken off in the fall.

The only peaceful sight in the church was the altar of the Blessed Virgin. Her statue stood untouched looking down on the scene with an expression that seemed to remember the words of the prophet, "And there shall be in the temple the abomination of desolation" (Dan. 9:26).

We went out the back way, down the hill, silent with our own thoughts. A solitary hen was proudly picking her way through the new exciting piles of rubbish in the meadow. This particular hen had always liked to be independent and wander off alone. Now all her fellows had been eaten or used for target practice. She was the sole survivor. Nothing that happened had put one crimp in her strut. It gave us a much-needed lift watching her, so alive, so natural.

On the St. Lawrence Road we heard the sound of horses' hoofs and iron wagon wheels coming toward us from the direction of Stolzhagen. They brought me my first sight of a Soviet commissar. There were three of them pressed together on the front seat. Their bloated and twisted faces looked horrible. They were written all over with the drinking and raping that had gone on through the night. Anticipating a question about why we were walking away from the village, I shouted out as they came abreast and told them something about going to Stolzhagen to find out if Father Langwald was safe. They waved us on without even slowing their trotting horses.

But when the Stolzhagen road dipped into the valley and we stopped at the farm of the Werrs, Ursula's family, I found that I would have to wait for news of Father Langwald.

Mrs. Werr led me to the chicken coop and pointed to a mound of freshly turned earth. "Please bless them, Father. We had to bury them here."

The soldiers had compelled them to bury Ursula and her father at once and this had been the only ground not frozen solid.

"Father," said Mrs. Werr, "there are some dead in every house around us. There is work for you that will take days. Why don't you stay at our house while you are doing it?"

We went back to the house past a cow and two pigs that had been slaughtered and left lying with only a few cuts taken from each, the land of waste that is an unforgivable sin to those for whom three animals mean food for a year. Inside the front door the house was in the same condition as the other ravaged homes we had seen. The Werrs had decided to leave it that way to discourage other marauders.

Monica, the most talented and vivacious of the four Werr daughters, told me of their second experience with the Russians.

Just after they had buried Ursula and her father a detachment of three hundred men arrived at the farm. The officer in charge came at once to the door and assured them no harm would come to them from his men. He assigned the women one small room as their quarters and set three guards to protect them. Perfect order was maintained all night and this proved to be the only room in the whole village that was not pillaged.

After Mass next morning Sister Imelda and I started out to bury the dead and comfort the living, or at least to try. At every farmhouse we heard variations of the same story of looting, destruction, rape, and murder.

We learned that our first occupation directive had been issued. It began with a long preamble that the joyous day of our liberation had arrived; we were on the threshold of a bright new world. Then it went on to say that no one was to leave the village, no one was to travel on any road, no one, in fact, was to leave his house. We were to await further orders. I could not let that stop me from going to my parishioners. But when we slipped safely back to the Werrs that night I told Sister Imelda that she must not come with me anymore.

During the next few days I was able to come and go. My only trouble came from a single group of three Soviet officers and it started one evening after I had returned to the Werr home.

A captain and two corporals came stamping up to the door and strode right past me when I answered it. They walked whistling through the debris from room to room. Back in the living room, they thumped the piano with their mittened hands and seemed quite at ease as they accepted bread and butter and coffee from Mrs. Werr. But the captain's eyes kept roving around the room. He was particularly intrigued by my cassock hanging to dry beside the stove and the crucifix sticking from my jacket pocket. I did my best to explain I was a priest and produced some liturgical books in evidence. The captain, however, proceeded to make his own inquiry by digging into my pockets. He appropriated my last pencil and a couple of handkerchiefs. Then he came across a little booklet provided to Russian workmen in Germany. This was a very practical little dictionary carrying Russian and German words under an illustration of what they stood for. He was so delighted with it that he began studying it at once.

When he went back to his search he found my graduation and ordination certificates and my doctor's diploma. The last one was the hardest to explain. He straightened up at the word "doctor" and could not be convinced that a doctor's degree in theology had nothing to do with medicine. He put the first two certificates aside, folded up the doctor's diploma and prepared to leave with his two companions. But on an afterthought he picked up the graduation certificate, tore three pieces from it and passed them to his fellows. The smooth paper had attracted him. They grabbed for their tobacco pouches, poured tobacco onto the paper, rolled it, licked it, and lit their *papirossi*. As I watched the certificate of which I had been so proud go up in smoke, I thought of the ceremony at the coronation of a new pope at St. Peter's in Rome, when a batch of flax is burned before him with the words: *Sic transit gloria mundi.*

At dawn next morning we had more news of our three friends. One of the tasks that lay before us that morning was finding a burial place for the body of a neighbor, Mrs. Kastellan. Before we could get to that another neighbor, Mrs. Neuwald, came stumbling to the door on half-frozen feet. The same three officers had visited her home after they left us. To escape the captain, she had leaped from a window and hidden in a peat bog until she could get over to us.

A little later there was noise and shouting at the front door. I went over to see what it was about. The minute I stuck my head out, it was whacked by a thick, heavy strap. I was so dazed that it took me some time to understand that the wrought-up men were our visitors of last evening and they were shouting, "Ruki vyerkh." (Hands up.)

The captain's face was distorted with rage and he waved a pistol threateningly. They ordered everyone outside where they lined up all the women, including some refugees sheltered in the back rooms. Then the captain came over to me. Pointing his pistol at my breast, he shouted furious and unintelligible words. Every few phrases were punctuated by stinging slaps on my cheeks with his leather gloves with which he kept gesturing toward the Neuwald farm. It dawned on me that he wanted Mrs. Neuwald. He had not recognized her in the line of standing women and she was apparently unaware of her danger. I had to think fast.

Pointing to the body of Mrs. Kastellan, I said as calmly as I could, "That dead woman you see there is not from the farm you are pointing at. She is from that other one over the hill."

He was taken aback for a moment. Then he worked up his temper again, struck me several times with his gloves and smacked me over the head with the butt of his pistol. He pointed more emphatically than ever at the Neuwald farm and ordered me to tell him where the woman was who had jumped out the window the night before. He said he was interested in a live woman, not a dead one.

Just as definitely I repeated what I had said. "Even if you were to shoot me, it would still be true that the dead woman on the hillside does not come from that farm but from that one."

Very angry, and obviously suspicious of my stupidity, he snapped the safety catch on his pistol, walked around behind me, kicked me in the seat of the pants with his heavy boot and prodded me toward a pile of straw between the woodshed and the chicken coop.

The faces of my people were white with fear. I gave them my last blessing and recommended them and all my parishioners to the Good Shepherd. On my way to the straw pile I walked past Mrs. Werr and could hear her saying over and over again, "Jesus, Mary, and Joseph; Jesus, Mary, and Joseph."

I thought of the Mass I had said less than an hour before and tried to surrender myself to God's holy will. Strangely enough, I was not conscious of any overwhelming fear. I felt rather calm. Against all the rules of the catechism, I forgot all about saying an Act of Contrition. In what I thought would be my last minute I just managed to say half aloud, "Glory be to the Father and the Son and the Holy Ghost; as it was in the beginning, is now and ever shall be, world without end. Amen."

At the straw pile the captain made me turn around and face him again. With cold emphasis he repeated his question, telling me that this was my last chance. "You can shoot me if you want to," I told him, "but the woman lying there is not from the farm you are pointing at. She is from the other one over the hill."

For a moment he hesitated. The tense stillness was broken by the sound of a carriage rattling into the yard. Two officers, the elder a commissar of higher rank, stepped out. In brusque military tones the commissar asked the captain, "What are you doing there?"

Since the first hundred hours of license were over and military discipline was supposed to prevail, the captain did not dare say what he had really been about. He gave an involved answer in which I could make out only that he was claiming to have discovered that I was a *vratch*, an army doctor.

I jumped at the chance to get away from the captain's pistol. I called out to the commissar, "Nix vratch...pope, documenti!" (I'm not an army doctor. I'm a priest...and I have papers to prove it!) I took out my driver's license, the only paper I had left in my pocket, and walked over to the superior officer holding it out.

He took it in his hand and pretended to read it. Then with an air of superiority he ordered the captain: "Let him go. He's just a foolish harmless priest, not worth a grain of powder."

When they had gone we went back into the house and I asked everyone to join in praying a Te Deum with me.

I spent the rest of that day helping to grind meal, as we were almost out of bread. The business of doing ordinary things while knowing that at any moment someone might decide to jump in and shoot you was fantastic. Not all nerves could stand it. It was the Neuwalds, of all people, who decided that my presence was bringing danger on them all and it would be safer for everyone if I would leave the house. Mrs. Werr, on the other hand, insisted as before that I remain for at least one more day. She argued that my sudden disappearance would bring more trouble on them. Nobody objected when after further discussion the Neuwalds decided that they would leave.

While we were threshing a batch of grain in the barn that afternoon Monica provided us with a diversion. She burst into a fit of laughter and threw herself down on a pile of straw. She could hardly control herself enough to point to the cause of her outburst. A long-handled bedpan was lying in the straw at her feet. This household veteran of many years' service in the sickroom had evidently been recently raised to a new dignity. The Russians had used it as a frying pan.

That evening the Soviet captain and his officer friends returned as nonchalantly as if nothing had happened. As on their first visit they walked whistling through the house, thumped on the broken piano and sat down to a glass of milk and some fresh baked bread. But they weren't hungry. They got up and left as abruptly as they had come.

Next day we learned that more men had been taken away. They included our seventy-three-year-old burgomaster, Mr. Fugh, the blacksmith, Mr. Gorgs, and sixty-year-old Mr. Greif who was so ill that he had to be abandoned to die in a ditch just five miles outside the village.

The Mass of Quinquagesima Sunday gave us in the Gospel these words for our meditation: "Behold we are going up to Jerusalem.... And they understood none of these things, and this saying was hidden from them; neither did they get to know the things that were being said" (Luke 18:31ff.).

The next week's round of similar experiences was broken by

two notable happenings. A poster went up containing our "further instructions" and a Russian doctor arrived in the village.

After studying the miserable, barely legible print of the poster, we made out the following:

(1) The commanding general of the Second White Russian Army ordered under penalty of long imprisonment or death that all people of the village appear before the new Komendatura in Wernegitten to be registered.

(2) All men between the ages of seventeen and fifty would be drafted into the Second White Russian Army. They were to bring along a set of clothing for winter and another for summer, a mattress, and food for fourteen days.

The doctor was the first our village had ever known. He set up shop in Bertha Poschmann's house and people reported that he was as friendly as he was busy. The only trouble so far had been that all his patients, about thirty-five of them, died during his first week with us.

I decided to pay him a visit and try to find out from him what the notice meant. Did they really expect everyone—the children, the women, the aged, and the sick—to go in person to Wernegitten to be registered?

At the door of the Poschmann home I found an elderly soldier tinkering with a bicycle that was very familiar to me. I had fallen from it the night Bertha Poschmann raised the alarm. A guard ushered me into the "operating room." The big dining-room table had been opened to its full length. At the far end stood two pails. A handful of surgical instruments and a bottle of disinfectant lay on a chair and there were some more bottles on the window sill.

Lying in the middle of the table was a naked Mongolian soldier undergoing an abdominal operation and groaning in pain. He was held in position by another brawny soldier with very dirty hands. When the doctor noticed me he motioned with the surgical knife that I should go into the adjoining room.

After the operation he stepped briskly in to join me, asked me to sit down and offered me a large piece of newspaper and some tobacco to roll a *papirossa*.

When I told him I presumed that he would be the ranking officer here and that I was relieved at the thought of some authority being established, he smiled approvingly. I then asked for permission to bury the dead.

"Bury all you want," he said. "I'm glad somebody's taking care of that. It could cause pestilence."

He pointed through the window to a Russian soldier lying near the ruins of a burned house. "Would you be kind enough to bury him too?"

When I said I would, he went on, "But don't give him an honorable burial or a decent grave. He was a criminal."

We had quite a long talk and I was chilled at the direction it took, at its evidence of evil producing evil. The horror of it was symbolized by the doctor's fingers, as grimy with blood and dirt as his once white coat. He spoke with brutal candor about Russia's answer to Hitler's criminal policies toward the Slavic and the Jewish races. He gave the impression of patiently explaining something to a child as he multiplied stories of SS brutalities. He did not seem to have any realization that Germans, Christians as well as Jews, had been the first victims of Hitler's brutality. It became frighteningly clear to me how we Christians were caught in these devastating floods of common guilt. Forced to suffer punishment of the guilty, our only chance to break the onslaught of evil was by accepting the suffering and atoning for its cause.

My host went on, "Your women are the booty of the Russian soldiers. Hitler tried to build a race of his own invention. Stalin will destroy that race. German women and Russian soldiers will produce a good race."

I asked him about the order for all to report to Wernegitten. He said there could be no exceptions.

"May I reopen my church?"

"That is not in my power. You will have to ask the Komendatura in Wernegitten about it."

On my way out I saw that the patient was still stretched out on the table. His naked limbs had turned blue and his groans were weaker. Even a healthy man would have turned blue if left to lie naked in that frigid room.

On Ash Wednesday morning I blessed the ashes made from the willow branches which take the place of palms in our country. As I made the sign of the cross with ashes on their foreheads, I prayed over my people, "Remember man, that thou art dust and into dust thou shalt return." Then I reminded them that faith always looked forward from things present to those that are to come, to the joy of Easter which always follows Lent and Good Friday.

In Wernegitten I went first to look up Father Teschner. I found the old priest in the attic, very much alive and eager to have an audience for his dramatic story.

"The first of them to come," he said, "were Siberian guards and their commander was a devil out of hell. As soon as he found out I was the priest he waved at a soldier and yelled, 'Take the old so-and-so out and shoot him!'

"The soldier kept prodding me with his rifle till he had me up against the door of the chicken coop. But all the time he kept saying, 'Don't worry, little old man, don't get excited. You're going to be all right.' Then he lifted his rifle to his shoulder, sent three shots whistling past my head and then whispered urgently, 'Get inside that chicken coop, you fool.' I scrambled inside and he went back to the house to tell the commander he had shot me.

"After dark I got off into the woods and stayed at one of our farms till the next commander let me come back to the rectory."

The good old man warned me not to go near the Komendatura or I would never get out of it free. But that was why I had come to Wernegitten.

I walked toward the Komendatura headquarters at the school-house and my first meeting with established Soviet authority as opposed to the passing individuals and groups we had known so far. These would be the people who would determine what would be done with us. At the door I heard the lively notes of an accordion and by heading in the direction of the music I found an official. He was a sergeant wearing the green and red insignia of the Soviet secret police, the MVD. Sitting very close to him was the accordionist, a Polish girl whose only uniform was a cook's cap. There was little sign of law or order here.

Although the girl held no rank and had apparently been picked up as an interpreter, she seemed to run the place. The sergeant told me that the notice meant exactly what it said. All the men would be drafted, everyone must come to Wernegitten to register. There would be a postponement because the registrar was too drunk to write. But all must report on the date set, a matter of three or four days, or soldiers would come to get them. I thought I might as well state my own case at once. The rules of the Red Cross Convention forbade my being drafted into the army on two counts. I was a pastor active in my work. I had only one lung functioning and my physical condition was such that not even Hitler had drafted me.

The woman gave me my answer from behind her accordion: "In Russia we don't need any popes and in Russia there are no invalids. They'll grow you a new lung when you get there." I left feeling certain that we would be deported and that there were only a few days left.

The next few days were even worse than those that had gone before. They were filled with the stink of death.

Most of the day was spent in burying the dead. At night we gathered where we could and offered Mass when the Soviet soldiers were too busy carousing to bother us. One of the tragic scenes of those days had a macabre irony of its own. It was in the home of a wealthy farmer who had been notorious in his mistreatment of refugees and the Italian "Badoglios." We could get into the place only after a series of looting bands had finished with it. A pig and a calf were making themselves at home in the parlor. Fine clothes and family pictures were covered with their filth as was the paper money, including thousand-mark bills from the days of Kaiser Wilhelm which strewed the floor. Between the parlor and the next room lay the bodies of the farmer, his wife, and his elder brother. The animals had obviously been clambering over them and tearing at them. Cupboards that had been stuffed with sacks of freshly spun wool lay open. The looters had cut open the sacks in their search for valuables, flinging aside the huge balls of soft wool. Some of the balls had rolled up against the corpses so that the wool the avaricious man had refused his freezing refugee tenants kept clinging to him even in death.

A handful of old men went silently with me to the hill called Ziegenberg at the entrance to our village where our soldiers had made their last stand. About half a dozen still lay there unburied. When we examined them for identification we found that someone had already looted them. But even for those who no longer had their dog tags we found some letter or notebook with their names and addresses. From the letters we could tell that most of them had served throughout the whole war and that they had families back home waiting for them.

The grandeur and the misery of the human race were both represented in this handful of men on the hill. Each was different and each revealed himself in his possessions. The personal effects ran from medals and rosaries to prophylactics and lascivious pin-up pictures. They all went into a common grave with one cross of white birch above it.

On the way back from picking up these bodies we found the body of a Russian soldier who had been run over by the treads of a Russian tank. It had been so pressed down into the mud that it had gone unnoticed till now. As a precaution I went to the Russian doctor and asked for someone to accompany me and identify the body. I recognized the friendly old Siberian guard he gave me. He had walked into Mrs. Hirschberg's kitchen while I was giving Holy Communion to the family, timidly asked for one egg and gone quietly away. Now he waddled beside me over the fields telling me mournfully about his wife weeping and waiting for him in Moscow.

When we got to the body the old soldier did not even notice it at first. A German rifle had caught his eye. He picked it up, tested it like an expert, shot it off and then threw away his Russian rifle and kept the new one. With the bayonet he dug out the body.

It was no wonder the man had been run over by one of his own tanks. They could not have seen he was a Russian. His uniform was buried under two blue civilian suits and a thick fur coat that had belonged to a German motorcycle courier. Every last pocket was filled, but with two items—dishes and razors. Evidently he had specialized in his looting. The old Siberian did not even bother trying to identify the soldier. He merely poked around with his bayonet repeating, "*Voÿna ssla!*—War is bad! His mother will be broken-hearted!"

The burial place was a mass grave which already held thirteen other Russian soldiers. A marker had been carved from a beam and looked like a Cleopatra's needle, about three feet high and six inches square at the base. It was painted blue with a small red tin star at the tip. Several names were inscribed on it and our Siberian friend took great delight in being able to read them off for us. Every Russian mass grave or single grave I saw was decorated with a similar marker.

The First Sunday in Lent would be our last Sunday in Suessenberg. Its liturgy once again spoke like the voice of God in our souls. The Epistle I read my people that morning said: "Let us conduct ourselves in all circumstances as God's ministers, in much patience; in tribulations, in hardships, in distresses; in stripes, in imprisonments, in tumults; in labors, in sleepless nights, in fastings...as dying and behold we live, as chastised but not killed, as sorrowful yet always rejoicing, as poor yet enriching many, as having nothing yet possessing all things" (2 Cor. 6:4–10). The Gradual of the same Mass renewed an eternal promise: "He has given his angels charge over thee, to keep thee in all thy ways. In their hands they shall bear thee up, lest thou dash thy foot against a stone... thou shalt not be afraid of the terror of the night" (Ps. 90: 5, 11).

The "terror of the night" seemed indeed to be upon us. Despair and fear in the soul, misery of every kind in the body, desolation all around. All of us had loved ones dead or sick or violated or still in danger. But in the midst of this death we had supernatural life, faith, rising like a green tree on a grave in the churchyard. We could understand, however vaguely, that suffering has an end within itself and that end is mature faith. Where we suffer God, no suffering from elsewhere can reach us, and to suffer God is joy, peace, and consolation. It even brings a renewal of natural courage and natural strength.

Next morning I said Mass at the Zyball farm, which had been the scene of another gruesome slaughter followed by a Russian act of tenderness. Two Soviet soldiers had come to the house with the usual "Uhrr, schnapps, deutscher soldat" demands. An old man, nervous, excited, and hard of hearing, had stiffened with fear and begun making the sign of the cross. They shot him down before he could finish it. Then they ordered Mr. Zyball and a refugee named Mr. Krause to carry the body to the barn. The soldiers shot the two men in the back as they were bending to put the body on the ground. Grandpa Hippel and another old man about eighty had the misfortune to come into the yard just as the Russians were crossing it. They were ordered into the barn, made to stand beside the other bodies and then killed. The soldiers then took Mr. Schlegel, the only surviving man in the house, and shot him beside the rest.

Shortly afterward another group of Soviet soldiers, led by an officer, came to the farm and asked Mrs. Zyball for her husband. Mrs. Zyball took the officer to the barn and showed him the gruesome sight.

The officer shook his head. "This must be a crime of the SS."

"The SS was not here. Russian soldiers shot down those old men."

The officer still shook his head, protesting that Russian soldiers would not do such a thing. Then he left and came back with a sled loaded with three sacks of wheat flour, two sacks of sugar, and a large side of bacon. He brought it in to Mrs. Zyball and said, "Don't you worry any more. You will have plenty now to feed your children. *Voÿna ssla.*"

Final word had come during the night that all the men in the draft order must report to Wernegitten the next day. We arranged to meet at nine o'clock next morning in the center of the village.

Each of us went off to make his preparations. Back at the old farmstead, Uncle Franz and my Aunts Elizabeth and Anna had gathered together for me all the clothing and food they could manage. My cousin Josef's wife had prepared more canned food than I could get into my knapsack. Mr. Braun, the watchmaker, had added a ten-pound slab of bacon to the pile, but I couldn't take it along.

When I gave them my blessing in the morning Uncle Franz and Aunt Elizabeth had the same last message for me, "We'll meet again in heaven."

"What about you, Aunt Anna?" I asked.

"Oh," she said, "I'll be seeing you again here on earth. I'm going to survive."

I made a last pilgrimage up the hill to the little church I had come to so hopefully just five months before, to "my" church. Kneeling on the altar steps, I recommended my scattered flock to the Good Shepherd. I asked Him to remain present in the hearts by faith and love even though He could no longer be with them in His own home. "And please," I prayed, "in Your mercy and goodness bring us back together in this place some day from wherever we may be driven over the face of the earth."

I took a last leave of the church of my village, loving it even as it stood now—the shell hole in the roof and the broken windows; the rectory littered with debris; my study, its treasures thrown out the windows; the processional paths leading from the three neighboring parishes; the once peaceful meadow; the path on which I used to walk saying my breviary; the sunny hillside garden.

On the road to Wernegitten began the blessed reality which continues as I write. I became, not the parish priest of a settled little village in an all-Catholic land, but a pastor of the Wandering Church "which has no remaining city."

CHAPTER V : "...Into the Pit"

WE WALKED THE THREE MILES TO WERNEGITTEN STILL trying to believe that the registration would only be a counting of heads and that we would be assigned, as we had been told, to some work in our own region. If some of us realized that this was an empty hope, we were at least certain that some of our group could not possibly be of any use to the Russians. The young man I was walking with, Heinrich Schmidt, for instance, who had lost his sight and one leg in World War II, would surely be sent home.

Our imprisonment began quietly. All the Suessenberg men were directed to a vacant house where we waited until we were called to the schoolhouse Komendatura. There we were lined up to wait our turns to go in for registration in the teacher's living quarters. I led Heinrich before the registrar who was seated at the teacher's desk. Behind him stood the commandant and seated beside him was the girl I had seen playing the accordion a few days before. Over their heads on the back wall hung a large schoolroom reproduction of Hoffmann's "Child Jesus in the Temple."

The girl was knitting as steadily and implacably as the *tricoteuse* who watched the work of the guillotine during the French Revolution. The procedure was all but unbelievable. The registrar asked the questions while the commandant, wearing a very solemn expression and a most imposing uniform, stood stock still behind him. When the questioning was finished and it came time to decide if the man should be taken, the registrar turned and looked, not at the commandant, but at the girl. She answered with a swift downward swish of the knitting needle. I did not see her make any other gesture.

I took Heinrich up to the table and stated the obvious facts that he was blind and had lost a leg. The registrar paused and I looked hopefully toward the woman. Her knitting needle went down as usual. I protested that he was a hundred percent invalid. She answered like an automaton, "In Russia there are no invalids."

I was next. Since I still had two eyes and both legs, I did not bother mentioning things like lungs.

The registration consisted of listing the names and ages of all the men from the villages under the Wernegitten Komendatura. When it was over we were divided into work groups. Most were assigned to looting teams and sent out on wagons to empty the houses in a given area while their inhabitants were in Wernegitten for registration. This gave us a firsthand experience of one version of something that is covered in treaties by the official term "reparations."

Father Langwald was there with his people from Stolzhagen. Both of us were assigned to unloading the loot as it was brought in. The horse-drawn wagons were loaded with furniture, pianos, washing machines, wall clocks, sewing machines, butter churns, farm tools, mattresses, old rusty pumps, and even doors taken off their hinges. We carried into the schoolhouse bags of rye, oats, and barley. I saw many familiar names stamped on them: Zyball, Werr, Funk, Fischer. This was the grain they had been saving for seed in the spring.

Our next job was to get rid of the small mountain of junked cars, carriages, and farm tractors that had been piled up the previous day and were now in the way of newer booty. We had to push them over a steep embankment and let them roll down into the meadow below. Some of them rolled so well that they finished up in a stream at the far end of the meadow. By nightfall the meadow was littered with ruined machines.

The hard physical work might have had the effect of easing sorrow, or at least bringing forgetfulness, were it not for the occasional vivid reminders of what was happening to us. Old Mr. Schmidt, Heinrich's father and the tailor of Suessenberg, led me to a heap of sewing machines and pointed out his old Singer. "Look, Father," he said, "that's mine. For fifty-two years I worked on it to raise and feed my nine children." He had not been on the disposal detail and I did not tell him that after a few days of standing in the snow it would probably be thrown over the embankment with the rest.

Father Langwald and I got another promotion. We were appointed to the burial detail, gathering bodies and disposing of them in a mass grave. In the meadow behind the schoolhouse garden we found six civilians, four of them very young girls, one an older woman. The body of an elderly man was in a pig pen. In a rain barrel behind a farmhouse was the corpse of an old woman. Then we found Mathilde, youngest daughter of the Kramers from Wernegitten. She was lying on her left side in a furrow of a roughly plowed field. Her rigid right arm stuck straight up in the air and a rosary dangled from her frozen fingers.

We put fifty bodies in the mass grave, only fourteen of them soldiers.

ONE morning two guards with drawn pistols entered our quarters and ordered all the men outside. Grabbing my knapsack and my leather bag, I joined the procession and we were lined up two by two in the middle of the road. About ten MVD men were milling about swinging long leather whips, the notorious *nagaÿka*, relics of the time of the tsars. They were arguing vehemently among themselves but we could make no sense of the rapid Russian except for one soldier who was counting us with the help of an abacus. He checked and rechecked and always came up with the same answer: twenty-two.

We had no idea of what was going to happen to us and when we were marched behind a barn we feared the worst. But they only wanted to do a little pilfering out of sight of any superior officer who might pass by. The arguing went on and we stood there for two tormenting hours. Then a horse-drawn wagon loaded with half a dozen bicycles pulled up and some of the guards climbed on. They ordered us to fall in and march behind the wagon as it rolled down the street. There was still no word where we were going or why.

When we were passing the schoolhouse Mrs. Lemke came running out in tears, waving her arms wildly in front of the sergeant who brought up the rear. Pointing to her husband, she said he was sixty-nine years old and begged the soldier to let him stay. Without a word, and without drawing the attention of the other guards, the sergeant called Mr. Lemke out of the ranks and told him to go back to the house with his wife.

We were on the road that led to Heilsberg and marching at such a brisk pace that my three layers of clothing, topped by Mr. Werr's old fur coat, left me bathed in sweat at the end of the first mile. Some of the older men were soon groaning with pain and exhaustion. But we had to march on. I prayed that wherever this march led I would be given some of the opportunities of acting as a priest that had come during the last days in Suessenberg.

We passed through a suburb of Heilsberg and I could see St. Michael's golden statue atop the church steeple shining brightly in the late afternoon sun. The red tile roof of the bishop's castle behind it glowed like fire. The snow sparkled in the sun. But the streets were littered with abandoned sleighs, carriages, carts, beds, luggage, and dead horses.

In Heilsberg the guards stopped the wagon and ordered us to throw our luggage on. Two more hours of fast marching brought us to Grossendorf. We were halted in front of an MVD headquarters and left standing in the cold that had come with the setting sun. The combination of chill and our sweat-drenched clothes soon had our teeth chattering.

We were marched senselessly several times from one end of the village to the other and then back to stand in front of the MVD and wait again. Somebody was going to question us that night but no one seemed to know who. So we went from Pilate to Herod, from Annas to Caiaphas, until someone was ready. A new set of guards took over and had a great time making fun of us. Vodka had loosed their tongues and in their taunting they let slip something we had not been told before: "When you get to Moscow you'll really find out what work is like." All the Russians till then had told us we would be given labor tasks in our region.

It was well into the night when we were herded into two small rooms in the basement of a bombed-out house. The rooms were already occupied by thirty other German civilians and a few Lithuanians and Poles. The cement floor was covered with a thin layer of dirty straw. Since we were locked in and not allowed out, one corner had already been reserved as a lavatory. The stench was nauseating.

In spite of everything I could not help smiling at what I saw in one crowded corner. Father Langwald was seated there, and propped up against him, his head on his shoulder and snoring loudly, was the pastor of Reichenberg, Father Podlech. From his seminary days, Father Podlech had been famous for his stolid nervous system. He could sleep anywhere. It was like living with the familiar again to find him so calmly and characteristically asleep.

One of his parishioners told me of some other aspects of Father Podlech's stolidity. The Russians had tried to force him to tell where some women and girls of his parish were hiding. When he refused they put him up against a wall and fired a dozen bullets around his head. He remained unmoved. They beat him and still he would betray no one. With drawn pistols they drove him through the length of the village and then locked him in a cold barn for four days without food. When they brought him out and questioned him again he told them only that he had appreciated the much-needed sleep. The frustrated Russians had finally set him free and he had continued working for his parishioners until he was shipped off like the rest of us. I was grateful for his healthy snore that night in our basement prison. It made a good cover for the whispered confessions that brought me the consoling conviction that God wanted me where I was.

About two in the morning a guard stomped into the room and ordered us out to the yard. We were sent to an attic at the other end of the village. It had been splintered by artillery fire and was cold and drafty. There was a room boarded off at one end of the attic and we waited to see what it would hold for us. The only one to break the silence was a sixteen-year-old who moved among us repeating with suspicious insistence that he was a prisoner just like ourselves and offering advice:

"The commissar is in the room down there. He has all the records of everything right in front of him: who was in the party, who worked with it, the military lists. Personal information about every one of us, our families, who we are, what we are, what we did, what we own. He knows it all exactly and he's just trying to catch us in a lie. If we tell him the truth everything is all right."

A name was called and the first of our men was led to the room for his hearing. I noticed how many of the men had been drinking in everything the boy had been saying. The boy claimed to be from one of the large bombed cities but his accent told me he was from the countryside in our own region. When the guards called him over to share their greasy soup I started to pass out cautious warnings against him.

Father Langwald was the only one among us who felt in any way optimistic about the interrogation. He was putting great confidence in the hope that his Polish Nationalist League membership card would prove he had worked for the Poles in Germany and clear him of any accusation of collaborating with the Nazis. From my experience with Gestapo investigations I knew it was always dangerous to give information you are not asked for. "It will make them suspicious and they will try to trap you," I told him. "And anyhow, your sentence has already been fixed and it won't do you any good."

I heard my own name called and walked toward the little room. When the door was opened a rush of hot air hit me in the face. A stove was going full blast in the rear of the little room. I was motioned to a chair right beside it. The stifling heat after the ice-cold attic made my head swim.

Across a small table I looked into the face of the commissar. A pair of dark, intelligent, and piercing eyes looked me over thoroughly. Before getting down to business, the commissar poured tobacco into a piece of newspaper and rolled himself a cigarette with his delicate, manicured hands. He made a tidying gesture on his well-pressed green uniform, ran his fingers through his hair and, after spreading four long pages on the table in front of him, motioned for the interpreter to proceed.

The interpreter sat at the right side of the table, between the two of us. He spoke German with a Polish accent. His opening was about what I had expected and prepared for.

"Your name is Gerhard Fittkau?"

"Yes."

"Tell us all about yourself."

I had made up my mind to be accurate and detailed in giving my personal history. I felt that a complete first statement I could repeat on any point would save me from being badgered in cross examination. I named the places I had studied, the subjects and my appointments after ordination.

The interpreter was obviously in trouble. This sort of thing was out of the run of what he had been handling. He apparently had some general idea of what it meant to be a priest but all the different places of study baffled him. And he had no idea of what I meant when I spoke of the time spent in writing a "doctor's thesis in theology."

They started pounding at my years of study outside Germany before ordination. What was I doing in Austria? Italy? Switzerland? I explained, but did not get anywhere. They kept coming back and back on the same questions. Then they shifted to something that seemed to puzzle them even more. How did I explain the years of postgraduate studies in Breslau *after* ordination?

They finally threw the direct accusation that I had been engaged in some sort of special service assignment for the Nazi government. They pinned it particularly on the graduate years in Breslau.

I explained patiently, while the burning hot stove made sweat run down my back, "I don't think the Nazis were in the least interested in a study of the concept of Mysterium according to the mind of St. John Chrysostom."

"But what else did you study there?"

"For my certificate to teach at the university I passed an examination on the Patristic background of the modern liturgical movement. I don't imagine Hitler could have made much use of that."

There was no comment when I added that publication of my dissertation was forbidden by the Nazi laws.

They turned to my family and I gave all the names and occupations, including the rank of the brothers who were in the army. The questions even extended to my uncles and aunts and the size of their farm. It was on this point of capitalists or noncapitalists that the commissar seemed to resolve his doubts about me. Both he and the interpreter looked favorably impressed when they learned that my father's livestock amounted to only one cow and mine to a few hens. I was glad my father had recently lost his second cow and that the goat I ordered had not arrived. It might have put me into another category. The commissar became quite genial and the next question had to do with my becoming a useful member of the constantly expanding Union of Soviet Republics. All that training of mine could surely be put to good use.

I was asked very pleasantly, "Couldn't you give up all this priest business and do something useful in Soviet administration?"

They added by way of explanation that a job as a priest would not fit into the new order. The conversation took me back to one of my Gestapo sessions. Nothing could have made more clear to me the basic similarity between National Socialism and Communism.

It was no help that this time I had to reach the commissar through a fumbling interpreter and could not even present my side of the question decently.

In an evidently well-intentioned attempt to instruct me, he passed along the information that modern science had unmasked the superstitions of Christianity and had indeed proved that Christ had never lived. He went on, "The very foundation of Christianity contradicts itself. You have two Bibles and one opposes the other."

I gathered he meant the Old and the New Testaments. So I told him that I had studied both rather carefully for ten years and never found two Bibles but only one. "The Old Testament," I said, "is to the New Testament what the cellar is to the rest of the house. Only a man who has read neither could speak the way you do."

He admitted he had read neither. I replied since I had read both I thought I would keep my job as a priest. "Christ was not only the greatest figure in history," I continued, "but He still lives. You know that your own Russian people testify to this in their Easter greeting, '*Christos voskresye*—Christ is risen.'"

"Oh, yes," he replied, "I know that somebody started that rumor about resurrecting. But the Jews got it hushed up by paying thirty rubles."

He was quite nice as he closed the interrogation. "You have nothing to worry about. They will release you at the next Komendatura."

"Then why can't I go now?"

"That's not in my jurisdiction. At the next Komendatura there will be a medical commission to examine you. When they find you are not physically fit for the work they have in mind, they will send you back home."

I was still in Ermland at that moment and those words had a hopeful sound. But the phrase, "the work they have in mind," sounded sinister.

When they brought me a four-page transcript of my interrogation I asked for a translation. It sounded harmless enough so I signed without any hesitation.

Father Langwald was having his interrogation when we mustered for return to our cellar prison. He stumbled out just before we left and slumped down behind the chimney. One look at him told me that my examination had been easy indeed. It turned out that his troubles started with the admission that his parish property included three hundred acres of land—sandy land that only had brought him trouble with the tenants among whom it was divided. That had classified him as a capitalist. Then his precious Polish National League card had backfired. It had infuriated the Polish interpreter who turned it into an accusation that Father Langwald had been spying for the Nazis and for the "reactionaries in London." The fact that it was dated before there were either Nazis or a Polish government in exile had meant nothing. They had kept pounding at him for a confession that he was both a capitalist and a spy.

Back in the cellar we got our first Russian meal. It was a five-gallon milk can filled with dirty water from a nearby pond with pieces of ice still floating on top. Father Podlech woke up long enough to pass around a small loaf of bread from the pillowcase that served him as a knapsack. I was able to contribute a few slices of cold bacon. Vomiting and dysentery were the result of this unsatisfactory meal and the reserved corner of the room was frequented more than ever.

New groups were pushed into the cellar until there was no longer any standing room. Then about forty names were called off and
we were ordered outside, lined up in twos and marched back to
Heilsberg. Again we reached our destination bathed in sweat and
again we had to stand around in the cold for two hours.

The misery and helplessness of men completely at the mercy
of others who seem to take delight in toying with them and keeping
them in suspense is something that one who has not been through
it would be completely unable to understand. We were cold, tired,
hungry, sick, and apprehensive. Our wretchedness was driven home
to us by the derisive bullying of two boy guards, one a swaggering
sixteen-year-old, the other a boy about twelve brandishing a rifle he
was hardly big enough to carry. When Father Podlech sat down on
his pillowcase-knapsack the twelve-year-old kicked him to his feet.

We were finally herded into a courtyard where we found some
two hundred fifty victims worse off than ourselves. They were old
men, cripples, boys under sixteen, dressed in dirty rags, tired and
dispirited. Some wore wooden sandals but many had only rags
wound around their feet. The better dressed had blankets around
their shoulders.

After dark we were herded toward another basement entrance.
Elder men who lagged behind were urged on by the tips of leather
whips playing on their backs. A guard threw the door open but the
space before us was already so filled that we could not advance.
Whips kept cracking over the men in the rear until they began
pushing forward with all their weight. The mass of bodies in front
of us gave way and we pressed inside. We were on a steep stairway
leading down to the cellars but we were jammed so closely together
that it was impossible for anyone to fall. The place was so dark that
I could not see the men next to me. I could feel them pressed tight
against me and hear their groans and cries. When we got downstairs
we learned from previous arrivals that we were in the district headquarters of the MVD.

Body heat made the packed basement very warm. In spite of this, or perhaps because of it, I snatched several hours of the first sound sleep I had known in three days. But it was not uninterrupted. A systematic shifting of groups from one compartment in the basement to another went on all night. Men would hear their names called and would have to push their way out of one cell to be marched to another. They seemed to be trying to break up the original groups and put strangers together. After the third of my four moves I found a comfortable resting place on top of a coal pile, only to be called out again. This time I could make out only one familiar face in the room, but I was happy to find that it was Father Langwald's.

He introduced me to two men sitting on the cement floor with their backs against the wall. The first was a man about sixty-five with friendly gray eyes and a forehead full of wrinkles. A white Vandyke beard set off his chiseled features. His hands were folded calmly in his lap, though his head drooped from weariness. He grasped my hand warmly and greeted me with a quotation from the psalms. I finally recognized him as the Reverend Pastor Ebel, Lutheran minister from Roessel.

The Reverend Ebel was well known for his refusal to bow the knee to Baal in the Third Reich. A member of the "Confessing Church," he had chosen to jeopardize his position and his salary rather than to carry out the orders of Hitler's "German Christians" who had been put in control of governing bodies of the Protestant churches in order to replace the Cross of Christ with the swastika. He had once enraged local party officials by offering prayers in his church for his jailed Catholic confreres. Now, in this MVD cellar, he kept urging his fellow prisoners to join in prayer, praising God and asking for resignation to His will.

His companion was Brother Basil from the Franciscan monastery at Springborn. Instead of his brown habit, he was wearing a dirty peasant's coat and a pair of scuffed wooden sandals.

We settled down together and Brother Basil made us at home with Franciscan hospitality by passing around his snuffbox. I thanked him but refused on the grounds that I was already sneezing enough from the thick dust in the cellar. I made my own contribution to the little feast by producing a tin box of my sister's Christmas cookies, now reduced to crumbs. Over our snuff and crumbs the Reverend Ebel found words for what we were all thinking:

"Did the Russians have to come and teach us how to pray together after all these centuries? I can't tell you fathers how much consolation I have been getting from praying with Brother Basil here.

"I think we are getting another lesson in the mysterious ways of providence. Letting us suffer together is perhaps His way of teaching us what we have not learned even by common action against a common foe. It seems that God is using even the powers of hell to show us the way."

His untroubled serenity, the dignity of his words, moved us deeply. I took out the pocket New Testament I had rescued from the scrap heap and we read together the seventeenth chapter of St. John's Gospel, on Christ's farewell prayer for the unity of those who believe in Him.

A young Polish interpreter wearing an aviator's leather helmet came slinking over toward us. Everyone had been giving him a wide berth because he was always nosing around and was exceptionally friendly with the guards. He stood looking at us for a moment and then said, "Mr. Fittkau, come with me."

I pressed my sister's New Testament into the Reverend Ebel's hands and he accepted it gratefully. It was part of the subhuman condition we were going through that we knew that the summons might mean anything.

I followed the man outside and joined some other prisoners in the courtyard to find out that I had merely been assigned to a labor brigade. My first reaction was that it felt good to be out in the open air.

It was almost unnerving to discover that the guard assigned to us was a well-mannered and considerate young man. He marched us some hundred yards down the road to what had been a fine home. He led us to the woodshed to gather armfuls of firewood for carrying into the house.

Inside I got my first glimpse of a Russian bathhouse. The room had been stripped and the furniture thrown into the yard. Three walls were lined with washtubs placed every few feet along low benches. A huge brick oven encasing a farmer's fertilizer tank had been built along the fourth wall. In the center of the room a hole had been smashed through the floor so water could be dumped into the basement.

My working partner turned out to be a talkative young man whose background gave me something of a jolt:

"I was a member of the Communist Party for seven years. My father, a workman from Dortmund, was also a Communist. Under the Nazis we were outlawed and had to go underground. I was turned in by a comrade who had changed his coat for a Nazi job. I got a five-year sentence and afterward they barred me from the army and sent me to a farm in East Prussia."

"That record ought to land you on your feet now," I said. "Maybe you'll be the Communist burgomaster of Heilsberg."

"Does this look like it?" he asked, and pointed to the welts and bloody matted hair on the back of his neck. "That's all I'll ever get for seven years of giving all I had to the party."

I shook my head in disbelief and he rushed on, gathering bitterness as he spoke: "You know what they said? They said I was a traitor to the cause—I didn't do enough sabotage during the seven years. They said I was running away when I let them put me on farm work—I should have gone back in action with the underground!

"It's a swindle! The Nazis are a swindle! The Communists are a swindle! Everything's a swindle! I'm fed up with the whole lot."

I was learning that not all my fellow prisoners would be priests, ministers, and simple farm folk from Ermland.

My next job was with a clean-up squad in a four-story apartment house. It had been occupied by troops and the mess on every floor reminded me of what I had seen back home. After helping clean out the kitchen by throwing all the china out a window, I was sent to the attic with a load of feather beds. Rummaging around, I discovered a small crucifix and put it in my pocket. I found a *History of Germany* half the size of an unabridged dictionary. I recognized it and turned to the last page and read its promise that the Führer was restoring the German nation to its rightful place of honor and power in the world, and all the German people would enjoy an era of great prosperity.

A bright silk evening dress lay on top of the pile of rubbish. I used a piece of broken glass to cut out of it a generous handkerchief almost a yard wide.

Footsteps on the stair made me throw the dress down on top of the book, and in the sight of the two lying together I read a parable. The bright rich dress was a symbol of the glory in which Hitler had promised to clothe Germany. It was now a torn rag in which the maiden Germany could not hide her shame and stood exposed to the ridicule of all who looked on her.

I was sent outside to the water detail. This meant filling an old washtub with water from the dirty pond, pulling it on a sled into the courtyard and dumping it into a large scum-covered caldron. The dirty pond water stirred up the soot that had fallen into the open kettle the day before. This water with some sliced potatoes added to it was boiled to make our meal for the day.

From a basement window some prisoners were holding out containers. By watching our chances we could slip over with a ladle of water. I was trying this when one of the guards halted me with a quick gesture. I pulled up short like a frightened child. But this was a friendly guard, a youngster with a typical round Russian face and a kindly heart. He was merely pointing toward an approaching comrade, one of the lads who liked to beat up prisoners.

When the danger had passed I went over to the window and found a genial red-bearded face beaming up at me. There was a lively sparkle in the man's eyes as he said, "Don't tell me you don't know who I am!" When I explained apologetically that I did not have my glasses on and the light in the basement was too dim for me to make him out, he burst out laughing, "Shame on you, Father Fittkau, for trying to high-hat the pastor of Freudenberg!"

It was Father Josef Kolfenbach, a jovial and hard-working Redemptorist who was well liked by all his fellow priests. I was so happy at finding him that I went back to work with a lighter heart.

We carried more water, shoveled broken glass, and tried to keep out of the way of the more abusive guards until, at the point of exhaustion, we were led back to the basement for the miserable beginning of a horrible night.

So many more men had been packed into our room that the guards had to heave against them with their broad shoulders to make enough space to wedge us in. It was actually impossible to turn around. I had to remain for hours in the position the guard had pushed me into. I was pressed against a miserable wreck of a man who in turn was pressed against the wall. He was suffering terribly from dysentery and had no control of himself whatsoever. All night he babbled unintelligible requests. But none of us could do anything to help him.

I saw in him an example of the breaking-down process that was going on in all of us. The whole unbelievable experience was taking its inevitable toll on mind and body. I had a horrible feeling that everything was slipping away from me and I was becoming insane. I tried to keep my grip on reality by rationalizing that my dizziness was a physical reaction to be expected from what we were going through. My bowels had not moved for eight days. Normal body functions had no chance in circumstances like ours—all day long under whips and taunts and threats, boys throwing rocks at men old enough to be their grandfathers if they saw them trying to relieve themselves, no moment to relax or settle down, constant motion, pain, fear, suspicion, humiliation, and embarrassment that were bound to undermine the physical and moral force of the strongest.

As it began to grow light the cramped misery became even more desperate. I had been edged close to Father Langwald and I told him of the three consecrated hosts I had concealed in the buckle of my suspenders. He felt with me that the supernatural Bread might bring us the strength to keep from breaking down. I broke one of the wafers in half and we gave Holy Communion to each other.

All that day names were called out and new groups lined up outside. Sometimes we would hear the name of a friend we had not known was in the room with us.

Reverend Ebel's name was called and as he squeezed past me to the door he pressed the New Testament into my hand and said, "May the Lord be with you." Before I could make him take it with him he was gone. Erect and dignified, there was no trace of bitterness in his face. It was evident that there stood a man who had already won the fight within himself. His last glance toward me was so full of peace and purpose, so full of resignation, that it put me to shame for my own weakness.

The reshuffling left room for the rest of us to sit down and have a nap.

Among the next crowd pushed in our door were three bewildered boys, all about fourteen. We learned the reason for their bewilderment.

Gerhard, Josef, and Franz were from Bischofstein. They had gone out to get water for Josef's mother when they bumped into some Russian guards marching a bunch of prisoners down the streets. The guards had simply prodded them into line and taken them along too. Now, here they were in this cell after a fifteen-mile march, without knowing why and worrying about not having been able to get a message home to their mothers.

Josef still carried the small milk can he had been taking to get the water. It turned out to be a valuable asset which he put to work immediately. Few of the prisoners had containers of any kind and a water detail was still working outside our window. They made a place for Josef by the window and let him collect water from the passers-by. He would ration this out and receive in return a little piece of bread or whatever other kind of food they happened to have in their knapsacks.

So Josef was able to help his friends by intuitive application of one of the basic laws of prison-camp life. Any small possessions that others might use become a man's capital and he was entitled to make profit from them. A knife earned you a sliver of any food it was used to cut. A needle could be rented for anything the man who wanted to use it could pay.

The boy's position of privilege enabled him to get me a place near the window too. I was there drinking in the fresh air when I saw Father Kolfenbach. He was threading his way behind the fellow in the leather helmet over the boardwalk of varnished doors and broken inlay that had been stretched across the snow. His six foot three swayed from side to side and he was having a difficult time to keep from plunging headfirst into the mud. Even his red beard seemed tired. But in spite of his clumsy walk and the strange surroundings, his thick fur cap, Roman collar, and long black overcoat made him look dignified and clerical. My hand crawled into my pocket and started passing over my rosary, for he was being headed toward the MVD interrogation room.

It was three hours before he came out. The lads, who had been in the same cell with him for a few hours, were delighted to discover that he was being brought this time to ours. He came in rubbing the dripping perspiration from his forehead with his sleeves. He was so exhausted that all he could tell us at first was a hoarsely whispered, "None of us will ever get out of here alive."

The three boys squeezed over to make room for Father to sit on the floor. I pulled over one of my two bags to make a cushion for him. Josef held his milk can to the priest's mouth and gave him a refreshing drink. Everyone offered him something. Father Langwald, after diligent rummaging in his satchel, finally came up with one last dried-up hamburger. "How are we going to divide this?" he asked plaintively. "Six mouths and one little piece of meat."

But the boys refused a share. "We can get all we need with our magic milk can."

So Father Langwald solemnly divided the hamburger into three and we priests had a feast.

"I have a message to give you two," Father Josef said when he had recovered a little. "It comes from the interpreter. He says all priests are going to be released very soon." Then he added in a tone of dry disbelief, "They like to play with us—cat and mouse."

The slinking Polish lad came back again, leather cap still flapping over his ears. This time he had come for me.

He marched me along the alleyway between two rows of dustbins toward a table where another Polish interpreter was sitting. The helmeted lad stuck out his hand and demanded whatever personal papers I had left in my possession. That meant the driver's license that had saved my life, my ordination certificate, and a paper issued by the vicar general identifying each priest of the Ermland diocese.

He handed the papers to the other interpreter and withdrew. When this official looked up his face was friendly and his manner respectful. "I see you are a Catholic priest?"

"Yes. My parish is in Suessenberg."

"Well, I am glad you are going with us. We will need a priest."

"Going where?"

"I'm surprised you haven't figured that out yet. They are not going to release anyone here." Then he added very slowly and softly,

"I was in the Communist Party for five years. This afternoon I had to deliver all my papers just as you did."

The sneaky interpreter came back, handed a fistful of papers across the table then motioned brusquely for me to follow him.

My head felt clogged and the blood was throbbing at my temples. I tried to muster some energy and gather my wits. I did not find it hard to pray, "Take my life into Your hands, O God, and do with it what You will."

It was another small, overheated room with my seat right beside the stove. Another silent officer was in charge and there was a different interpreter. Scarcely was I seated on the stool under a low-hanging, glaring light bulb when the same set of questions as before were hurled at me. I handled them smoothly enough until I was asked what I had preached about in church. When I told the officer I couldn't remember my talks in detail but he could find them in my sermon book back in the rectory at Suessenberg, the interpreter leaped from his chair in such a state of excitement that he came as close as any man I have ever seen to literally foaming at the lips. "You obstinate fool! You liar! I'll help you remember! I'll tell you what you talked about! You were all the time agitating against the Red Army! Against the Soviet Union! Just like every priest!"

The silent officer at the end of the table kept writing steadily, completely undisturbed and showing no sign of excitement. I thought I might be able to calm the crazed interpreter by a little change of direction in my answer. "I'm sure you know better than that. Your German is so good that you must have lived for some time in this country."

"Yes," he came back, "I did, and that's exactly how I know about you priests. I made a point of going to hear the priest in Roessel. I know what I'm talking about."

Roessel! Reverend Ebel's town where the two Catholic priests were jailed for opposing the Nazis? I decided to throw his accusation right back at him.

"Never once in any church in Roessel did you hear a single word against the Russian people."

"Shut up!" he yelled. "I'm doing the questioning here, not you." Then he took a deep breath and, pointing at me once more, with a great deliberation said, "I'll give you just one more chance. Now tell me, what was it you said in your church against the Red Army and the Soviet Union?"

I answered him quietly, "All I ever did in church was preach the Gospel. I do not remember ever having said one thing there against the Red Army or the Soviet Union."

He glared at me and shouted once more, "I'll help you to remember!" Then he dashed out of the room.

He was back in a moment with an MVD captain who started right in to demonstrate his power and prove that he would stand for no nonsense. He picked up a log about a yard long and shook it threateningly over my head saying, "You realize, of course, that I can beat you to a pulp if you keep on telling lies?"

I answered with more boldness than prudence and with more courage than I felt, "If you can prove that I have told you one single lie, I'll give you permission to beat me all you want."

He was a short, thin man and he had the unpleasant trick of holding his face just two inches away from mine when he spoke to me. I could smell his breath and see his glaring pop-eyes without lashes staring right into my own. A few black stumps of rotted teeth did nothing to enhance his beauty.

In a lisping dialect he began a half-hour oration on the glories of the Soviet Army. When he wanted to emphasize a point he gave the log a swish past my head. Between his manner of speaking and my own dizziness I could not make out a word of the speech, except for one refrain that was repeated so often and so forcefully that I could have said it myself at the end. Every couple of minutes he would make a rhetorical pause, thrust his clenched right hand into the air and proclaim triumphantly, "The great Red Army has destroyed Hitler's swine! Now it will go on to wipe out all priests and all other pigs!"

It seemed ages before he came to an end by jutting his face even closer to mine and sputtering at me, "What do you have to say to that?" I asked the interpreter what it was the man wanted. The translation seemed a little brief for the speech but it probably covered everything. "He wants to inform you that the Red Army and the Red Army alone has been successful in smashing and crushing Hitler and all his pigs. And he tells you that it will also smash every single person who helped Hitler in any way."

Then the captain came back and ran through another flurry of words. All I could make out this time was that the Americans had done something.

When he stopped for breath I looked helplessly toward the interpreter. He bowed sycophantically to the MVD man and then said to me in an oily voice that was in contrast with his previous harshness, "Mr. Captain would like to know if you think the Americans will be able to stop the final victory of the Red Army."

The question took me off balance. I showed my bewilderment in my answer: "But I don't know what you mean! The Americans are your allies. They're your best friends. They gave you the trucks you rode into our towns. Why should they stop your victory?"

That set the interpreter into another stamping rage. When he had himself sufficiently worked up he leaned over and spat out between his teeth a single word which he evidently intended as a vile epithet, "Diplomat!"

Then, like a man who felt cheated because he had done his best and got no reward, he turned away muttering, "You are lucky we are so good-natured, otherwise you would be smashed to bits right now."

The captain strutted around the room showing off the shiny tight-fitting boots that looked as if they had belonged to a German officer. He seemed well pleased with his speechmaking although his bald head was red with excitement and he was clearing his throat in a way that showed it was tired and dry from all his yelling. From the far end of the room he flung the log toward the woodpile, dangerously close to my head. Using his broad hand like a squeegee, he wiped the sweat from the top of his head and left.

I thought the interview was over. Then the interpreter suddenly wheeled and pounced on me like an animal catching his prey by surprise. "We know you were a member of the Nazi Party. We know you had connections all the time with the SS. They sent you out of Germany with special orders to spy for the Nazi government."

My eyes were burning from the blinding light. The heat from the stove was nauseating me. My temples were pounding and my eyelids were heavy. I felt rather than understood that this was to be the same thing again, machine-gunning out the same old questions in the hope of drawing different answers. "My God," I prayed, "help me to think and talk straight."

I heard the answers pass my lips as I had given them in the last interrogation. But I seemed to be far away, listening to myself talk.

The interpreter refused to be satisfied. Time after time he came back to the charge that I was sent out of Germany by the Nazis for espionage.

Finally I tried to shake my head clear and reason with him. "Listen! I can prove I had no connection with the Nazi regime. When I went to Rome in 1930 there was a liberal and democratic government in Germany. It was before the Nazis took charge. I was ill in a sanitarium in Switzerland when Hitler came in. How could they have sent me out of Germany to spy or anything else?"

"All right," he spat back, "you say you were not a Nazi. But it still doesn't do any good to play dumb with us. Your people in Suessenberg told us all we need to know about you." Then he got very excited again and pointed a finger dramatically in my face. "You are hiding a book because it is full of lies about the Red Army!"

I couldn't even laugh. "Before writing that book I spent five long years making a careful study of eighteen big volumes of the works of St. John Chrysostom. Not once in all those books did I find a single mention of the Red Army. St. John Chrysostom died in the year 407, fifteen hundred and thirty-eight years ago."

The man's capacity for showing temper seemed endless. He crouched with rage, shook both fists under my face and hissed, "But you are against communism, aren't you?"

"I'll tell the truth even to that," I said. "Yes, I am against communism as it is against our Christian religion. As for the present war policies, I am not informed enough to pass judgment."

There was a signal from the silent officer and I knew my three hours of grueling were over.

I was in no condition to think about it then, but the contrast between the disciplined officer in charge and the crude, ignorant mountebanks who did the questioning leads me to believe that such men are used deliberately as blunt instruments to deliver a psychological beating, a modern equivalent of the thumbscrew and the rack.

The sweat was running down my face and neck onto the soaked fur collar of old Mr. Werr's overcoat. My stiffened legs hardly responded when I was given the signal to get up.

I was told to sign my name to another four long pages of writing. Since they were again in Russian, I once more asked for a translation before signing. When the interpreter had finished his harmless summary I said, "If that is all you have against me why don't you release me? My people need me."

"Keep quiet!" he ordered. "You should be satisfied that you weren't beaten to death for your stubbornness. Nobody needs you in that foolish job. We'll give you a chance to learn how to do some real work."

I felt suddenly ill and weak and disappointed. If they had only given me a sentence so I would know what I had to face.

The guard had difficulty getting me back to my cell. Half-dazed, I wobbled across the courtyard, snatches of Psalm 90 from my last Mass running through my head. "God has given His angels charge over thee, to keep thee in all thy ways." I knew that no matter where these men would lead me, God would be there to protect me.

Father Kolfenbach had no time to offer me the comfort we had given him before he was called away for further questioning. He handed me the bags he had been guarding for me, but before I could get over to the place he had left someone else had slipped into it and I had to find another spot to slump down and rest.

When I had recovered a little I looked around at others who had returned from their interrogations. The usual technique had been to follow the first questions with a few heavy blows and lashes on the back of the head. A little of this and the poor victims began saying whatever the questioners wanted, "confessing" that they had been either Nazis or capitalists. When I looked at their welts and bleeding cuts I realized that my interrogation had been a very "humane" one after all.

Father Langwald had also been deeply moved at seeing these broken men coming back to the cell wet with their own blood. He, who had always been undemonstrative and shy about offering prayers in public, started praying out loud, slowly and in a low voice, repeating the Credo, the Pater Noster, and the Ave Maria for all those who were to be questioned this night.

Just before dawn we heard trucks warming up their motors in the courtyard. A guard appeared and called out a list of names. Father Langwald was on it. When he shook my hand before leaving he left in it a small phial of castor oil and whispered, "Take this about an hour before the next feeding." He tried to smile at me in his mild and quiet way, but his nervous blue eyes betrayed the realization of what lay ahead. "God be with you," and he was gone.

They marched him close by our basement window on their way to the trucks. All we could see were slow-moving feet and legs and the sorry assortment of bags, knapsacks, pillowcases that the more enfeebled men dragged along behind them. None of us inside said a word. We just gaped, and listened to the weird shuffle and bumping of the feet and bags. There was a short pause, then a sudden whir of motors and the noise of trucks rolling out of the courtyard. Then everything fell silent again, both outside and in.

I made good use of Father Langwald's parting gift and felt such wonderful relief that despite all that was going on I sat down cross-legged on the floor and got some good solid sleep. When the next man came back from questioning I let him have my place. I was so relaxed I could sleep even standing up.

CHAPTER VI : *Lambs for the Slaughter*

DAYBREAK THE FOLLOWING MORNING BROUGHT MORE
trucks and another roll call. Near the head of the list was "Kolfenbach, Josef." I prayed fervently that I would get into the same shipment with Father Josef. But the list was alphabetical and "F" comes
near the end of the Russian alphabet. I had to sweat out the fear
that I would be left behind. When I finally heard "Fittkau, Gerhard," I grabbed my bags and ran almost joyfully to catch up with
my fellow priest.

About one hundred fifty of us lined up in a fresh fall of snow
to be loaded into canvas-covered trucks. Our driver raced over the
cobbled streets of Heilsberg. Through the open back of the truck
we caught glimpses of Russian guards, two small boys pulling a cart
and the golden statue of St. Michael looking out over the ruins and
the few living left among them.

We passed through Springborn and saw Brother Basil's Franciscan monastery. Out in the country, we saw no more wayside
shrines and crucifixion groups and knew that we had passed the
boundary of Catholic Ermland.

The truck finally unloaded us before a red brick building surrounded by high walls in the town of Bartenstein. The building was
familiar to some of us. It was the state prison in which my predecessor and other Ermland priests had served their sentences in the
tender hands of Hitler's "justice."

We were marched upstairs and into the prison chapel, now strangely hollow. They let us sit in the stalls the prisoners had used while we waited our turns to go into another "little room." It was a luxury to be able to sit on a real bench with a back to it. As we sat down heavily, sighing with relief, Father Josef and I caught ourselves smiling at the same thought—how often we had seen the canons in the Cathedral of Frauenburg going through the same motions after singing the Office of the day.

As the men came out of the little room we noticed that some of them were holding empty knapsacks but all of them were holding up their pants. We had run into some more *kultur soldats!* To speed things up a guard came out and ordered us all to take off our suspenders and belts and have them ready to hand over.

This was doubly embarrassing to me. Before I even thought of how I was going to hold up my three pairs of underwear and two pairs of pants, my hand went up to my heart, over the suspender buckle in which the last two consecrated particles of the Holy Eucharist were hidden in a tiny piece of linen no larger than a postage stamp. No one had found that hiding place but I could think of no other as secure. There was not much time, so very quietly and discreetly Father Josef and I partook of the particles, receiving Holy Communion right there in the old prison chapel. For Father Josef that Communion was to become his Viaticum.

We were still thanking God for His great goodness in being with us, in going the Way of the Cross before us, when a guard motioned the two of us into line. Father Josef was carrying very little, so he took one of my two bags so that I would not appear to be a capitalist. He went in first.

When my turn came the looting officer eagerly pulled the suspenders from my hand and laid them out neatly in a large wooden box on top of Father Josef's belt. Then he dumped out my knapsack and started sorting the contents. Thread, needles, buttons, and nail scissors were thrown on one pile; my little box of cake crumbs on another; my blanket on a third. He held up the cold cream jar I had filled with cotton soaked in sacred oil and asked, "What's this?"

"Medicine," I said.

He opened the jar, smelled the contents and threw it on the floor. Then he made me hold up the knapsack by its straps while he slashed the straps from both sides of the bag.

"Now hold the bag open," he ordered.

I had to stand there holding it while he cut several times through the rope that ran through the hemmed mouth of the knapsack.

Angered at this wanton destruction that left me without any supports for carrying the bag, I fumed at him, "What was the sense of doing that?"

Without showing any emotion, he answered laconically, "Germania kaputt."

I was allowed to keep the cold cream jar. But no amount of pleading could get back the bottle of Mass wine or the carton of unconsecrated hosts. I still had my red handkerchief, a piece of hard, dried-up ham, half a can of grease, an ounce of bacon, my gloves, and a can of food without a label. In exchange for my warm clean blanket I was given a dirty horse blanket. Father Josef had managed to get by without giving up my missal, a hymnal, a towel, and a pair of socks.

I fashioned a belt out of a red woolen scarf slit lengthwise and tied front and back. There were no belt loops on my pants and I found that by walking very carefully I could make about a hundred yards before having to stop for a pulling-up and re-tying job.

The sun was setting when we were paraded out to the trucks again. The crowding was worse than before, and for the first time we had women and girls mixed in with the men. We had to hold whatever cramped position we had landed in for the three or four hours the journey lasted.

When the truck stopped and the guard dropped the tailgate I

slipped off the truck and landed on my feet, but they were so numb that they buckled under me and I went sprawling in the snow.

I could tell by the sky line that we were in Insterburg, near the border of East Prussia and Lithuania. The dark quiet of the night and the thick, softly falling snow made a peaceful scene. But the peace was shattered by a sudden weird whining like the call of a hyena or a jackal in the wilderness. It was the sound of a Russian locomotive whistle. We could make out a large building and a door-way leading from its courtyard down to railroad tracks. We could hear men shouting to dogs that growled and snapped in answer. Then we could make out that they were herding a long procession of people, mostly women, out of the gate down to the tracks. As we drew closer, I could hear men and women crying out to relatives, calling them by their first names. While we stood there the procession was kept moving relentlessly toward the screeching locomotive we could hear but not see.

We were getting a general idea of where we were going and a specific idea of how.

When the procession ended we were driven into the court-yard through the same gate. We were lined up, counted, and taken into the building, which turned out to be the dread Insterburg Penitentiary.

We dragged our feet and our bags into a huge assembly hall. It had obviously been used at some time for religious services. Part of a pulpit and an altar remained, but the only other furnishings were large herring barrels standing at the end where the organ had been. They were intended for use as toilets but overuse brought about by dysentery had filled them.

There was a stage at the altar and with Russian officers coming and going across it as new groups, about three quarters of them women, kept streaming into the hall. We guessed that this was a distribution center where we would be divided into groups for deportation.

The only question now was whither. It might be to "rehabilitation" work comparatively close to home or it might be to relatively bearable assignments in farms or factories in the eastern part of the Soviet Union. On the other hand, it could be the death camps of Siberia or the Russian Arctic. We were still waiting.

Father Josef and I walked around the hall trying to spot a familiar face. The first I saw belonged to Gertrud, the valiant housekeeper of our bishop's vicar general in Frauenburg. When I greeted her she threw up her hands and cried out, "My God! Can this be Father Fittkau?"

"Why not?" I was honestly surprised at her reaction.

"Because the curly sideburns, the dirty beard, and the red scarf round your waist made me take you for a Russian Jew."

The tall thin woman next to her was her sister Lena. I had just time to get some news from our cathedral city—Bishop Kaller had been taken off by the SS just before the Russians came; there were rumors that he was dead; the vicar general and half-a-dozen other priests were still in the MVD cellars—when a tall, friendly looking Russian officer stepped to the center of the stage and called for attention. He had a sheaf of lists in his hand and he instructed us that when we heard our names we had to come up to the stage for assignment to groups. He made fun of his own mispronunciation of our names. When he saw bent-over old men dragging themselves up the stairs to the stage he went over, took them aside and did not put them into groups with the rest.

We were taken out into the courtyard and lined up twelve abreast standing at attention, or as close to that as we could come. We heard our names called again against the whining background of the locomotive. We were all excited. This was our call. We would be going somewhere definite and all this miserable business of uncertainty would be over.

But we were marched to the cells for three more days of waiting, answering similar roll calls twice each day, just before sunrise and just after sunset.

Those three days were terrifying. All night we could hear the cries of women in the neighboring cells as guards came to choose their victims. They would pound on our walls and call out the names of their menfolk: "Erich, Erich!" "Hans, Hans!" "Josef, Josef!" There was no way of helping them.

In our cell matters were not much better. The mingling of groups had brought us a new type of fellow prisoner—the criminal and the bully. These were mostly Russian civilian toughs and "liberated" ex-prisoners of other nationalities. They set about establishing their dominance of the prison world by taking whatever they wanted and beating up anyone who resisted. Then they would fight among themselves and establish little gangs around ambitious leaders. They throve on the helplessness of the older and more resigned German prisoners. The guards, far from stopping them, protected them for a share of the loot. In one of the fights I was openly robbed of the bottom half of my beat-up canteen. The thief was a young Russian who had been put in with us because he had been caught as a well-fed farmhand on a German farm.

During one of the quiet moments, while hundreds of us were trying to rest from our exhaustion on the filthy floor, one man who kept himself bolt upright, as though unwilling to soil the trim uniform which showed he was a Prussian state forester, suddenly yelled out, "We know whom to blame for this dirty mess we're in. It's the Pope and the Jews!"

The crowd remained silent at his words and I answered him, "If you still don't know who led us into this mess you'd do better to keep your mouth shut. You better thank your Führer for having brought on you and on himself exactly what he had planned to do and what he has already done to the Jews and to the Christians as well." To his surprise, several prisoners applauded.

We were called out into the hall during the night for another little private looting by the guards. One of them took a fancy to the six-inch crucifix I wore on my breast inside my overcoat. Without taking it from my neck, he held it up in the air for the other guards to see and yelled out, "Alleluia!" in mockery. I echoed the "Alleluia," though I was aware that liturgically it was out of place during Lent. I thanked God for still making His presence known among us. The guard did not take the crucifix, but let it swing back into place.

Our sunset roll call the next evening was another false alarm, but we were called out again after midnight for the last time. We went through the doorway in a repetition of the scene that had welcomed us to Insterburg three nights previously. Another crowd had just been unloaded from trucks. They were peering through the darkness toward us as we had peered toward that other dark procession. The human cries they were hearing from separated families were coming up this time from our ranks. I could hear them all around me. I could also see and hear the dogs and the solid double row of flashlight-carrying guards who made an avenue of no escape. This time I was in the procession that shuffled off into the dark to where the long line of boxcars dwindled endlessly into the distance.

CHAPTER VII : *On the Way of the Cross*

A GUARD'S FLASHLIGHT FLICKERED AROUND THE WALLS
of the boxcar in a last-minute check. The heavy door began sliding
shut. Two men on the inside had to lend their weight to lock the
door of their own prison. A dead silence fell on all of us as in the
moment of closing a grave. Each man strained his eyes through the
darkness toward the door. We all heard the dead click of metal on
metal as the outside latch fell into place. Then came queer scratch-
ing and clinking noises as of wire and chain making doubly sure
of the latch. It was the early morning hours of Tuesday, March 6,
1945.

Father Josef and I eased ourselves to the floor. The air was bitter cold, so I unfolded my horse blanket and draped it from his
head and shoulders to mine. When all our partners in misery also
attempted to sit down, trouble began. Quarrels started in every corner of the car. In the darkness it took us two hours to understand
that the lack of floor space was not due to the malice of people who
wanted to take up too much of it. There were simply too many of us
for the size of the car. Like most Russian freight cars, this one was
less than one-third the size of the ordinary American freight car.
There were forty-nine of us cramped into it.

All of us were exhausted, some of us were very ill and we were
locked in together in circumstances under which no man could be
at his best. But everyone was anxious to get settled in some way

before the train started. It wasn't long before a voice spoke up and it wasn't much longer before we began learning a little more about human nature and the ethics of survival.

The voice spoke with authority: "There is enough room in this car for all of us. I have a plan."

I recognized the voice. It was the old Prussian forester who had delivered his dictum about the Pope and the Jews back in the prison hall. And I recognized the type. The men belonging to it were efficient, energetic, strict, and without imagination. They had a talent for obedience and command. It had enabled them to serve Hitler's government as faithfully as they had already served the republic and the Kaiser. These men always have a plan. And they are always outraged when minds less methodical or obedient than their own refuse to fall in with it. I wondered what the plan would be and how it would be received in this company.

The voice went on, "Think of all the space we're wasting and how awkward it is. The man in each corner has the legs of the two men sitting next to him crossing his. The men in the middle are falling over backward and sideways across the legs of other men and starting trouble."

There was no response so he went on, "Here's my plan. We'll find out exactly how many of us there are. Then we'll divide the floor space equally and each man will have his own area. So we'll number off. I'm one..."

The plan was quite sensible, but it did not get anywhere. Any man who had his back against the wall didn't want to risk rolling around the middle of the car. Anyone who had maneuvered his bag to gain an inch on his neighbor was afraid to lose his advantage. Though we tried to argue that the plan would work, it soon became clear that it had no chance of being put into practice. The discussion was very soon dropped and we heard no more of it. It was to be every man for himself.

All night we heard the guards marching up and down the line

of cars. At regular intervals a heavy tramping over our heads told us that a patrol also marched the length of the train along the roof.

The only entrance for light or air was a chute consisting of two sideboards jutting out from a hole cut low in one wall, our latrine. By the time the first rays of dawn showed through the chute we found the iron strips on the walls and ceiling coated with frost from our breathing.

Suddenly the train started with a jolt that banged my head against the wall. I made the sign of the cross, following Father Josef's example, and recommended myself and all others in the car to St. Raphael, patron of travelers. With the light we could take notice of our neighbors and find out about each other. We could also see the tiny makeshift stove in the center of the car—a stove without anything to burn in it.

The first topic of conversation was where we were going. An old man with a flowing white beard had no doubt about it. He banged the cold stove he was sitting on and with his patriarchal beard accenting each word said, "It's lucky you have nothing to burn in this now. It's a lot colder than this in Siberia. You'll do a lot better if you get used to it before you get there." It turned out that he had been in Siberia for four of his sixty-five years during the First World War.

It was interesting to notice that most of the men could see the future only in terms of their past. Hermann, who had been manager of a brickyard, fingered a pair of horn-rimmed glasses and decided, "No. They are sending us to Stalingrad or maybe some other city like that. They'll put us to work making bricks. They need the bricks for rebuilding bombed houses." Karl, a tough old Masurian farmer, pushed his beaver cap a bit farther back on his head and said, "Not if they're smart. Not if they know what they need most right now. They need food. They'll send us to the Ukraine to work the farms. That's what we did with the Russians and Poles."

We had four German soldiers among us. Their spokesman was

Jan, an old Communist. In civilian life he had been a combination ditchdigger and landscape gardener from Emden. He took up more space in the car than anyone else because he insisted on lying full length with his head in the corner and his feet sticking out into the center. He was tough enough to get away with it. He had a little speech to make: "Poor people are used to hard work. It doesn't matter what kind of work they give us, we're used to it. It's the big boys that'll get hit. The boys that never worked but ate up the profit from the work we did. Now they're going to find out for the first time what it's like to work, and they'd better find out fast. In the Soviet Union if you don't work you don't eat."

Gregor was also a Marxist. He had been foreman of a submarine section in an Elbing shipyard. "They're taking us to the yards at Leningrad," he confided, "and the way I see it, it makes no difference whether we build submarines in Leningrad or in Elbing. A man who knows his job can get his vodka up there. And what's the difference between vodka and schnapps?"

Georg, a pal of Jan's, had been a prisoner of war in France after World War I. He was bitter and without illusions.

"Sure. We're all wonderful workers and they've just been waiting for us. Why don't you shake the cobwebs out of your head? Most of us will be dead before they find out how wonderful we are. We'll be lucky if we get to sweat on some collective farm. There we could scrounge some grist once in a while and mix it with grass to keep us from starving."

Many of the men in the car were certain we would never live long enough to reach Russia. They had already given up. But underneath all the fears and uncertainties was a definite feeling of relief that we were at last moving. For one thing, the swaying of the car shifted our cramped bodies and at first seemed to give us some comfort. But one man's movement would be another's chance to steal another inch and we were in a constant painful struggle for space. After a few hours our community pattern began to emerge. The more selfish and ruthless were clearly gaining the advantage. The others were sinking into even greater misery and hopelessness.

Hermann, the brickyard man, turned out to be a noisy and demanding bully. He constantly clamored and pushed for more space. On one side he pushed Franz, weakest of the three boys, tight into a corner. On the other he yelled noisily at Meister Kretschmer, an old butcher from Elbing, who could not possibly move farther since he was beside the lavatory chute. Hermann was apparently quite astonished when the old butcher not only refused to yield an inch of space but with fierce deliberateness gave him back more than he bargained for: "Do you see this little bit of lard?" old Kretschmer asked. He indicated a small can he had been clutching in both hands. "I know that when that's gone, it won't be long till I'm gone too. But as long as I live, even if I'm skin and bones instead of two hundred and fifty pounds, I'll always be strong enough to kick your teeth in if you don't stop pushing."

That put an end to that.

In front of Father Kolfenbach was Karl, the Masurian farmer. He proved that being a nice old man did not mean he could not take advantage of his neighbors. He was perhaps the most indefatigable in working for more room, quietly and cajolingly asking the men next to him to move over a little. When this finally got under their skins he would stop talking. But at every motion of a neighbor he would manage to worm himself over till he had made himself quite comfortable at the expense of those around him. When this became too obvious and the others started yelling at him, Karl would give in with an air of injured good will and yield a little bit of his territory. He brought even Father Kolfenbach to the limits of his patience by leaning back on him for hours at a time.

Herr Stramm was one of the most unfortunate inhabitants of our little world. He was sorry for himself because he had lost his hat getting onto the train and his coat collar wasn't high enough to keep his bald head warm. He was sorry for himself because every-body else in the car had a better place than he had. He especially pitied himself because he had not been able to escape in time with his wife and three small children. His great consolation was that he had saved a thermos bottle, now empty. It had become so precious to him that he would not put it in his sack for fear it might be bro-ken. He held it in his arms like a baby. He could not at all accept what had happened to him. Why to him? Alois, an old soldier badly wounded in World War I, tried to stop Stramm's constant whining about his three children: "Do you think you're the only one? What about the rest of us? What about me with my seven children all under fifteen? Why don't you be a man and stop crying? If you want to do your family any good make the best of what you have. Go find a place for yourself."

But the pitiful creature kept creeping around the car searching for a better place and never getting settled until he finished up lying at the feet of Father Kolfenbach and myself.

Talking about food became a substitute for having it. Some of the men could give graphic and detailed descriptions of the prepa-ration of particularly luscious dishes. Georg, a typesetter who had been living rather comfortably in Breslau, gave long dissertations on various types of onions to be used in frying potatoes. We could smell the onions and taste the potatoes.

One of our bully boys, a Lithuanian bricklayer named Ant-onas, kept chewing at a big piece of bacon he had stolen at Inster-burg Prison. He was strong and hard-hearted enough to brush aside the request and then the threats that came from those who thought he should share it with his hungry neighbors. He would sit comfortably on a tin keg of fat he had also managed to acquire, smack his lips over the bacon, tell us how many bottles of schnapps he used to buy every week, and complain about how he missed it now to help his digestion. It is an insight into this kind of life that all of us were forced to keep on good terms with this unpleasant character because he owned the only knife in the car, and we needed a knife to take an occasional sliver from the little bits of food we had left.

We had been thirty-six hours without water and without any real food when the first sun showed through the chute. Karl could tell by the position of the shadows that we were headed east.

I had more than food on my mind that morning. I was glad of the respite when the old forester put an end to the food chatter with an abrupt command: "Stop this nonsense! It doesn't help our stomachs any and it keeps us from thinking about what we should be thinking about. It's about time you fools realized that we are all going *kaputt.* We're through."

I was remembering the date. It was March 7, 1945. The anniversary of my ordination. I was back at that morning eight years ago when I, with the rest of my class, together with Bishop Maximilian Kaller, offered up Holy Mass for the first time in my life. I was hearing the words of the bishop's sermon. He had chosen the text: "Jesus...suffered outside the gate. Let us therefore go forth to Him outside the camp, bearing His reproach; for here we have no permanent city, but we seek for the city that is to come" (Heb. 13:12–14).

The first propaganda trials against priests were being held at that time and Goebbels was about to proclaim open war against the Church. The bishop had foreseen then what the rest of us saw afterward, what I was experiencing now.

Meditating on the bishop's sermon, I realized that being where I was now could be the fulfillment of our vocation as priests. I accepted all that was happening to me in that light and prayed God, "Please do not sell my skin too cheaply; let it be of some value, at least for my fellow prisoners."

My prayer was answered with startling suddenness. The rasping voice of the old Prussian state forester boomed out across the car. "Make room for the short priest to crawl over here. I want him."

The men were so stunned at this call for a priest from such an unexpected source that they let me creep over the tangle of arms and legs without cursing too much. I took the old man's hand and noticed he was very weak. "What can I do for you?" I asked.

"Pastor," he said, "I'm going to croak."

I took a long look at him. Time was short and I would have to talk to him as he would want to be talked to.

"So are we all. But if it is your turn now, you must know that a man can't just die like one of his dachshunds—creep off in a corner and have it all over with. Do you think there's nothing to come after that tough life of yours? Why do you think you were living at all?"

"Maybe there is something. But how is a man to know?"

There was not time to go into a long instruction. "There may not be much time for talk but I suppose there's one thing bothering you," I said. "Deep in your heart you know very well that off and on you have acted like a *schweinehund*. The voice that bothers you is what we call conscience. It is the voice of the Creator and Redeemer you may shortly face, perhaps in a few minutes, to answer for everything."

The old man nodded. There was dead silence except for the clattering and rattling of the car while the old forester frankly and loudly answered a few specific questions about his past life.

"As long as you have a breath in your body," I assured him, "you can straighten these things out by asking God's forgiveness. You can be certain that He is more understanding than the best priest on earth could be."

As his breathing became more labored I told him: "All these things will not be the most embarrassing ones when you face your Lord. What will you say if He asks, 'How much did you do in your whole life to render thanks and praise to the One Who created and redeemed you?'"

The rest of the men were listening intently as I tried to lift the spirits of the dying man.

"Even if it happened that you lived like an animal and paid no attention at all to God, He is still willing to forgive you. He knows how little you were told about Him. He hasn't forgotten one single good thing you have done in all your life. He has promised us solemnly in the Bible that He will take you back right now if you can say these words and mean them in your heart: 'My God, You know what a pig I've been. But if You want to, You can make me clean and take me back into Your house like another prodigal son!' We have it on God's own word that there is more joy in heaven when one old *schweinehund* like you comes back than there is over the arrival of ninety-nine people right from the front pews of the church. And I'm sure that for an old forester like you St. Peter will muster a bugle band of angels to blow a special salute."

He squeezed my hand and swallowed hard.

"The only way to come to terms with God now," I went on, "is to talk to Him personally, that is to pray. Do you know the Our Father?"

Straightway, in a voice that still had its boom, he let it ring out through the car right down to the old liturgical ending, as the Protestants still use it, "For Thine is the kingdom and the power and the glory forever. Amen."

I improvised simple acts of faith, hope, and love and packed the sins we had just gone through into a prayer of contrition. Then I gave him a final boost by saying, "Right now those angels are practicing that special salute for you."

He squeezed my hand again.

"If you want to fall right in and be in step when you get there," I added, "you might as well learn the salute yourself. It goes like this: 'Glory be to the Father, and to the Son, and to the Holy Spirit, as it was in the beginning, is now, and ever shall be, world without end. Amen.'"

Three times he repeated the doxology, but just before the final Amen his voice broke. With a last effort he rallied strength, got out the Amen, raised his head high, took a last deep breath and slumped his head over on his knees in death.

Then I began reciting the Church's prayer for the dead. The final prayer, in which I asked all the prisoners to join, was for the man in the car who would be next to follow the old forester.

We had our first corpse as fellow passenger in the crowded car. But in my heart there was some happiness. On this anniversary of my ordination Our Lord had assured me that I was in the right place.

During our third waterless and foodless night in the boxcar the door next to the chute jarred loose about an inch. It not only let in fresh air and some good snow, but also gave us a fine though narrow view of the countryside. During the same night our knife-owning comrade Antonas prepared the old forester for his last rest by relieving him of his shoes, coat and knapsack. It was this same Lithuanian bully boy who recognized the place when we stopped next morning on a siding by a big railway station. We were in Kaunas, his home town.

We heard the wires being loosened on the latch, then a pounding on the door for help in sliding it open. Before it was half open two guards with fixed bayonets were shouting orders I could not understand. But Antonas jumped to the door and reached down for an old rusty milk can holding six gallons of water. Antonas tried to take charge but the men mobbed him. We tried to see that each man got a pint of the water. About a dozen were left with none but what they could beg from the rest. A small riot broke out against Fritz, a sixteen-year-old shepherd boy who had somehow contrived a second helping.

I held my portion in the aluminum frying pan which was left of my mess kit. I took it a few drops at a time, holding it in my mouth a while to warm it. That dirty water tasted as good as the finest Rhine wine.

We were also given a blanketful of stone-hard cornbread cut into small squares. The Russians break these bitter crusts of *sukhari* into their cabbage soup. A careful count proved that we could have two squares each and a spoonful of crumbs. We sat down to dinner, but only the prudent who had saved a little water could swallow the crusts.

We were moving again and Alois, a disabled veteran of the first war, seemed to be building up as bad a state out of bitterness as Herr Stramm had out of self-pity. "Why did I let them take me? Why didn't I shoot at least one of the swine? I hope if they come near our house my wife is waiting for them with a rifle and lets them have it. She will too." He kept digging himself deeper into moroseness. "We're all going *kaputt*."

I tried to lift him out of it.

"What good would your shot have done? Kill one, more come on. What good does hate ever do? How do you know the man you shot might not have more children back home than you have?"

But his bitterness was eating him up. "That doesn't make sense," he retorted. "Nothing makes sense."

I took a sideways look at him. I felt I was beginning to understand the man so I decided to try something, half-fearful it would bring his boot crashing against my chin.

"You'll never find sense in anything," I told him, "till you get some faith in you."

I waited, but he showed no anger. He just looked puzzled.

That made me certain I had estimated him rightly but thought it better to wait a while before telling him that faith is a room in which things become transparent. It was enough for the moment to remind him of how he had told Herr Stramm to make the best of things and offer him some of my water.

I was pleased when he accepted it.

We had not gone far that night when the train stopped again. We began to hear, faintly at first, then more clearly, a strange chanting. Then we could make it out. It was the voices of women in the neighboring cars joined in a repeated rhythmic chorus, "Water! Water! Water!"

Some of our men took up the refrain and we all joined in. Herr Stramm had once been a band leader of a war veterans outfit. He swung his beloved thermos bottle like a baton and kept us in time with the women, a deeply moving prisoners' chorus.

Half an hour later there was a thumping on our door and we sprang to it, hoping for an answer to our cries. But the guard who stuck his head in had merely come to ask, "Is there anyone dead in there?" By this time others had completed the looting job Antonas started. The withered body lay naked except for the old forester's dirty underwear.

His unconcern making it plain that the sight was nothing new to him, the guard pointed to three men and ordered them to wrap up the body in a blanket and follow him. When the men came back all they would say was that they hoped they would never be picked for that job again.

That night the boy Franz was so weak he needed help even to sit up. He was shivering violently and moaning over and over again, "Water, please somebody. Give me just one little drop of water." We did not have any water, but in his condition it would have been murder to give it to him if we had.

My borrowed rubber boots were beginning to pinch my swelling feet. Franz had smaller feet than mine and the boots would help keep him warm, so I gave them to him.

After midnight the train started to pull out, then stopped with a jolt. We heard the pounding of heavy boots, loud shouts, and then a burst of shooting. We learned later that three prisoners had been killed trying to escape.

The train moved on again and we could see through the crack that we were traveling through forests. It was not until the next evening that the door was opened. Again we begged for water but the guard curtly asked for two men. Antonas by this time had appointed himself chieftain of the car. He told Father Kolfenbach and myself to go.

It felt wonderful to be out of the car, to be able to look around, to feel the blood circulating in our limbs. We were led over many tracks until we could see a ruined city sloping down a hillside toward a destroyed railroad station. The guard kept us going on through ruins that included what might have been a beautiful cathedral and some very Soviet-looking boxlike concrete structures.

We came finally to a line of prisoners waiting at a water spout still functioning on the damaged wall of a bombed building. Clean bubbling water was gushing out of it. When our turn came we found that the mound of ice formed by the spilled water left room for only one at the faucet. So Father Josef took our milk can while I stood looking over the railroad fence.

I watched a very old man come walking slowly along on the other side of the fence. His feet were wrapped in felt boots and he was so weak he could just drag them along. He stopped at the fence post beside the spout and stared at us. I greeted him and asked him where we were.

He slowly raised his arm and pointed to the destroyed city. As he stood in that position, like the gnarled stump of a dead tree, he fitted perfectly into the scene. I could read no anger in his face, just a sadness at our common fate. He pointed and said, "This used to be Smolensk."

Smolensk. That meant we had crossed White Russia and were pointed straight at Moscow and all that lay beyond it. But this was a major railroad center where we could branch off equally easily to Leningrad to the north or Stalingrad or the Ukraine to the south.

Father Josef was so much taller than I that we had an awkward time juggling the heavy milk can over the piles of rubble around the station. When we got to the tracks we had to stop and let a long freight train go past in the same direction we were headed. Through some half-open boxcar doors we could see women sitting on sacks with children clustered around them. There were also some elderly men in the car who looked like Russians. But they also looked as if they knew as little about where they were being taken as we did.

The water was for the women's cars. We could hear them crying, "Water! Water!" as we drew near. When we had opened the door and hoisted the milk can up, about fifty women leaped at it at once. They were mad with thirst. They pulled and clawed at each other and dragged each other away by the hair to get their own containers filled. The containers included china cups, cake pans, babies' bottles, medicine bottles, or just bare dirty hands.

Badly as this sight made us feel, matters got worse when some wounded Russian soldiers came hobbling up behind us and started to jeer at the women. They laughed and ridiculed and taunted. "Look at the cultured Germans!" Some children came running over to join in the fun. They had a great time laughing at the women. But three of the onlookers, Russian women wearing black babushkas, had sympathy and suffering written all over their faces. They would have liked to protect the dignity of their sisters. One of them protested quietly to the guard that the soldiers should be made to move on. It was the children who shouted down this request.

Without warning one of the wounded soldiers, thoroughly drunk, stepped forward and struck Father Josef squarely in the face with the palm of his hand. Among the curses that went with the blow we heard, "You Hitler swine!" This was too much for the guard. He grabbed the drunk by the collar and pulled him away, and then ducked just in time. His comrade had taken a swing at him too, accompanied by the same label, "Hitler swine!"

Under cover of the confusion I spoke to one of the calmer women prisoners. "How many of you have died?"

"Three," she said, "but there will soon be more."

After three more trips between the faucet and the cars we dragged ourselves wearily back to our own boxcar. We were locked up again and our jolting journey to nowhere started again.

CHAPTER VIII : *A Carload of Death*

THE NEXT DAY WAS LAETARE SUNDAY. THE CHURCH
marks this day in the middle of Lent for rejoicing in the midst of
sorrow. We used the Mass of the day to pray with our companions.
Father Josef and I gave short talks, taking our theme from the Introit: "Rejoice with joy you that have been in sorrow... We shall go
into the house of the Lord."

The first to thank us publicly for the service was Jan, the old
Communist. "I've never heard about these things, Pastor," he said
apologetically. "You should tell us more about them."

Some hours later Herr Stramm came up and whispered softly
in my ear: "That reminded me of services just before an attack at
the Somme in France back in 1918. The chaplain said something
about the words of God standing firm even if the mountains and
hills should fall. I remember him saying 'Thy grace stands.' I didn't
understand it then, but I think I do after your talk."

One of the men I had been doing what little I could to help
was a retired teacher, Herr Pietsch. He had buried his sorrow and
the evident fact that he was slowly dying under a strange obsession.
He lived in constant and anxious fear of breaking his glasses. He
held them firmly clutched in his hand day and night. He called
me over that night because he had become unable to attend to his
own needs. But even then, when I braced him in a sitting position
or worked him across the floor to the chute, he would not let the

glasses go. "But they are my glasses, Reverend! My glasses! If I should lose these glasses or break them, I wouldn't be able to read. Just think of that. I wouldn't be able to read." I had a difficult time getting him to resign himself. But he was not to be with us long.

During that night another man died.

At daybreak the train halted and a guard yelled in through the wall, "Is there anybody sick in there?"

We were all sick. But we all knew what the call meant, so the only one foolish enough to admit it was Herr Pietsch. He shot up his hand and starting waving it like a schoolboy in the classroom while he shouted back, "Yes, I am, sir!"

The huge door slid open and he was carried out. As they lowered him down from the car, he kept saying, "My glasses, my glasses. Be careful of my glasses."

He was taken to the "hospital," a car down the line on which you could just make out a faded and almost worn off red cross. There wasn't as much as a bench or a chair in it, let alone a cot. The only equipment was a can of water. It was a place to put dying people and let them die.

Locked in again but still on the siding, the men began to speculate on who would go next. Karl, the gentle but selfish farmer, stayed out of the conversation and slipped over to grab the space left by Herr Pietsch. Poor Herr Stramm noticed it. Feeling again that everyone was taking advantage of him, he protested bitterly. I was just consoling him with a few drops of water to break up the quarrel when Karl suddenly broke into a jumble of incoherent phrases. We could make out something about getting a sleigh ready to go home. Then he shouted at the top of his voice, "Karl! Karl! We're going home now." Then silence. Through the shadows I could make out his neighbor, Urban, slipping off Karl's coat and putting it on himself. When he had it on he announced to the rest of us, "Karl is dead."

More guards came to our door and ordered five men for a

burial detail. I was glad to get out of the car again, but I wasn't glad for long.

We were taken to one of the women's cars. The body of a girl about fourteen was rolled onto a blanket which we held. Then to the Russian hurry-up refrain, "Schnell, schnell; buystro, buystro," the guards prodded us forward with our burden. They gave us no time to arrange the body for carrying, so the head and arms dangled from the blanket as we staggered toward the end of the train. We were halted at the door of an immense boxcar, three times the size of ours. Laying the body down on the snow we put hands and shoulders to the big door. It seemed to be stuck. By jerking it a few inches at a time, we finally managed to shove it open on a gruesome sight.

For the entire length of the boxcar, a pile of bodies of men and women seven layers high reached almost halfway to the roof. The pressure from on top had squeezed out the bodies beneath. Our forcing of the door had sheared the hip and leg from the corpse of a woman on the second layer. The gaunt bone, still tight in the hip socket, was dangling over the edge of the car.

"Schnell, schnell! Buystro, buystro!" Other groups of pallbearers were lining up behind us. Two men from our group had to climb up the pile of bodies. We had to heave the girl's corpse up to them. They caught it, thank God, on the first laborious attempt. Then, like men filling a coal bin, they had to swing the body to the far end of the car where the pile was beginning to reach the ceiling. We had to make two more trips with two other women. We discovered that the three last cars were all being used for this ghastly freight.

All of us were numb with horror and shock. An old hard-looking peasant beside me started mumbling, "My God, my God, how can You look down on this without destroying the world?" He got a jab from the butt of a guard's rifle for talking.

On top of my disgust another thought flashed into my mind. I was sure we were all marked for death. They would not allow us to look upon an inhuman sight like this and live to tell about it.

Marching back along the cars our whole group, including the guards, was stopped in its tracks by a most unusual sound. It was the sound of women's voices. The same dry and hoarse voices we had heard putting up the water cry at every stop. But this was different. I could not make out the words but I knew the melody. They were singing "Holy God, We Praise Thy Name!"

The singing was the first of three joys that came as though to blot out the horror we had just seen. The next was our first hot meal. It wasn't hot when it got to us but at least it was something cooked—a kind of barley gruel. It made new men of us.

Then the guards brought us a splendid present: a bundle of wood for the stove. Antonas, of course, took charge of the wood against the day we might get a match to light it. He loaned us his knife to make small splinters for kindling and then decided that we should give up some of whatever paper we had in order to make sure the fire would really get started. My contribution was the envelope that had been holding dysentery pills. Most of the others contributed scraps of paper money.

At the next stop two of the three boys from Bischofstein, Gerhard and Josef left the car on a special detail. While they were gone Father Josef took advantage of the less crowded corner to hear the confession of their companion, Franz, and give him Extreme Unction. Franz lay there quite motionless, the rubber boots I had given him standing by his side. Father Josef could not shake him out of his listlessness.

The two boys came back in a couple of hours. Josef no longer had his precious milk can but they were bubbling over with the exciting news that they had been to the city. First they were taken to the Red Cross car and loaded with clothes and shoes the guards had taken from the dying. They carried these to the center of a small town where crowds of peddlers were doing a thriving business. It was apparently a regular stop for these trains. Shoes and pants were in most demand. They could be bartered for food, homegrown tobacco, vodka, or a homemade liquor called *samogonka*.

While the guards were doing business Josef had made a deal for himself. He got four small herrings and some matches for his milk can.

The two boys gobbled all the herrings themselves except for a tail they graciously presented to Father Josef. They promised me that I would get a tail too the next time they got a herring.

They gave Antonas the matches and our hopes sank when we saw that they were book matches with no abrasive on the packet. But one of the men dug through his pockets and came up with a small piece of the necessary abrasive.

Getting the fire started was a great adventure. Everyone was breathless until the splinters caught fire from our donated paper. Just seeing the fire made us feel warm and happy, and most of us just sat staring into it. But soon Jan sidled up to the stove, carefully suspending a small aluminum kettle of water in one hand. It was a mystery to whom the water belonged because we had all seen Jan drink down his share. He broke up some of his dry, hard bread into the pot and from a deep pocket pulled out a piece of bacon, which also went in. The bacon must also have been requisitioned from someone. Jan had absolutely no food when he entered the car. From time to time he would stir the concoction.

Others quickly followed his example. Small cooperatives were formed. One member contributed his kettle, another some water, a third a slice of bread and another a pinch of salt. The biggest capitalist of all was Joachim, another Masurian farmer, who had hidden away in his underwear a small packet of saccharine tablets. Breaking each tablet in half, and sometimes in quarters, he would give a piece to the cooperatives in exchange for a good share of the brew. But I did all right too. I had a little bar of concentrated pea soup, so everyone was willing to do business with me. Soon Father Josef and I were enjoying a bit more than the wonderful odors.

All night long the fire burned. To keep it going we dismantled piece after piece of the wooden beams on the ceiling and inside walls. The walls of the car remained coated with frost. Still it was a great blessing. It gave everyone in the car something to do, something to look at, something to dream about. The little fire gave us another lease on life.

In the course of the next two days we became painfully aware that not all the effects of the fire were blessed ones.

"Who is the pig that brought all these damn lice into the car?" Jan pushed his way through the crowd, heading straight for the stove. He stripped himself naked to make a search for the little creatures in the poor light from the chute. He swore with satisfaction as he cracked the first one between the nails of his two thumbs. When Jan had finished his job and returned to his place Alois came forward and gave the rest of us detailed instructions on how to hunt down and exterminate our new "fellow travelers." Soon we were all busy at the hunt and I became quite expert at it.

The next morning, through the crack in the door, we could see a glimpse of a large city. There were no indications of bombing, only drab and dirty buildings and backyards such as you see from any railroad entering a big city. The train stopped and for several hours nothing happened. We could hear much coming and going of guards, shouting and the typical hacking cough of the Red Army soldier. We decided we might be in Moscow. Hermann put on his glasses and gave a solemn discourse about distances, direction and elapsed time to establish this conjecture as a fact. There was a tremor of excitement through the car about what would happen to us now.

All that day the only action was the frequent shunting and switching that bumped us all over the car. Once the guards came around asking if we had any dead bodies. Then the switching started again. Someone had the grim thought that they were uncoupling the three last cars to dispose of the bodies in them. They would probably have to be counted to guarantee that the train delivered the same number of prisoners as it had received.

That night we received our third warm meal since Insterburg. This time there were scraps of fish in the thin barley gruel. The next day each car got two cans of cold water.

We stayed there two and a half days during which we could draw water from a fire hydrant down the track. I was fortunate enough to be assigned to the water detail. It gave me a chance to take a look around, and it also let me meet a group of fellow prisoners who had come to the hydrant from the other train. Most of them were peasants from Romania and we only had time to exchange a few words in broken German before the guards chased them away.

A procession of haggard women came trudging down the track toward us. They wore black babushkas and dirty quilted dresses, and their feet were bound tightly in felt wrap around boots. Slung over their shoulders were heavy iron picks and long wrenches that fitted the bolts on the tracks. They dragged themselves over the ties through a soggy layer of melting snow. One of them spoke to us very cautiously in German, "Are you Germans?" When we nodded, she said only, "Oh my God!"

We later learned that these women had been deported from old German settlements in the Black Sea district of Soviet Russia. The settlements had been established under Catherine II, one hundred fifty years before.

The puddles of water around the hydrants were a temptation I could not resist. It would be the first time in four weeks I had a chance to wash my face. But the guard did not think my beard was dirty enough yet, and when I stooped over to scoop up some water, he let go at me with his boots. I did manage to get one handful and rub it over my eyes. It felt like balm and was well worth a few kicks.

We carried the last milk can of water to the Red Cross car at the front of the train. All we could see beyond the tracks were some ugly buildings around a big modern concrete plant six stories high.

A large sign on the structure read "Kombinat." We heaved the can up to the car. It was received by a woman wearing the long black cloak of a nun.

It was Sister Imelda of the Gray Sisters of St. Elizabeth, going about her work of mercy here as unconcerned as if she were in Suessenberg or back in her own convent.

"My God, Father," she said, "what a sight you are!"

"That's so I'll fit better into the Soviet Union. How about yourself?"

"As bad as it is, at least I have some chance to help. Every day about a dozen die here. There are always a few who are glad to have somebody help them face it."

"Do you have any medicine or equipment?"

"Just the cans of water you bring. But a commissar made an inspection and promised improvements. He wasn't pleased with what he found. Too many are dying on this transport."

I thought of the things that happened to so many of the women and I asked, "Doesn't anyone bother you?"

"No. There is one good guard who sees that nothing happens to me. I must have a hard-working guardian angel."

My joy at seeing the familiar face of Sister Imelda was mixed with sadness that my people of Suessenberg had lost her. Before I could ask what happened to the other women, a guard dragged me away. But through the rest of the long journey and for many months to come I could remember the haggard yet still cheerful features of this brave nun. She was a living pledge that God could give us strength to live up to our calling even under the most impossible circumstances.

We thought we would be moving on soon. But at midnight the doors were thrown open and we were ordered to pick up our bags and get out. Why did so many of the moves have to come at midnight? I was half-asleep and annoyed when I hit the ground and joined the line standing by for the next order. One of the last figures leaving the car slumped across the doorway and could not rise again. I was surprised to hear the fallen man whispering my name. His head lay sideways on the dirty wet floor of the car, and in the darkness all I could see were the whites of his wide-open eyes and the outline of his pain-twisted face. I was near the doorway and shifted over slightly. The man lifted his arm as though it were lead and held something out to me.

"What is it you want, Comrade Stramm?"

In a low, hoarse whisper, stretching his treasured thermos bottle toward me, he said, "Take it...thanks for everything...now I know what it means...'Thy grace stands'...my wife...my children... if you see them tell them...'Thy grace stands.'"

Then he pointed to the thin overcoat he was wearing and gestured for me to take it. His staring eyes followed us as we marched off. He knew he was being left to die.

We had to get down on our hands and knees at some stages of the march to get over mounds of dirt covered with wet, slippery snow. Our destination was a large hall in a long one-story white brick building. Men and women assistants dressed in blue and white were standing around. Half a dozen long carts with lengths of pipe laid across the top were waiting for us.

An assistant came along with an armful of strong wire hoops and told us to take off all our clothes and string them on the hoops. I strung up a fur coat, an overcoat, two sweaters, three sets of underwear, two pairs of pants, a small pillow, a blanket, two shirts, and a knapsack. Then we had to hook the hoops to the pipes and the carts were wheeled away.

We shivered there naked on a slimy tile floor. I was shocked to see how noticeably Father Josef's ribs and spine stuck out. The giant was becoming a skeleton. Miserable figures shifted from one foot to the other and wrapped their arms around their bodies to keep warm. It was an hour before anything happened.

Large doors at the far end of the hall opened and two women

came out. As we approached, naked and hesitant, we could see that their faces were expressionless and they seemed to be disgusted with their job. Each had a half-gallon tin can under her arm. Passing them we had to hold out two fingers onto which they scraped a small lump of semiliquid soap from the ends of spatulas.

In the next room there were perhaps five hundred showers row on row. There were no faucets. After another half hour a slow drip of water began. I did not yet start smearing the black fish soap over my body for fear I might never get it off. When the drip increased to a steady trickle I started cautiously to use it, and the water actually kept coming and changed from cold to lukewarm. When the water stopped we rushed across the hall toward our clothes, but they weren't ready. Another woman came and lined us up to stand, wet and cold, for another half hour before we were marched in to dress. Thus I had my first experience of a delousing station. I had been inside my first Soviet building, and that in the capital itself.

It was a different boxcar this time. The same size had to do for more men. Only Father Kolfenbach, the three boys, and Alois remained from my former car-mates. Franz was in terrible condition. He had been too weak to wash himself in the showers. When he got to the car he couldn't climb on, so the guards took him by the scruff of the neck and the seat of the pants and threw him on. He landed helplessly face down on the muddy floor close to our feet. He turned his head enough to stare up at me. There was an expression of intense mental hurt and physical pain in the wide-open eyes. No picture I had seen in the past weeks and months was etched more deeply into my soul than that boy's wretched position and terrible look. He was our misery personified.

At noon we were ordered to change to another car. Franz was unconscious and we had to leave him there to die.

Father Josef had also become frightfully weak. The agonizing sharp pain he was suffering from his kidneys made him shout when he was pushed from one man to another in the scramble for places in the new car. In this move we lost the friendly boys from Bischof-stein and got in exchange a gang of teenage toughs who started in to terrorize the whole car.

There were about ten of them under an eighteen-year-old leader whose mocking nickname was "The Pastor." They started right in to prove their toughness by jockeying for the best places. The train had just pulled out of Moscow when they showed that they had studied gangster techniques. They started a miniature riot claiming that somebody had stolen a pair of gloves from one of them. The leader quieted them and announced that there would have to be a thorough investigation. Everybody's baggage had to be searched. We had all to move back and leave a clear space where all the luggage was to be deposited. Then, with a cry of triumph, the gloves were discovered in the knapsack of the youngest and most harmless member of their own gang.

A little hunchback took special pleasure in the embarrassment of the alleged thief. He started clamoring that the thief be beaten up as an example to all the rest. The bewildered young victim started to cry. Lothar, a quiet lad of about seventeen who did not belong to the gang, spoke up.

"If you are going to beat up anybody, beat up the hunchback. I saw him put the gloves in the boy's knapsack."

The four days we spent with this gang were not easy ones. Father Josef sank perceptibly under the abuse he got from them. I was not made any happier by what the shadows told us about our direction. We were headed northeast and north, climbing toward a region I had once read about in a magazine report. The report told of maximum severity penal colonies in the vast tundra and taiga stretches under the Arctic Circle in the northeasternmost corner of European Russia. The article had pictures and maps demon-strating that this area was worse than many parts of Siberia. The Soviets planned to develop the Komi district between the Petchora

River basin and the Vorkuta area by means of a sprawling system of forced labor camps. The plans were more extensive than those for the White Sea Canal built under the GPU ten years previously with half a million slave laborers.

We had left Moscow on March 20. On the morning of March 24 we were unloaded on a siding between two high fences.

Through a knothole I could see a series of snow-covered roofs that angled down almost to the ground. We were marched through a gate and along between two rows of these dugouts till we arrived in front of a log cabin. Several small groups of people made up of elderly men and children stood around looking at us without much interest. They were dressed in rags, obviously Russian and thoroughly miserable looking. They appeared to live here and from the size of the camp there were probably thousands of them.

A fat woman ordered us into a small room where three dirty men sat on stools with a bench in front of them. We were told to strip, bundle our clothes, and throw them into a heated chamber, and while we stood naked the three men went about their business. In four or five sweeps the first man clipped our heads and faces leaving us like plucked chickens. The next man poured a few drops of water into our hands instructing us to moisten whatever hair we had left on our bodies and stretch out on the bench. The third one shaved our bodies with a straight razor at the same speed the other had shorn our heads.

After this humiliating procedure we got the usual dab of soap from the woman and were pushed into the next room where we washed from a dozen wooden buckets filled with lukewarm water. On the way out we found that our clothes had been heated so well that each of us was missing at least one piece of clothing. I lost a sweater and an undershirt. It seemed a poor setup compared to the Moscow delousing station, but I realized that this mass hygiene was a sensible precaution against typhoid. It might also make our louse hunting easier.

There were about sixty people jammed into our new boxcar, most of them strangers. We were relieved to have lost the boy gangsters but the relief was short-lived. The next few days were to be worse than any we had known so far.

The constant and increasing misery had brought about a progressive dehumanization of its victims. Most of the men had become as ruthless and brutal as animals. Everyone could see the sad state of Father Kolfenbach, yet no one would give him a place to sit down and rest. We finally had to sit down by the only open space, the lavatory chute. There was enough room between us for its use. St. Paul's words were in the minds of both of us: "As it is, it seems as if God has destined us, his apostles, to be in the lowest place of all, like men under sentence of death. We are made a spectacle to the world...we both hunger and thirst and are naked and are buffeted and have no fixed abode...we are made as the refuse of this world, the offscouring of all, even until now" (1 Cor. 4:90).

All night the snow blew up the chute and gradually covered us. We were so cold that it did not melt when it touched our bodies. I found some relief by huddling against my neighbor on the left, an old Lutheran teacher from Masuria. He had given up the fight and was quietly preparing himself for death.

After that cold night six of the older men were taken away to the car for the dying. That enabled Father Kolfenbach and me to move over and sit beside each other. We shared our blanket again, its woolen nap white with frost. It was impossible to believe we could endure this much longer.

Now was the time to use the precious can of food I had been saving for the last. The miracle that it had not been taken from me was probably due to the fact that it had no label. Two men eagerly offered knives to open it—and entitle themselves automatically to part ownership of the contents. Though I did not know what was in it, I was sure it would be something good out of Aunt Anna's pantry. The spicy odor of marjoram from her delicious liverwurst floated through the car and brought the men around me to their feet. A dozen hands reached out dry pieces of *sukhari* in a barter that cost me half the liverwurst. It was wonderful while it lasted but the meal was too rich for our "lower houses." We had to pay a bitter price for the delicacy during the following hours.

Another night and more snow; the journey had now lasted twenty days. That night we received our fifth and last meal aboard our prison train. The guards were in a greater hurry than usual in dishing out a gruel as thin as the first we had been given.

It was Palm Sunday, March 25, the beginning of Holy Week. Our thirst was almost as unbearable as the cold. For consolation I began reading to Father Josef the liturgy for the blessing of palms that would be taking place in churches around the world that day. "In the evening you shall know that the Lord has brought you forth out of the land of Egypt; and in the morning you shall see the glory of the Lord" (Ex. 16:6–7).

I wanted to read the entire liturgy of the day, but could not finish it because all I had to keep my hands from freezing was an old stocking and this was not too effective.

In this car our window to the outside world was a knothole. I caught a glimpse of a little settlement in a shallow valley. It had a typical Russian church with onion-shaped towers, probably a monastery of one of the schismatic sects banished by the tsars into these wastelands. For the rest, there was only endless snow broken by occasional and very sparse woods. Once in a long while we would see a modern log cabin built for the men who watched over this long, lonely stretch of rail.

We had lost the feeling that we were going anywhere in particular. Life had become a matter of not freezing, not starving, not dying from exhaustion or dysentery locked inside the four wooden walls of a boxcar. There wasn't anything else.

CHAPTER IX : *Column Seven*

THE TRAIN STOPPED AS IT HAD STOPPED SO OFTEN. WE heard rough voices outside as we had heard them so many times before. We were past speculating about what this stop meant.

The door was unlocked and pushed back and we were ordered to get out and bring our baggage. Another delousing? It didn't really matter. We were well conditioned by this time and we quite simply and unquestioningly obeyed. Many of us were so weak that we collapsed in the snow when we tried to scramble like sheep to where we were told to line up. The first sign that this was not just another stop came when the engine chugged off leaving six cars standing as still as empty boxes in the snow. Men were coming out of three of the cars, women out of the other three.

We clenched our teeth and started dragging swollen legs in the direction we were pointed. The powdered snow was so slippery and I was so tired that I fell face down and had to be pulled to my feet by Father Kolfenbach. Behind us an old man collapsed and nobody helped him up. We passed a rickety open shed piled with straw snowshoes and looked at the place we were headed for.

Ugly wooden palisades ten feet high enclosed a square compound with watchtowers at each corner. Snow-covered roofs showed over the top of the wall. Straight ahead of us a wide gate was surmounted by a wooden arch carrying in crude Russian letters the inscription "Column Seven."

So this was our new home. We did not have time to muse on it. "Schnell! Schnell! Buystro! Buystro!" We were hurried through the gate and under the arch by the impersonal harsh cries common to herdsmen the world over. If you don't shout and crack your whip the animals won't keep moving. "Schnell! Buystro!"

We were herded through the narrow door of a primitive structure built of logs that seemed to be more under the snow than above it. We found ourselves in a narrow isle about two feet wide lined on both sides by tiers of bunks fashioned from unplaned timber. The bed slats were cracked and warped planks. The only light came from four small openings covered with oil paper and the only air came through the door. An old oil drum set in brickwork in the middle of the floor served as a stove.

All of us had a single thought: grab the best place you can. We had had it ground into us by five weeks of fighting for sitting room in basements, bins, attics, cells, and boxcars. I wished for a place on the second tier. Father Kolfenbach followed me but the effort made him back down immediately. He knew he was too weak to keep climbing up and down. Three men jumped in beside me with their bags to share the six-foot width. I laid my head on my knapsack and stretched out my legs. After the boxcars this rude place seemed spacious and comfortable. Just being able to stretch out was an intoxicating comfort.

The man next to me had just leaned back to rest when the guards appeared and ordered us all down from the tiers with our belongings. These same guards had accompanied us all the way from Insterburg. They wanted to say goodbye by making one last search of our clothes and luggage. I felt resentment choking me. When a stupid-looking guard grinned and snatched a rosary from the man next to me I lost my temper. "Stalin says there is freedom of religion," I shouted. "That is a religious article and you are forbidden to steal it." Stalin was probably the only word he understood, but the vehemence of my words and gestures startled him. He dropped the rosary.

When the guards had gone a rough, guttural voice growled from the other side of the aisle: "Why did you have to get the guards against us over a silly superstitious thing like that?"

Before I could answer him a well-modulated voice cut in sharply from the top tier on our side: "Keep your dirty mouth shut, Fritz. I am not a Catholic any more than you are, but you should respect another man's faith. Better if you asked him to pray for you. I think you could do with it."

Those were unexpected words in this place. I climbed up to meet my unknown champion. A tall man, he was sitting in his bunk, bent over to avoid the low roof, sorting out his belongings. There was a fresh scar over his right eye which I noticed when he turned round with a little red-edged book in his hand.

"I see you have managed to save a book."

"My one treasure," he said as he held it out to me. "We call it the Grain of Mustard Seed edition of the Bible." He gestured at its coverless condition and went on, "The cover was destroyed in the Moscow delousing but the pages are all there. I'm glad I still have it. Along the line they've taken my last blanket, bread bag, container, and even the picture of my wife and three children. It is good of God to leave me my Bible."

"Who are you?"

"Theodor Goebel, Evangelical pastor of Burgsolms, in Hessen."

"How wonderful! That makes us stepbrothers in Christ. I'm a Catholic priest, from Ermland. Come on down and meet another one of our faculty, Father Josef Kolfenbach."

Father Josef was as happy as I to meet this fine minister. By one of those coincidences, it turned out that Pastor Goebel's wife had lived next door to Father Josef in a small city on the Rhine and they had played together as children.

While they talked I went to my bunk and came back with my own most precious possession, my missal. Pastor Goebel and I agreed to exchange our books and we made a pledge of friendship

that has never since been broken. We decided to make an attempt
at some sort of Holy Week services. If we could possibly manage it
Pastor Goebel would give a sermon on Good Friday night and I
would speak on Easter Sunday.

The meeting raised our spirits to some extent. Even Father
Josef, though obviously becoming weaker, talked vivaciously as the
three of us sat on his bunk till another order sent us outside.

We walked along a path with snow piled more than shoulder
high on either side to a long barracks in the center of the compound. On the way we had to stand aside to let pass an emaciated
panje horse, his head hanging down, slowly pulling a strange load
in an open sled. In the twilight I thought at first it was loaded with
logs, but looking more closely I saw the frozen bodies of half a
dozen men and women, heaped up in the most ghastly positions,
some with their glazed eyes still open. As the horse padded off
toward the main gate we filed into the mess hall, a long, dark cabin
with rows of tables and benches running to a partition cutting off
the kitchen from the dining room. Three German girls came out of
the kitchen and stood beside a panel in the center of the partition.
The panel slid open to give a glimpse of a man wearing a white
chef's hat. Our expectations ran high.

We reached greedily for the freshly baked loaves of bread the
girls carried on trays to our tables. But one mouthful was enough
to disillusion us. The loaves which looked so inviting tasted bitter
and musty. They had been baked from some coarse grain and were
soggy with water. The second course brought us each a tin spoon
and a clay bowl filled with lukewarm water. At the bottom of the
bowl lay pieces of turnip with leaves and roots still attached. The
turnips had been neither cooked nor seasoned, merely cut up and
thrown into the warm water, but we managed to swallow the soup
because we were so thirsty.

We were surprised to see the girls coming with their trays a third
time. This time the dishes held two tablespoons of coarse yellow

maize and half a teaspoon of a thick waxlike grease. Very few of us had been able to get down the bitter bread, nor could we stomach the maize. Nevertheless, this food gave us reason enough for a prayer of thanksgiving after the fare we had received in the boxcars. Bread, soup, and gruel were to be our diet for the next four weeks.

On the way back to our barracks we saw seven nondescript men come shuffling through the fence surrounding the solitary confinement shack. We were told they were the only survivors of a detachment of three hundred men deported from the White Russian and Ukrainian sections of Eastern Poland when the area was annexed by the Soviet Union after the Hitler-Stalin Pact of 1939. As the first victims died off, the camp had been refilled with Ukrainians and Tartars accused of collaboration with enemy forces during the time of the German occupation.

It was impossible to guess the age of this handful of men trudging across the yard. They were ragged, dirty, and pinchfaced. They walked with the feeble gait of eighty-year-olds. But they might easily have been in their forties.

Waves of heat engulfed us when we reached our quarters. At first the warmth was wonderful, but, lying on the top tier near the low ceiling, I soon found it unbearable. The fire was consuming all the oxygen; the heat and the foulness of the air became a torture. It was a night of near suffocation.

A tall, thin official woke us in the morning. His bursts of violence seemed to come from a man driven by some dark inner conflict. He cursed the man who was sleeping nearest to the entrance and threw his baggage and clothing on the floor. We were bewildered by his tirade and his actions until we realized that he was our doctor and did not want us to sleep bundled up in our clothes. He gave a general order that we were to sleep with our clothes off for better blood circulation. He did not say how we were going to put up with the wet, rough boards or with the icy blasts that blew in every time the door opened.

His long, ungainly limbs and the black hair he habitually wore bare to the weather earned him a nickname, the Black Stork.

The third man the doctor tried to kick awake didn't react at all. The Stork tore off the coat the wretch had wrapped himself in and found him dead. He was not the only one. Three others had died in our barracks that night, unnoticed even by those who slept alongside them. The bodies were piled up to be taken away by the sled that was going for the day's supply of bread. The men who took them out to a cabin behind the mess hall reported that six other corpses had been found that morning in other barracks.

When our newly appointed barracks senior ordered us to turn out for breakfast, six men were unable to get to their feet. The Black Stork stalked around trying to kick them into activity, but some of them absolutely could not move. They were carried away to the same cabin with the dead bodies. This cabin was supposed to be the camp hospital.

At breakfast we noticed the strange appearances of each other's faces—puffed and swollen, the eyes half closed. It must have been the effect of all the liquid after five weeks' thirst plus the heat of the barracks after five weeks' cold. The swelling was probably the result of a desperate attempt by our weakened hearts to accommodate our systems to the new conditions.

While the bread was being served, the political commissar of the camp, a Volga German named Helwig, gave us a brief instruction. In genial tones he advised us to eat the bread but to avoid drinking water. This would have made more sense if the bread itself hadn't been loaded with water. Next he gave us a lesson in table manners—we were to take off our caps while eating. Slavishly we dragged them off in spite of the biting cold. As soon as he had left, apparently well satisfied with himself, we put them back to keep us warm during our turnips and water and yellow maize.

The first thing I did after breakfast was to move down from the top tier to a space left by one of the dead. It was close to Father

Josef with only an old Masurian between us. We asked the old man if he would change places with one of us, but he wouldn't budge. All he would say was, "I'm not interested in making any change."

We felt less harshly toward the old man when we learned the story of the woman's sweater of green wool he hung onto so desperately. It had belonged to his wife who had still been at the farm when he was taken away. He had recognized it on one of the women prisoners and learned that his wife had died during the first three days in the boxcars. Now he kept to himself, nursing his grief, his bitterness, and clinging to his wife's old sweater.

On that same first full day in the camp, we got our first and our only official statement of where we were and what we were to do. In a feeble attempt at military procedure the senior ordered us to line the aisle and stand at attention. Three officers walked down the narrow space between the two lines of prisoners. The central figure was a short fat man in the familiar uniform of the MVD. The visor of his cap was pulled far down over small tight eyes and he strutted down the aisle with his hands in the pockets of his black leather coat, looking us over and muttering a few unintelligible words. When he had finished his inspection the interpreter went into a set speech. The parrotlike words put an end to all our uncertainties, all our waitings, just as a death sentence does for a man in the dock: "The high commander welcomes you as coworkers in a most important project for the Soviet Union. This work has already done much for victory in the Patriotic War. Your job will be to improve the great Petchora railroad system. This is the system that brings coal and oil from Vorkuta to feed the famous industries of Leningrad, Gorki, and Moscow." Then the interpreter, who was one of those who interspersed their translations with little cringing bows toward the boss, hammered home with unpleasant directness a lesson we had already absorbed from one day in Column Seven. "This is an immense project and thousands of workers have already given their lives to it. You must not be sentimental if some of your group make the same sacrifice. Be clear about one thing from the start: this is not a health resort; it is a work camp. And remember you are in the Soviet Union and living by its rules: those who work, eat; those who don't, die."

The officers then wheeled out, leaving us to digest the dismal fact that we had been swallowed up by the vast forced labor camp system of the Komi region between Petchora and Vorkuta. My fears on the train had been justified. This was the area I had read about—a district larger than all of Germany, under exclusive control of the department of forced labor in the Soviet Ministry of the Interior. We began to exchange what slight information we had on this vast area: the Petchora was a river flowing into the Barents Sea about five hundred miles northeast of Archangel…an enormous system of slave labor projects…worse conditions than most of Siberia…

The lugubrious conversation was interrupted by the return of the interpreter. He had some more details to fill out his little speech: "That officer was the high commander in charge of all work camps in the Knjashpogost section of the Komi Republic. Here is your work task: you will be digging a canal on the far side of the railroad tracks. The canal is necessary to relieve danger from ice and flood water to a railroad bridge over the Izhma River. The Izhma is a main tributary of the Petchora.

"Your work on the canal will be hard work. You are to have ten days of rest before you start it. Use it well to build your strength.

"Now everyone must immediately go outside in the sun. The barracks is to be cleaned."

There was an odd kind of satisfaction in knowing exactly where we stood and having some kind of specific future mapped out for us. But there was little consolation. The men who had died beside us last night, the others who were dying around us, our own consuming weakness made a mockery of the promise of ten days of "rest" before we were given hard physical labor in the subarctic cold.

It was about ten o'clock in the morning when we went outside and the sun was shining strongly. It melted the top snow on the roof and sent water dripping down the icicles spiking from the overhanging eaves. Everyone tried to get a place leaning against the sunny wall out of reach of the dripping water. Men who were too weak to fight for a good place dropped down anywhere in the wet snow. Among these was Father Kolfenbach, shivering from cold, inside an overcoat now twice too big for him. The rest of us leaned, weak and tired, against the wall, blinking at the snow glare and watching the water drip from the eaves.

Not all of us were listless. A little energetic red-faced fellow named Max Abromeit made a great business of trying to liven us all up. He hobbled up and down in front of us, using a cane to drag his stiff leg through the snow, and shot out a barrage of advice: "What's the matter with you all? Get moving! Walk around a bit. It'll make the blood flow and you'll feel a lot better. And take deep breaths. You're done if you lose your fight. Look at me! Two wars didn't kill me. Do you think they're going to break me down here? I've got a bride at home and I'm going back to her. You just wait and see!"

A young lad named Horst squatting on his haunches by the wall gave a little cheer. "You've got the right idea, old fellow, but the wrong technique. The less you do the longer you last. Every stitch of work you do that isn't absolutely necessary is plain and simple suicide. I know what I'm talking about. I'm alive today because I deserted the army and did three years for it. See these fingers?" He held up a long thin hand. The first two joints of the forefinger and the first joint of the middle finger were black with gangrene from frostbite. "They don't look nice and they don't feel so good. But these fingers will get me through this summer and someday I'll be back home in Berlin."

This same Horst had his bunk on the far side of Father Josef. When we were back in the barracks again, he came sidling up to me. "Your friend is practically done for," he whispered. "Why don't you let me take his coat and shoes before *they* get them?"

His talk was interrupted by a racking cough and I looked at him quietly and said, "Let's not rush it. Suppose we wait and see which of you goes to pieces first?"

When he left I discovered that the half-tin of food we had saved from the boxcar was missing.

At supper that night I was so sick that I could only nibble at the crust of bread, and merely looking at the turnips and maize made my stomach turn. But I received a pleasant surprise when I passed the kitchen on my way out. One of the girls, a young evacuee from the Rhineland by the name of Lili Glaser, who had been caught in Elbing, stopped me and brought out Gertrud, the vicar general's housekeeper I had last seen in Insterburg.

Gertrud looked flushed and worn out as she greeted me. "I'm so happy, Father, that we have a priest. That's the first good news I've had since I got here."

I congratulated her on having a job in the kitchen, but she shook her head sadly: "The men around here want more from the women than work. I don't think they'll keep anyone long who doesn't give them what they want. Pray for me, Father."

I asked after her sister Lena.

"She's still with me but I'm worried. She's getting very weak."

A guard broke up the conversation.

The next day was Holy Thursday, the day of the Last Supper when Christ on the eve of His Passion and Death instituted the Sacrament of the Holy Eucharist. There could be no Holy Eucharist for us, but we found consolation in the liturgy of the day.

Father Kolfenbach had barely managed to make it back to his plank after breakfast. The old Masurian lay in his bunk, too lifeless even to go to the mess hall. Leaning against the corner so that light could fall on the missal, I started reading to Father Josef from the Introit of the Mass: "But it behooves us to glory in the Cross of Our

Lord Jesus Christ, in whom is salvation, life, and resurrection, by whom we are saved and delivered..." The Epistle offered a meaning for the boxcars and Column Seven: "...we are being chastised by the Lord that we may not be condemned with this world." The Gradual told us, "Christ became obedient for us unto death, even to the death of the Cross. Therefore God also has exalted Him..."

Together Father Josef and I, in full knowledge that physical death would separate us very soon, read the Offertory prayer: "I shall not die, but live; and shall proclaim the works of the Lord."

I was just noticing that our old neighbor was sitting up against the wall listening attentively when Father Josef's eyes warned me to look to my right.

The political commissar was standing there. Instead of the outburst I feared, he said quite politely, "Am I disturbing you?"

"Not at all."

"You were praying, weren't you?"

"Yes. We are both priests and this is a great feast day in our Church. Do you object?"

"Not at all. These are your free days and you can do what you want. Besides, you must know that the Soviet Union gives full freedom of religion. Anyone can worship as he wishes."

"I am glad to hear that. But I don't suppose that is what you came to tell us."

"Well, no. I have something for you to do. Can you write Russian?"

"Only the alphabet and only the capital letters—and I'm not too quick with them."

"That's good enough. Here's what I want. Moscow has ordered that we make a list of all who die in the camp—names and dates of death. I want you to list the nine men who died from your shipment."

I thought fast. This could provide an opportunity for making a census of my "parish" and getting around to visit it.

"That will be difficult," I objected. "I don't even know my neighbor's name let alone the names of the men who died the first night. I will have to go around and ask. And it will be easier to keep the list up to date if I take down the names of all the living."

He agreed to this and took me out to find some writing material. This gave me a peep at the camp outside the beaten path from barracks to mess hall. Leaning against the outside wall of a hut that served as the doctor's office and was labeled "Ambulatorium," I could hear the noise of a heated discussion. Finally the commissar came out with the Black Stork who handed me a piece of cardboard and a pencil, saying, "God help you if you don't bring this back tonight. If I lose it I can't keep up my work."

With the help of our senior I managed to discover the names of seven of the nine men who had already died. Then we started on the names of the living. My instructions were to ask for the surname, first name, father's first name, date and place of birth, and former occupation.

I would have liked to add another question, "Religion." But I really did not need to go beyond the questions given to make a safe guess at the answer to the other. Since Germany is divided into rather clear-cut religious areas, the birthplace alone was a significant clue. Furthermore names like Alois, Franz, August, Josef, Anton were usually avoided by Protestants, who preferred Willy, Fritz, Kurt, Horst, and Max, while a few names like Hans and Georg were interdenominational. I stood a fair chance of learning the religion from their own and their father's first names.

So I was able to visit my "parishioners" and let them know that, in spite of my unpriestly appearance, I was a Catholic priest bringing them a chance to make their Easter confession. We made arrangements to meet at various places: my bunk, behind the toilet shed or inside it, or to go out and saw firewood together. After the first few confessions I took the pencil back to the Black Stork thanking God for the marvel of grace that an order from Moscow should have brought together a priest and his people for Easter confessions.

That night Father Kolfenbach took a turn for the worse. The bread had given all of us another severe bout of dysentery. It was more than Father Josef could stand. I roused a guard and begged for medicine. All I got was abuse and curses. Pastor Goebel and I could do nothing more in our helplessness than take turns watching by his bed and helping him out to the shed. I crushed some charred wood from the stove into powder and tried that old-fashioned remedy. With great effort Father Josef managed to swallow some of it but it did not help.

It was pitiful to sit and watch this once big and strong man, a man not yet in his forties who had never known a day's illness, lying there so helplessly weak, and dying for lack of a little medicine that might have carried him over the crisis and enabled him to survive.

On one of my watches I dozed off and awoke to see Father Josef stumbling by himself along the bunks toward the door. Before I could reach him, Pastor Goebel had leaped from his top tier and half-carried him out.

On Good Friday the morning routine was as merciless as ever. Even those like Father Kolfenbach who could not stir for breakfast were forced to get up and report outside for roll call afterward. The Black Stork dragged them from their beds like logs of wood and kicked them on the floor till they got up. All but one responded to this. He was unconscious. We were able to help Father Josef outside. When we got back from roll call the unconscious man had been dragged to that day's pile of corpses.

The next item for this "rest day" was sick report. We were marched in groups of twenty to the "ambulatorium," ordered to strip and wait in an adjacent room until we were called. Through the door we could hear the monotonous repetition of questions: "Dysentery? With or without blood? Stick out your tongue. Turn around." Then another voice would announce the classification of each prisoner. In descending order of fitness each was labeled as group one, two, three, or "OK." We were soon referring to OK's as KO's. That classification meant you were "without category," unfit for heavy work even by labor camp standards.

Pastor Goebel and I held Father Josef between us to face the examining committee. There were four members. The chairman seemed to be an elderly fellow with tin-rimmed glasses, graying hair and a long, cynical knife-slit of a mouth. His deep, clever features, showing both intelligence and jaded satiety, reminded me strikingly of Holbein's "Erasmus." We came to call him "Brillen-August" a German nickname for people who like to wear glasses for their scholarly appearance.

But a white-uniformed woman who toyed continuously with a stethoscope seemed to be running the show. Her well-fed appearance and her make-up made it seem likely that she had just come from Moscow.

Third on the committee was the Black Stork and the fourth was the political commissar who had been so concerned over our religious freedom.

The commissar grinned broadly at us and then at his companions, as though looking for their applause, and said to us, "You're the lads who blessed the Nazi guns, aren't you?"

Pastor Goebel looked straight at him and answered for all of us: "I don't remember ever blessing any weapon. But I do remember going to jail for refusing to salute the Nazi flag. And I remember being drafted and sent to the front even though I was a working pastor with bad lungs. My Catholic friends here have records that read the same."

We were given the usual questions and testings. Then the woman doctor put a question to me: "Why is your thorax deformed?"

"I had tuberculosis and they collapsed one lung."

Our first physical examination since we had been taken into custody ended with all three of us being classed with the OK's. That meant assignment to work inside the camp as a general rule and outside in the canal only under particular circumstances.

After this ordeal was over Father Kolfenbach was near complete exhaustion. I tried to read to him the Gospel account of Our Lord's Passion from my missal, but in spite of himself he could not help dropping off into comas. I would stop and wait for him to recover. When he did, he would beg me to keep on reading. Once he said, "Now I begin to understand something of what Our Lord must have suffered."

After the noon meal the Black Stork ordered everyone out and again enforced the order with his dragging and kicking routine. It was another delousing, this time in a drafty log cabin even more primitive than the last place. Again we stood naked and shivering till we were sent to another room in groups of twelve and given ten minutes to wash ourselves.

Poor Father Kolfenbach had to struggle to keep his balance. That was the full extent of the effort he could make. Too weak to wash, he suffered the added public humiliation of no longer being able to control his bowels. A rough-voiced prisoner kept railing at him for not cleaning himself. I looked at him in his helpless condition and saw another picture. His bones were plainly visible through his skin, the skin itself hung in lifeless folds on his cheeks, the tendons of his throat were taut like a very old man's. I saw standing behind him Christ before the mob on another Good Friday when Pilate pointed and said, "Behold the man!"

I finished as fast as possible and washed Father Josef as best I could with a piece of linen torn from my shirt, actually preparing his body for burial. His exhausted whisper of thanks was calm with resignation: "He was obedient unto death. Even if it doesn't make much sense for me to go on like this, I want to obey these people to the end...."

He could not go to supper that night. I brought him back a piece of the herring we had been thrilled to find in our bowls. He could not manage it. We made him as comfortable as we could on his bunk and Pastor Goebel, sitting on his second-tier bunk with his legs dangling over the side, began his Good Friday sermon. He read from his tiny Bible about the Good Thief who had been crucified with Christ. His clear, manly, warm voice reached every bunk. The prisoners stopped fidgeting with their belongings and fell silent. The only sound besides the pastor's voice was the crackling of wood in the barrel stove. He praised the mercy of Christ in forgiving the Good Thief, opening heaven to him in his last hour by the merits of His own innocent suffering. He invited his listeners to join the Good Thief and abandon the blasphemous thought that was the devil's temptation to us now: the thought of blaming God for all this suffering. To place such blame was to make man as if he were God and to hide the great sin of mankind which is unbelief. We should rather lay that sin bare before Him by sincere searching of our consciences. The pastor closed his sermon with a prayer to Our Lord to be with us in our desperate condition and to say to us also when our hour would come, "This day thou shalt be with Me in paradise."

He came down then to talk to us. Father Kolfenbach thanked him for what he had said and asked for his prayers.

Neither Pastor Goebel nor I had strength enough to stay awake all night, but we kept watch, allowing each other to doze for intervals of a few minutes.

Father Josef knew he was dying. We decided to hear each other's confessions. I put the small pocket stole around his neck and shoulders. The flickering fire from the stove cast long shadows over his fine priestly hands, now thin and bony as they rested on his knees. At the absolution he could not lift his hand. With the wrist resting on the knee, he managed to raise two fingers and shape a small sign of the cross. Then I took the stole.

He asked if I would administer the Sacrament of Extreme Unction. I took from his pocket the one book he had saved, a small *Ritual*. Then I found the cold cream jar of cotton soaked in holy oils.

These oils had been blessed just a year before, on Holy Thursday, in the cathedral, by our bishop. Who could have thought then that that blessing would be reaching into this place?

By the fitful light of the stove I read aloud the soul-strengthening prayers of the last anointing: "Through this holy anointing, and His most tender mercy, may the Lord forgive you whatever sins you may have committed."

I made a small sign of the cross with the holy oil on his bloodshot eyes, his ears, nose and his cracked lips; on the hands which so often had been raised in blessing; and finally on the weary shepherd's feet.

My dying friend was engulfed by a wave of misery as his mind wandered back to his home and family. He struggled to speak through his heavy breathing: "My mother...worked all her life to give us an education...I owe her my vocation...if you get back... give her this cross...this rosary...tell her...I died with them in my hands...my brother...he's missing...his wife and six children...help them."

I promised that if I survived I would try to do everything he asked. In return I asked him to use his place in heaven to win me strength to get through what was ahead. I thanked him for all he had given me in the way of help, consolation, and especially in his wonderful example of generosity in helping others.

He brushed aside my thanks and started finding fault with himself: "I remember...in the boxcar...I lost my temper with him...told him not to act like a spoiled child. I'm sorry for it...now I know what he was going through.... Don't ever forget, Gerhard, we can never, never...be too merciful to others."

I asked him if he had any regrets that his superiors had assigned him to the eastern province and caused him to be caught up in our enslavement.

"No, no! I never once regretted obedience... I don't regret it now...just thankful...greet my parishioners for me...tell the

provincial...thank the community...for making me a Redemptorist...tell them I give my life to God in praise...thanksgiving...
atonement."

"Josef," I whispered, "it is almost midnight, almost Holy Saturday. You'll be there in time to sing the triple alleluia with the angels."

There was the trace of a last smile on his lips as he answered,
"That would be fine."

He looked at his hands and I could see that his mind was far
away. We sat there silent, looking into the dying embers in the stove,
until his sagging body told me he could sit up no longer. I called
Pastor Goebel to help me lay him down on his bunk. I was too weak
to do it alone.

He passed the night, sometimes unconscious, sometimes delir-
ious with a thirst he could not satisfy. At one time he said, "If I
could only have one sip of lemonade through a straw..." I wiped the
heavy sweat from his brow and he went on repeating, "...through a
straw...through a straw."

Holy Saturday morning I had to go to breakfast. When I got
back I started reading to him from the liturgy of the day. Three
times I repeated a text from the day's Epistle: "You have died to sin
and your life is hidden with Christ in God. When Christ, your life,
shall appear, then you too will appear with Him in glory."

But he was so weak that listening was too great an effort. He
begged me to stop. "I can't listen any more, Father. That's enough...I
can't follow any more...I never would have believed...it could be so
hard...for a priest to die." The moment of death that he had always
been willing to face with such faith and courage was proving to be a
far more bitter trial than he had been able to foresee.

He closed his eyes and sucked in air through his open mouth.
The agony had set in. I gave him the last blessing with the plenary
indulgence for the hour of death and repeated the prayer, "Jesus,
Maria, Joseph." I pushed aside the stubborn old Masurian who still
held his place and crawled down his plank to Father Kolfenbach's

head. Pastor Goebel was in the aisle on the other side of him holding his left hand while I held his right. We put the *Ritual* on his
chest and together we prayed the prayers for the dying: "Into Thy
hands, O Lord, I commend my spirit. Lord Jesus Christ, receive
my soul…"

We were at our prayers when the Black Stork came in and
started his morning routine of dragging bodies from bunks to floor.
Our senior tried to head him off as he approached us. "You can see
he's dying, doctor. Let him die with his two friends. He's a pastor
and so are they."

"Priest or no priest," the Black Stork roared, "he has to die in
the infirmary like the rest."

With that he grabbed Father Kolfenbach's feet and dragged
him at an angle off the bunk so that his head and shoulders hit the
floor. Weak as I was, I felt so enraged that I could have flown at
him. But Pastor Goebel and I were struggling to keep our hold on
Father's arms enough to prevent his head from cracking too hard
on the ground. The Black Stork strode away and the senior helped
us put a blanket under the dying priest. The three of us started to
carry him to the "Infirmary" but his one hundred fifty pounds was
too much for our shriveled muscles. The best we could do was drag
him on the blanket down the aisle and across the snow. We reached
the infirmary door completely exhausted and stood wondering how
we could get our burden up the four icy steps.

While we were struggling in vain to do this, the medic in charge
of the infirmary came to the door. He was a repulsive-looking man,
fat faced with only one eye and a small slit where the other had
been gouged out. He had a smirk on his face as he dragged the
unconscious body up the steps saying, "Come on, hurry up with it.
There's plenty of room in our salon."

We went through a vestibule into a horror chamber that sur-
passed the wildest words we had heard about it. In a space about
fifteen feet square there was a low platform with about twenty dead

and dying lying on it one beside the other. Some of the corpses were stacked in two layers, some extras lying on the floor. We could not find place on the platform for Father Kolfenbach but One Eye merely grinned, wedged open a narrow space between a corpse and another wretch in his last agony, and heaved Father into it.

Father's body was so long that his head sagged over the back edge of the platform. I stepped over the corpses to get to the head and support it, just in time to close his eyes as he breathed his last. I said the liturgical prayers for the moment of death, and then took the cross from around his neck, his finger rosary, his notebook, his fur cap, and his overcoat.

We were supposed to leave right away, but I turned to One Eye and asked if there were any Catholics in the room.

He answered most affably. "Sure," he said. "I'm one myself. I used to be an altar boy and I played the trumpet in our parish band. I can even play the organ."

Would he point any dying Catholics out to me and call me after this from the barracks when he knew a Catholic was dying?

"Gladly!" he said. "We have some work for you right now. Here are two men from a village near Braunsberg. They're going fast."

The two were good Catholic farmers and overjoyed to have a priest come to them unexpectedly at the last.

While I heard the confessions One Eye was busy "preparing" Father Kolfenbach's body for burial. He left him with nothing but his soiled underwear. When he had finished Father Kolfenbach's head was sagging back again, his mouth agape, his ribs sticking high in the air.

My first reaction was to wish for the gifts of Goya or Hieronymus Bosch to paint this scene that would horrify all civilized men. Then I thought that Father Kolfenbach would want this looked upon with other eyes than theirs. As he lay there he was fulfilling another last feature of the Passion of his Master who hung ignominiously on the cross as the soldiers divided His garments.

There was a feeling of unreality, of nightmare, around me as I stumbled back to the barracks. It would be about nine o'clock on Holy Saturday morning, the hour when the great triple alleluia was echoing to heaven from the churches of Christendom. I fell on my bunk and kissed the cross I had taken from my dead friend. I was still too dazed to think very coherently, but in the midst of all I was conscious of an undercurrent of that deep Christian joy Our Lord promised would not be taken from us even in the hour of our greatest suffering.

I gave Father Kolfenbach's overcoat to the senior and offered his blanket to Pastor Goebel. The pastor at first refused, feeling he could not allow himself to profit materially by the pain and death of a friend. He accepted it only when I made him realize that Father Kolfenbach would have wanted him to have it. I added in a rather strained attempt at humor that the blanket would not make a Catholic out of him.

One Eye had promised to let me know when the body was to be moved. But he never did.

CHAPTER X : *The Labor of Slaves*

BY THE TIME OUR "TEN DAYS OF REST" WERE OVER WE
had become familiar with Column Seven and had also learned
something about its place in the Soviet system of forced labor
camps. But I never did learn exactly what category of prisoners I
was supposed to be in.

Column Seven itself was simply a collection of barracks like
our own arranged around a central square or parade ground. The
living quarters were all built on the same pattern; one story structures about twenty-two feet wide and seventy feet long, made of
logs with the chinks between them stuffed with a peat plaster. On
the inside they were lined with the same double tier arrangement
of rough wood bunks, with upright poles spaced along each tier to
support the roof. One or two crude stoves stood in the middle of
each.

There was a mess hall and kitchen, the "ambulatorium," the
death house of an infirmary, the isolation barracks at which we had
seen the seven beaten men, the delousing station, the guards' quarters and the little shacks that served as latrines for each barracks.
There were also some open sheds for storage and various kinds of
work.

The building that had been pointed out to us as the isolation
barracks was a prison within a prison. The wooden wall that surrounded it was topped by two strands of barbed wire stretched on

iron supports leaning inward. Another fence made of billows of barbed wire lay in wait for anyone who should manage to scale the wall. Such an inner prison is standard equipment in all closed camps. Perhaps it had some meaning in camps situated near free settlements, as in parts of Siberia and other places, but it had no meaning here.

The entire apparatus had been inherited from the tsars and Sovietized. It bears little relation now to the relative freedom of the banishment to Siberia we read of in Dostoevsky. All the hardships and cruelties have been retained and most of whatever humanity there was in the old system removed. It is now an essential part of the Soviet economic system, supplying up to ten percent of its labor force.

All camps are governed by the Central Camp Administration in Moscow, known by the abbreviation GULAG. Enforcement is in the hands of the police of the Ministry of the Interior, once the Cheka, later the OGPU and the NKVD, now the MVD.

In theory there are two types of camp: the ITL or "corrective labor" camps and the *Katorga* or "forced labor" camps.

Our Petchora-Vorkuta district, in the subarctic adjacent to the western top of Siberia was a Katorga area. Actually, the term "corrective labor" camp was a euphemism used by the Soviets because they had at one time proclaimed the abolition of the Katorga. When World War II restored the Katorga concept with its more severely enclosed imprisonment there was not much difference between one type and another except for the disciplinary camps for the recalcitrant or the death camps for the hopelessly ill. The type of camp had no bearing on what kind of work you were assigned, what kind of masters you had or who your fellow prisoners were.

The practice of mixing criminals with political prisoners which we had already witnessed in the boxcars was also used in the camps. And in the camps too it was the criminals or *blatnoÿ* who bossed the place and survived at the expense of the rest. They were an additional drag in the labor camps because they were as expert at avoiding work as they were at stealing extra food. And the food they stole came from prisoners whose rations had been reduced to a minimum because the *blatnoÿ* had caused them to fail to meet their work quota.

We were inducted into the work routine by being lined up around the square, all facing the center. The camp officers stood there in all their dignity. The *natchalnik* or commander, a stupid man but an efficient executive, was short and heavy set. He wore an officer's beret and long leather overcoat, highly polished leather boots, big gold epaulets, and the insignia of a first lieutenant. The staff around him consisted of a fat sergeant in charge of the guards and two men in working clothes: the work overseer, or *dessyatnik*, Mr. Norman, and the bookkeeper, a wrinkled pock-marked man called Crooked Boot because of his limp.

We were divided into brigades of twenty to thirty men each, each brigade named after its supervisor or "brigadier." The commander's talk was based on the golden rule, "If you don't work, you don't eat." This was no moment for us to feel sardonic over our knowledge of how much work was done by those who ate best in the camp. The rule was being spelled out for us. In whatever work we were assigned to digging the canal, shoveling snow, sawing wood or anything else—we would be assigned a norm for the brigade to accomplish each day. If we fulfilled our quota one hundred percent or better we would receive our full daily ration of twenty-one ounces of bread plus the soup and maize that went with it. If we failed to reach it we would get less; if we exceeded it by fifty percent we would have a corresponding increase in our ration. We would start with a small quota, the commander told us, so we could show our good will by doing more than was required. He ended with a classic remark, "We Russians are very humane people. But even our humaneness has its limits when people do not want to work."

The delousing station was the supply center for our prison

work clothes. We stripped once again and strung our civilian clothes on the familiar wire hoop. Then we lined up before a little wicket opening in a partition. As each prisoner stepped up we could hear a rough, tired voice wearily repeating, "One, two, three, four, five, six, seven." At each number an article of clothing would come flying out the wicket without anyone as much as taking a look at the man they were meant for.

"One" was a shirt. The few shirts that had backs on them at all were cut off just below the belt. Our predecessors had supplied themselves with handkerchiefs.

"Two" was underpants, originally long but with legs cut off either at the knee or the hip.

"Three" and "Four" were the most valued: brand-new cotton-quilted pants and coat that made a warm overall called *bushlat*.

"Five" was a *shapka*, a cap of the same cotton quilting, sometimes trimmed with fur.

"Six" was *vatchinki*, cotton-quilted stockings to be worn like boots.

"Seven" was a pair of new straw shoes supposed to be tied on by straw straps at the back of the heel.

We had five minutes to get dressed in the ill-fitting assortment of articles that had been thrown at us. I was lucky enough to come close to the collectivist plan's universal idea of a worker. My only real trouble was with the straw shoes, which were far too short for the straps to tie around the heel. But others were less fortunate.

When our time was up there were still some standing helplessly with their clothes in their hands. Others made such comic spectacles that the rest of us burst out laughing. Max Quandt was six foot seven. He had got into a shirt that reached just to his chest and he could not get into his pants at all. Adalbert, a truck farmer from Vienna just five feet tall, made a quick exchange with him just as we were being ordered out. The size was better, but poor Max was hustled out with the rest of us before he could struggle into them. Back through the snow he marched with us to the barracks, naked except for the straw sandals and the shirt that came down to his chest.

Before going to bed we paraded before each other in our uniforms and laughed at ourselves for looking like a bunch of Eskimos.

Next morning I wished my fellow pastor Theo Goebel a Blessed Easter and we formed ranks for our first day of routine work.

Three of our five brigades were sent out to the canal. We were with the KO's assigned to shovel snow from the camp. My brigade was supervised by Warkowski, a tall cynical Pole with water-blue eyes. He took us to the tool shed and gave each of us a crude wooden snow shovel. When we heard our quota we knew we could not possibly reach it in our condition. At any given moment at least a third of our dysentery-ridden crowd was lined up outside the little shed. Most of the others exhausted their strength in the simple effort to keep standing on their feet. The sharp arctic air was so full of oxygen that it seemed to burn our chests as we breathed it in.

Our job was to shovel away the snow piled seven to nine feet high around the kitchen. The winter's wash water and garbage thrown into the piles had frozen and had to be chopped out with picks. With all the strength I could muster I could just manage to lift the pick and let it fall back again on the ice. We did not make very rapid progress, but when we thought of the men in the canal we realized that this was easy work indeed.

I tried to meditate on Easter but my voluble companion Max Quandt managed to keep thinking up things to talk about all day long. Although he was sixty years old and had lost over eighty pounds in five weeks, he was still the strongest and the most optimistic of us all. He sucked on the cold stem of an empty pipe and told us endless tales of the taverns he had known in the three counties where he had worked as a teamster.

When someone expressed surprise that he had belonged to the Communist Party and the German National (Conservative) Party at the same time, he shrugged his shoulders and said, "What could

I do? My friends were in one party and my customers in the other. I couldn't let either of them down."

My other workmate was as sick and silent as Max was energetic and talkative. His hands and feet were terribly swollen. Even his eyes and cheeks were bloated with water. Polite and considerate, he was obviously a man of culture and education. After telling us he had been a soldier, he went on with some bitterness: "I'm not a man to refuse to work as a prisoner of war, even for the Russians. If this made any sense I could take it. But look what we're doing. We're moving this pile a couple of feet. It'll freeze again and we'll have to do it all over. And that ditch they call a canal! Any engineer would laugh at it. What good is anyone getting out of my starving to death here while my wife and children are bombed out back home?"

We shoveled on till dark and a number of the men in their numbed weakness came near despair at the thought of having to wrack themselves to this day-long physical effort day after day with no end in sight. Max rewarded me for being a good listener by moving over beside me and helping finish my share of the work.

After supper we were initiated into a moving game that became part of our new routine. One brigade was taken out of our barracks and another brought in. I was sorry to see Pastor Theo in the group that left.

When the newcomers had finished their fight for places and quieted down a little, I climbed to a log on top of the banked stove where everyone could see me, even from the upper tier, and asked for five minutes of silence to give my Easter talk.

They were all attentive as I opened my missal at the Gospel for Easter Sunday and read to them: "Who will roll back the stone from the entrance of the tomb for us?"

I addressed them as the fellow prisoners we were and referred the question in the text to the entrance of this camp in which we had been buried alive. I went on to speak of God, who had permitted us to be taken here as the answer and ended something like this: "Almost all here have been baptized Christians, but how many times have we not buried Christ alive in the tomb of our heart, and sealed it with our many sins? This then is our Easter message: that we are entombed here in these coffinlike shelters only to learn that there is a much more terrible tomb of our own making within us. Let us pray for grace and strength to break the scarlet seals and roll away the stone from our hearts that Christ may rise to live in us once more. Then only will we find the meaning of our suffering and the light of our darkness."

Then I offered a heartfelt prayer for our fellow prisoners, their wives, their children, and all their relatives.

I climbed down from my unconventional pulpit but the silence hung over the room for a few minutes more. As I was poking the warmed log I had been standing on into the fire, an old Protestant peasant and an old soldier who had been a freethinker came over to thank me for the sermon.

The freethinker said, "That's the first time I've ever heard anything good said about Jesus Christ. You should tell us more about Him."

That night there was a peaceful atmosphere in the barracks. The men shouted less and didn't quarrel so much with their neighbors. I was happy to think that a few rays from the light of Easter morning had reached into this dark corner of the world.

At roll call the next morning the *natchalnik* was pacing up and down the square talking seriously with Helwig, the political commissar. When they stopped Helwig stepped forward and announced in solemn tones: "The commander has been informed that religious services have been held in this camp. He wishes to make clear that the Soviet constitution grants complete freedom of belief and worship to every man in the Soviet Union. So for the preservation of this liberty of conscience, and to avoid interference with each individual's religious persuasion, it is prohibited to hold group services in this camp. Those concerned are hereby warned never to hold such services here again."

A man at my elbow muttered into his beard. "I'd like to get my hands on the pig who turned you in." The man speaking was the old freethinker.

The commander himself seemed indifferent to the whole matter. I rather got the impression he privately despised the commissar's parroting of the party line though he had to back him up in public. Although of lower rank, the political commissar, or *politruk*, was the representative of the Communist Party and a power to be reckoned with.

We went on shoveling snow and being moved from barracks to barracks almost every second day. We were being shifted to a shelter next to the infirmary when a bearded old man in a black fur cap collapsed in the snow. I picked him up and half dragged him to our new quarters. It was the old teacher who had been next me in the boxcar the day before we unloaded.

He was groaning with pain. "I can't stand it any longer. I'll give you my wife's address. Tell her. Could you read me something from your Bible before I die?"

Theo was in our new barracks so I brought him over to the old man. We were settling him on a bunk when I discovered we were not alone. Helwig, the *politruk*, was standing over us. "Go right on," he said. "Don't let me disturb you."

Theo's answer was a little gem of diplomacy: "We're really glad to see you, Mr. Commissar. We've been wanting to thank you for the announcement this morning. We were glad to know that the Soviet constitution does grant religious freedom and we agree perfectly with you that no man's religious convictions should be offended."

Helwig smiled with pleasure and Pastor Theo kept right on. "That's a very Christian point of view. Do you think the commander would let us pray with those who spontaneously ask for it?"

The commissar was eager to respond to our sensible reaction

to this announcement but he had his doubts about the question. "If you got that permission, how would we know that you wouldn't sabotage our work by talking politics?"

"You could come to the services yourself and stop us if you heard anything like that."

To keep Helwig from a quick refusal, I threw in a question. "Is it politics to tell the prisoners that Christ has risen and still lives?"

"That would demoralize the men and destroy their will to work," he answered.

"How do you make that out?" I insisted. "Believing in life after death doesn't make a man weak. It gives him a good motive for working hard here on earth."

Helwig looked unconvinced, so Theo tried again. "Would there be any objection if we prayed for strength so we could get better and get our quota done every day?"

"These are difficult points of policy," the *politruk* answered. "I will have to take them up with Moscow. But in the meanwhile, I warn you again, don't hold any religious services. Will you have a smoke?"

I took some from the pack of makhorka tobacco he offered and he gave the rest to Theo along with a piece of newspaper for rolling. When he had gone I gave my share to Theo, who was a heavy smoker. But he was so downcast at not getting around Helwig that he did not take much enjoyment in his makhorka.

He brightened up a bit when he thought of a new strategy. We were not forbidden to read the Bible to any individual who asked for it. We could simply read it loud enough for the others to overhear!

A voice called to me from the tier above, "Father, I'd like you to get me ready."

Although I barely recognized him, it was Heinrich Nitsch, a man who had talked to me at one time about his two babies and his worries. He was trying to sit on the edge of the bunk but was too weak to hold himself upright. His legs were swollen into straight cylinders. The ankles were so enlarged he could not move his feet and at the instep the flesh mounded from the toes into a great puffy ball.

There was no bitterness or fear in his voice as he made his confession. I sat up in the bunk with him and helped him not to fall. He tried to fold his swollen hands in the accustomed manner but could do no more than interlock the fingertips. His face in the firelight showed the structure of what had once been clean-cut features with a classic profile. You could see that through all the squalor and suffering he had preserved a lot of dignity. I had seen the same expression on Pastor Ebel as he marched out of the cellar in Heilsberg, an expression radiating inner peace that rose above the sordid surroundings.

The next day I felt a surge of well-being. My private cure for dysentery, keeping an almost total fast for an entire week, was working. I felt stronger and my body was giving unmistakable signs of adjusting to its new regime. I was actually in high spirits as I got that day's assignment. Four of us, including Max, the talkative teamster, were detailed to provide water for the kitchen. To get it we had to go out the main gate, along one of the outside walls, down a steep gorge and break the ice in a frozen creek. Our quota was six barrels before lunch and six more before supper.

After our third trip we got a windfall from the head cook, a well-fed, good-natured Ukrainian criminal named Stjepan. He gave each of us a bowl filled to the brim with thick gruel and let us in through the back door to the wood bin, where we enjoyed the most delicious and nourishing meal any of us had tasted since we were taken prisoners.

My pleasure was ruined by the sight that lay before us on our way to and from the creek. We could see the three brigades of our fellow prisoners working on the canal and it was a scene from the grimmer cantos of Dante's *Inferno*.

The canal itself was a wide band of dark earth through the

white snow. Its sixty-foot width had to be dug down to a depth of twenty-one feet. The implements were picks, the same primitive shovels we used for clearing snow, and wheelbarrows so antiquated the ancient slave drivers of Egypt or Babylon would have scorned them. Our predecessors had reached a depth of nine feet, which exposed the arctic permafrost and made the workers' picks bounce back from the hard earth.

Men and women swarmed through the ditch and along its banks in a planned but patternless movement like a colony of ants in slow motion. Some of the pick wielders were too weak to lift their tools while standing. They were kneeling on the frozen ground. They would lift the pick laboriously to one shoulder, rest it there for a moment and then lunge forward with a body movement, letting it fall into the ground, the body following the arc of the pick and remaining for another long moment bent in exhaustion, gathering strength to go through the motion again.

The shovelers had to complete the work of loosening the dirt, then dump it into wheelbarrows that took the black earth up the far side of the ditch and the sand up to the railroad tracks that ran along the near side. The bank of dirt grew higher with every foot the brigades dug down.

The runways for the wheelbarrows were planks laid loosely on uneven ground. An experienced, able-bodied working man with a good wheelbarrow would have needed all his strength and balancing skill to push a load up the steep incline. These unskilled and prison-weakened slaves had to do the job with barrows that were no more than big clumsy wooden boxes mounted on a tiny iron wheel no more than four inches in diameter. They simply could not do the impossible, so wires had been attached to the front of the wheelbarrows and two people pulled like horses while a third walked between the handles and pushed.

I watched three women struggle up the bank this way with a load of sand. The wheel went off the plank and the three of them wrestled with the heavy load trying to get it back on. Their super-visor—a prisoner like themselves—strode over to earn his position of privilege by yelling at them, "What's the matter with you? Hurry up! Get moving! Get moving!" They were falling far behind their impossible quota of three and a half cubic yards per person per day.

The picture was right out of the story of ancient slaves, the building of the pyramids, the Great Wall of China, Roman roads, the palaces of pagan princes. Here every mark of the individual personality had been suppressed. All dressed alike, all labored alike, they had no age, no sex, no separate meaning; nothing but a com-mon existence as units in a swarm of slaves.

ONE morning Helwig announced that we were to be put through another "interrogation" session. We remembered the ordeals at Heilsberg and shuddered.

An elderly man came in carrying a folder under his arm. Two prisoners followed him with a table and chair which they set down in the center of the barracks. Someone brought an oil lamp for the official and we were called up to the table one by one.

When my turn came I was impressed by the features of the man who sat before me. The lines etched into his face spoke so elo-quently of deep-held suffering that I thought I had seldom, except in the great paintings, seen a face so expressive of pain.

Slowly, in a sympathetic voice and with a fluent Swabian dia-lect, he went over the same list of questions I had been asked three times before. He seemed vexed at having to put the questions and closed his eyes sadly after each. He was content with the answers as I gave them and what had twice before taken three exhausting hours was over in fifteen easy minutes.

I made bold to thank him for his courtesy, praise his fluent German and ask him where he came from. He smiled, a little embarrassed, and said quietly, "We're Lutherans from the old Ger-man settlements on the Volga. Please don't repeat it to anyone, but

I have heard that the rest of my family is in Siberia." He detected my surprise at this confidence and added, "We're forbidden to talk with prisoners without witnesses present. But you are a priest and I know you won't betray me."

I promised to pray for him and his family that they might be brought together again. The last look from his tortured eyes stayed vividly with me all that night.

There must have been hundreds of thousands, perhaps millions, of Russian citizens scattered through the slave camps for no other reason than war had provided an excuse for the state to categorize them as "foreigners" and ship them out of the border regions to do forced labor. They were descendants of Germans, Poles, Lithuanians, Latvians, Estonians, Ukrainians, Hungarians, and various Tartars and Caucasians who had settled in Russian territory sometimes centuries before. But now, unless they were useful for other purposes, they were simply unreliable "foreigners" and fodder for the man-eating state machine. Imprisonment and deportation was more bitter and senseless to them than it was to us.

All Easter week I kept to my fast from anything with a high water content (which meant everything except whatever dry crust came on my ration of bread). Although the fasting made me feel better inside it did not help the swelling of my feet and legs very much. But my condition was something to be thankful for compared to what I saw around me. The first thing that had to be done after breakfast every morning was carry to the infirmary steps the stiff, frozen bodies of those who had died at work the previous day or in their bunks during the night. The bakery sled hauled them from there to a hut near the tool shed. When ten or twelve bodies had accumulated a larger sled would haul them to a mass grave in a sandy pit deep in the woods.

Our friend Alois was on the burial detail. The old soldier was neither a sentimental nor an emotional man, but he shuddered as he told us how the dead were buried. They had started trying to lower the bodies carefully with ropes and lay them side by side in the pit. The Black Stork had impatiently grabbed the ropes from their hands and shown them how this business of dumping corpses was to be done. He went over to the sled, grasped a body by the ankles, dragged it through the snow, swished it round in an arc and pitched it headlong into the pit. When all had been treated this way the detail sprinkled a thin covering of sand over that deposit of bodies and the work was done. The men were not allowed even to put an identification number on the pit, much less raise a cross.

Alois told me Father Kolfenbach had been buried that way with eleven others earlier in the week.

I told him that if he ever needed another helper to ask for me so that I could at least bless the ground.

On April 9 fifty of our sick OK's were marched off to a waiting boxcar and told they were being taken to a hospital camp where they would be sufficiently restored in health to come back and work in the canal.

My routine was much the same those days except for a change of barracks that brought me under a senior called Walter. He was a man of about my own age with a crippled right hand and a warped mind. He seemed to take devilish delight in making life as hard as possible for me. In an attempt to get me to do or say something he could report, he told me his wife was a Catholic and he himself a convert to the faith. We found out he had been an SS sergeant in the Oranienburg concentration camp near Berlin.

One of my jobs was bringing water to the delousing station. We were provided with handleless buckets which had to be clasped to the chest, drenching the carrier with icy water. But the work hardship was nothing compared to the abuse we had to take from Gorba, sadistic assistant to the syphilitic boss of the delousing station. Though a prisoner as we were, he cursed us incessantly. If he saw one of us resting he would fly into a rage and strike the offender, something he was forbidden to do.

At the end of one day's work I passed a line of women and girls marching from the delousing station to the barracks vacated by the fifty OK's who had been shipped out. I called out to them, "Any Catholics there? Anyone from Ermland?"

A voice called back "Thank God you are still here, Father." It was Gertrud, with her sister Lena beside her. Gertrud had become as thin as her silent sister since I saw her in the kitchen that first day at the camp. I fell in step with them for a little way and learned that she had lasted only two days in the kitchen. They were just coming back from two weeks in a small camp about three days' journey north. Their work had been to fell trees all day long, standing up to their waists in snow. At night they had to put the logs on their shoulders and drag them back to camp. A third of the women died during the two weeks. A district inspector found the survivors so weakened and their shoulders so lacerated that he ordered the camp vacated and the women returned to Column Seven. Lena was being put into the women's section of our expanded infirmary, but Gertrud had been declared healthy and fit enough to join the Third Brigade on the canal.

A new officer arrived to take over the work of the Black Stork, who was reported to be leaving us soon. He was young, healthy, good-looking, and not at all rough. It was he who conducted the next medical examination. He took one look at my puffed hands and swollen feet and ordered me to the infirmary. There was no great pleasure in the thought of being under One Eye's tender care, but at least it would get me away from Walter and Gorba.

CHAPTER XI : *The Camp Infirmary and May Day*

DRAGGING MY BAGS ACROSS TO THE INFIRMARY, I WAS not different in my wretched appearance, in my physical misery, in my struggle to stay alive, in my material helplessness than any prisoner in the camp. Yet my priesthood gave purpose to every day of my life and saved me from the pit of futility and despair that swallowed up those who could find nothing to live for in an existence wrenched out of the context that had given it meaning. Stripped of a church, formal ceremonies, respect, dignity, the naked priesthood still could function.

The fruits of God's victorious grace, so visible in the man who had died in my arms the other night, in Pastor Theo's invincible courage, in Father Kolfenbach's sacrificial death, in the serenity of women like Sister Imelda and Gertrud—all were grown in the garden of Christ's agony. To be called to accept not only my own share of it and help others to take theirs, but also to suffer a good measure of it vicariously for many others, known only to the infinitely merciful God, was worth any price I had to pay during the following ordeals.

One Eye's domain had been enlarged and improved since I saw it last. The death chamber in the middle had been white-washed and there were bunks around it. There were two wards on either side, one for the men and the other for the women, where the sick had a chance to recover before they were given up as hopeless and dragged into the middle chamber to die. But there was still a rule of thumb about admission to the infirmary. The number brought in always tallied exactly with the number of deaths during the preceding week.

We newcomers were greeted by the one-eyed master of the infirmary with his usual oily affability. Passing through the vestibule, I noticed two bodies lying on the floor, naked feet sticking out from a cover. I pulled back the blanket and recognized Jan, our tough friend from the boxcars. The bullying and pilfering that had enabled him to thrive in our boxcar community had finally failed. He had died two days previously from pneumonia.

A gentleman, as he liked to protest he was, One Eye asked me what bunk I would prefer. I pointed to one in the far corner, near one of two oiled-paper windows and as far away as possible from the open bucket that had been placed on the floor as a convenience for those too feeble to go outside. That bucket did a lot to take the joy out of such luxuries as whitewashed walls and a brick stove with a brick chimney. The stench actually made the room less livable than the common barracks.

As treatment for my swollen feet and legs I was ordered to put a log at the foot of my bunk and rest my feet on it so that they would be higher than my head. Crude as it was, the treatment was effective. The water drained from my legs so well that I had to go out ten times that night instead of my usual five. I could not bring myself to use the bucket.

Being able to go out into the clear night was something of a treat in itself. I could pump my lung full of fresh air and also hold the door open long enough to change some air in the room. I could stand for a few minutes and enjoy the luxury of being alone with the bright stars of the clear, deep northern sky. Bathed in the clean beauty of those arctic nights, the camp itself lost its squalor. The merciful cover of the soft light of night made it for the moment a place of peace. I had never before seen the stars in such brilliance and splendor. There was a meditation in the paradox that I was getting my most inspiring glimpse into the great beauty of creation while standing in the center of this concentration of man-made misery. For how many of us, I wondered, had God used these prison camps to reveal His beauty more clearly than we would ever have seen it amidst the cheap comfort of our lives back home?

Little Max Abromeit was in the ward, as lively as ever in spite of the fact that his lame leg was now giving him less trouble than other complications. He mixed no words in his short sketch of how things were run in the infirmary:

"Did you see Jan and the other fellow lying out there?"

"Yes, I did."

"Do you know why they're still there?"

"No."

"So that one-eyed pig and his hunchback helper can keep drawing the rations of the corpses."

Max went on with a few more pointed observations about the sole excuse for the existence of the infirmary being the continued survival of those two bloodsuckers.

I knew that Max had good grounds for his indignation. Control of the infirmary food plus first chance at the clothes and belongings of the dying had made One Eye a major capitalist in the black-market barter economy of prison camp life. His position also gave him a sense of power that he exercised at every opportunity.

My routine as a patient was not very complicated. A welcome item was washing in the two small buckets provided. We would line up naked on the floor waiting our turns, spending the time the while searching for lice. But the patients who refused either to wash or hunt lice kept us from ever reaching any approximation of hospital cleanliness. One Eye assigned us the chores of emptying the two wash buckets and the other bucket, but for obvious reasons he kept the task of carrying food from the kitchen for himself.

We received the same three dishes as the workmen plus a special course for the sick. This did not come to us without one more pin-prick of irritating humiliation. One Eye, like a politician disbursing public relief as though it came out of his own pocket, would first make a pompous little speech reminding us how generous it was of him to give us this treat. Then he would proceed ceremoniously from bunk to bunk placing in every outstretched hand a piece of egg cake the size of a small soda cracker. It was made of powdered egg that was rumored to have come from America. We waited impa-tiently through the homily and then ate the delicious nourishing morsel in utter silence as though performing a sacred rite. It did lift us out of our misery for a few brief moments once a day.

The Black Stork came in after breakfast and gave us all a quick examination. He let loose his customary diatribe against sleeping with clothes on and then ordered two patients into the death cham-ber. Their loud protests against what was usually a death sentence resulted only in their being dragged out at once. I took the oppor-tunity of helping them in order to get into death's waiting room.

Conditions were better in it. The bucket in the center of the room had a lid on it, the bunks were covered with bags of sawdust to absorb the waste from patients who had lost control of themselves. But the stove was fireless and the room bitter cold. I made a note of the empty stove as a possible means of future entrée and introduced myself as a Catholic priest. I added that if anyone wanted to speak to a Protestant minister, I could get a message to Pastor Goebel.

My old companion, Hermann the butcher from Elbing, was there, shriveled beyond recognition. Though he had to force every breath he drew, he answered my question about his own condition by pointing to his neighbor and saying, "I'm nothing but skin and bones. I can't last much longer. But he's worse than I am."

The neighbor was another butcher from the same city. His whole body was monstrously bloated.

"Help me over to the bucket, please, Pastor," he begged and then went on to prove his extremity had not taken all the fight out of him. "That oaf just wants us to die so he can get our stuff. We're animals and they want the hides. But he's not getting this." He was clutching a delicate porcelain pitcher from the old Majolika works of Cadinen, decorated with a bright flower design. "You help me to the bucket and I'll give it to you."

I shook my head, let him lean on me and did the best I could for him. I got him to the bucket and back as far as his bunk leaning heavily on me. When I tried to get him up again he sucked in a deep rattling breath, sighed out, "O my God!" and went limp in my arms, dead.

The dead body was too much for me so I called for One Eye. He barged into the room, saw at a glance that the man in my arms was dead, strode quickly to the head of the bunk, picked up the porcelain pitcher and attached it to his belt. Only then did he help me lift up the dead man and lay him out on the bunk.

There were two women in the death chamber, a middle-aged woman and a courageous girl named Maria so badly crippled from rheumatism that her legs were drawn up against her body as far as the knees could bend. At first contact Maria suggested, "Get into the women's ward next door as soon as you can, Pastor. Some of them are a lot worse than we are." The cold stove and One Eye's willingness to let others do the dirty work seemed my best bet for moving around the infirmary. When I went to him and volunteered to saw and carry wood—which he well knew to be part of his own responsibility—his callousness opened my way into the other ward. He accepted my help but ordered me to bring the fuel supply into the women's ward only. "The other ones are done anyhow. It'll do them no good."

It took a little black-market technique to get a decent piece of wood to cut up. Fortunately, I had some capital—the rations I had accumulated during my periods of dysentery. Behind the kitchen I waited for the Bulgarian who carted beams from a dismantled barracks for the cook's stove. I knew he was always hungry so I first helped him unload and then started waving half a day's ration of bread at him. He was a hard bargainer and I had to promise half of the next day's ration too before I got a log.

Waiting till the coast was clear, I rolled the log over toward the infirmary and Max Abromeit started to help me saw it. We had not cut one length when Walter came yelling over from his barracks. We had sneaked his personal ax and saw from their hiding place and he had spotted them.

I looked at him quietly and said, "Why don't you stop yelling and show us how to do this job properly?"

In an odd impulse of vain generosity and exhibition of strength he took the ax in his one good hand and sank it deep into the log. With the imbedded ax he lifted the whole beam into the air and in three mighty blows split the log into pieces. He preened himself and looked around for applause. We applauded so satisfactorily that he let us keep the tools for the next three hours.

The patients in the women's ward were dressed in the same dirty rags as the men. Some were stretched on their bunks, some shuffled around like ghosts, some stood about the stove trying to get a fire started. The One Eye of the women's ward was easy to pick out. Her name was Dora and she never changed in appearance or manner all the time I was in the camp. A tall, well-built woman with brown almond eyes, she was wearing a pair of soldier's breeches with two big black patches on the back. Always poised and serene, she had the bearing of a woman of birth and education. Though she never spoke to anyone of her past, her dialect told us she was from Berlin. Cool, clever, and affable, she was a typical military staff helper.

At the moment she was in a particularly happy mood. One Eye had just brought her some machorka tobacco as her cut in the barter he had made with the latest batch of clothes she had "organized" from dying women. She was glad to see my load of dry firewood. You always had to keep relighting a machorka cigarette and a burning stove was the best insurance for a good long smoke.

Lena called softly to me from her bunk on the second tier. She thanked me on behalf of all the women for the dry wood. They would be able to make ersatz coffee for supper and then boil their wash in a tin can. She told me she was doing well in the infirmary and was able to save extra food for Gertrud, who was still working in the canal.

Two girls who shared Lena's bunk thanked me for lending them my missal and asked me if I could come and hold services in their ward. I assisted another woman whose condition reminded me of Father Kolfenbach just before he died.

Then Dora called a warning from the window. The Black Stork was stalking across the yard. I was back in my bunk in time to hear his new orders. A detail was to pick up a load of pine branches from his office. The needles were to be stripped from the branches and brewed into a "vitamin tea" which would help our dropsy and scurvy. We were all eager to try the new medicine. The bitter green brew was not too hard to get down, but it turned out to be a horse cure that brought a new epidemic of dysentery and kept us miserable for the next twenty-four hours.

Gertrud and Lena came to visit me the following evening. They brought news that the woman whose confession I had heard in the ward had died during the night. She had been kept slaving in the canal until she had collapsed and been carried to the infirmary.

They brought me a dish of dried moss berries they had obtained from the rheumatic cripple Maria, who in turn had got them from Martha, the girl who acted as the Black Stork's servant. They had tried to make Maria eat them herself but she had said they would do her no good, whereas they might help me. We had a good long talk that lifted us out of our surroundings and carried us back to happier days in Frauenburg.

The death rate jumped, making room for a new set of patients, and this meant a new medical examination for all of us. My ten days of fasting plus the log beneath my feet had reduced the swelling and carried me over the dysentery crisis. I was dismissed from the infirmary and sent back to the barracks.

Walter gloated at having me back. I picked up the same routine of work at the delousing station and the kitchen to the accompaniment of abuse from Gorba, Walter, and their cronies. While Alois and I were sawing wood out in the driving snow we got a chance to know Martha, the Black Stork's assistant. Part of her job was to scrounge wood for his stove and she begged with such good humor and friendliness that we often drew down the wrath of Stjepan and Gorba when we were caught giving her pieces from our pile. She always had something to barter with hidden in her apron. It was usually her own ration of gruel which she could not eat because of her stomach condition. But she once tempted us by holding out in the palm of her tiny hand two small cubes of sugar, the first sugar we had seen since being taken into custody.

"We can't take that from you," I said. "Eat it yourself."

"Go ahead. Take it. I'll get more from the doctor."

My pastoral conscience gave a twinge at this. I respected Martha and I hoped that what I feared was wrong, but from what I knew of camp life I had to ask her, "Martha, I hope you don't have to pay too great a price for this sugar?"

She understood at once. "Oh no, Pastor. There's nothing at all like that. I wouldn't be there if there was. For all his rough show, he's really an honest man and he's very good to me. He gives me more of his own meals than I can eat. He's very sick himself, and awfully unhappy. I've seen him crying sometimes when he thought nobody was looking."

This was a new light on the Stork, but I could understand it. A tortured man near despair and filled with disgust at what he had to do could very well react with the violence he showed. I encouraged her to go on. "On Easter Sunday he gave me a twig of white birch with leaves on it. He had made the leaves sprout by keeping the twig in water on his stove. When he gave it to me he said, 'I know

Christians like to exchange symbols of new life at Easter.' I think he's a lot better than the new one. The new one trades with that one-eyed fellow in the infirmary. He stores away the clothes from the dead people. But the Stork has nothing. He works himself sick and hasn't even enough warm clothes for himself."

The news about the Black Stork was even more heartwarming than the sugar. We loaded Martha's arms with wood and told her we would do the same again any time we had the chance.

Theo was in the infirmary and, although it was against the rules, a few of us took a chance and went over to visit him. He was having a desperate fight against dysentery. Like everyone else in the camp he had his own pet cure for it and wouldn't put any faith in the water-abstinence treatment that had worked so well for me. So I gave him some "coffee" we had made from toasted breadcrumbs and delighted his heart by producing an old pipe Jan from Emden had left behind in the barracks.

His solemn procedure with the pipe was a touching demonstration of how much pleasure we got out of little things. He swung his swollen legs over the edge of his plank and eased himself down to the floor. Together we raked out some disinfectant One Eye had been given for the ward but never used. We poured it into a soup bowl and let the pipe soak for a while. Then Theo took a narrow strip of cloth and ceremoniously cleaned the stem. I boosted him back to the upper tier. He put the cold stem between his teeth and smiled through his swollen lips: "It's empty now, but as long as it's here there's hope it will smoke sometime. It feels good just to bite it."

It smoked a lot sooner than Theo could have hoped. Helwig the *politruk* appeared and didn't even bawl me out for being in the infirmary. Sensing his good mood, Theo started working on him at once: "How nice of you to come! It's been too long since we had a talk and I've missed you."

Helwig beamed at the compliment. Theo smiled innocently and looked from the commissar's cigarette to his own empty pipe.

"I know that a man in your position, Mr. Commissar, is always well informed on the latest developments. Have you any news you can give us?"

Helwig postured a bit, stamped out his cigarette and started to prepare another one. But first he passed around his makhorka and Theo started eagerly stuffing his pipe. My eye fell on the newspaper that Helwig was using for rolling cigarettes. It was an old issue of *Pravda*. There was a picture of Stalin, Roosevelt, Churchill, Eden, and some others seated around a table. I asked to see the paper and Helwig handed it over while he rolled his cigarette. There had been a conference at Yalta, Helwig said, to decide what the allies would do after the imminent collapse of Germany. According to Helwig's version of the *Pravda* account, Russia was on top of the situation and would have things just as she wanted them. All that could mean for us was an indefinite dragging on of our present situation.

Our melancholy brooding was broken into the next day when we were called out for an extraordinary roll call. It was announced that the whole camp would start preparing to celebrate the two great holidays of the working class, May first and May second. Part of the celebration was to be a competition between all the camps in the area with a special Stalin award going to the best camp. In order that we could all be proud of Column Seven, each canal worker's quota would be raised from three and a half cubic yards of earth to four and a half. To make a good showing easier, the OK's would be released from inside duties and allowed to go out and help the digging brigades in the canal. No mention was made of the fact that twelve women and six men had collapsed in the diggings the previous day. Our reward was to be an all-out celebration on the two Red holidays.

The big May Day drive was launched with all the Stakhanovite trimmings, including special privileges for "shock workers." A large chart was posted at the gate. The percentages of quota reached by each brigade, and by the best and the worst workers in each brigade, were posted every day. Each evening the top two workers from each brigade and the leader of the best brigade were signaled out for special reward. They ate on a raised platform at the end of the mess hall where everyone could see their servings of millet cakes as big as their fists. The special chart officer, a kind-looking fellow of Volga German descent wearing a clean uniform and a black fur cap, stood beside them and announced what they were getting. As our mouths watered at the sight of the food and the sound of the words describing it, he supplied us with such items of information as that each millet cake had been fried in three grams of fat.

The farce was played out in all seriousness in spite of the inescapable coincidence that night after night the same cronies of the brigade leaders turned up at the special table. The limit was reached one evening when an amiable big blonde who shared her favors regularly between the same camp officers was brought up in front of us and given a Stakhanovite eulogy for having exceeded 150 percent of her quota. Dispirited, disgusted, and exhausted as we prisoners were, this announcement caused a wave of laughter to pass through the ranks.

Ironically, we OK's who had been declared unfit for the canal were assigned to the heaviest work of all. Our wretched group were marched two miles down the railroad to the next siding. In a huge sand pit stood a train loaded with freshly sawn logs intended as fuel for the steam-shovel that gouged out the sand. The snow was three feet deep on either side of the tracks, which were themselves laid on a depressed roadbed with steep embankments on either side. The logs were piled high on two long open cars with sides four feet high. Each of the wet larch logs weighed about three hundred pounds. Our job was to climb up on the cars and unload the logs by hand onto piles clear of the tracks. Our quota was to unload both cars in two and a half hours. There were only twelve of us, all certified as too sick for the regular work brigades. It was quite impossible. None of us had any strength to speak of in our arms or legs. When the quota time had elapsed we were all standing there helplessly looking at the heaviest logs still lying on the floor of the car. Our best efforts working together could not lift them up high enough to throw them off. Alois came to our rescue with a plank to make a runway from the floor to the top of the side walls. With much tortuous straining and concerted effort we finally rolled the logs up the plank and pushed them over the side. By the time we had finished the job and dragged ourselves over the two miles back to camp it was long past meal time. Our reward for that day's achievement was the bunk without supper.

Another job took us three miles down the track beyond the canal system to dismantle an abandoned camp. As we were pulling down the beams of the last barracks, which was about six hundred feet long and must have housed a thousand men, my mind was filled with grim speculation about what misery and how many hopeless deaths this desolate site had seen.

In the canal we were given the job of sawing logs to make supports for the long wooden runways. This meant kneeling in the snow all day making agonized efforts to pull a dull saw across tough green wood. I got to the stage where I felt that I could not possibly make one more cut and that every cut I did start would surely be my last.

The heavy work proved I was far weaker than I had realized. My exhausted condition became so obvious that even Walter could see I was useless for the outside work. He switched me back to the firewood detail with Alois.

The big days were drawing near and the build-up toward them began having its effect on all the prisoners. Like children in some austere boarding school, we were tingling with anticipation of the break in the routine and the feast and entertainment. Alois did not even greatly mind when we were called out in the middle of the night before May Day to provide extra firewood for the feast preparations in the kitchen.

We were enjoying the peace and solitude of night in the deserted courtyard when a shrill voice started calling from the direction of the infirmary. "Why are you leaving me here? Why are you leaving me here?" the voice kept repeating. "I want to go home. Don't you see the sled at the gate? It's waiting for me."

Another one was cracking up. I called back across the yard, "We didn't see it yet. Who are you?"

"You'll say you don't know me. Nobody knows me. Anyhow you'll not take me back. None of you." Then a loud maniacal laugh. It was Lothar, the young fellow who had come to the help of the other boy in the boxcar. I went over and tried to speak to him. His eyes were glazed and fixed in a wide-open stare. He was running a high fever and quite insane. All I could do was take him back to the ward.

A large poster at the door of the mess hall the next morning announced the May Day menu: breakfast was to be oatmeal with sugar, millet gruel and three grams of fat; lunch: maize soup, millet gruel, bread, and an ounce of sausage; supper: maize soup, millet gruel, and a cutlet weighing a hundred grams (nearly four ounces) with three grams of fat.

Our eyes popped at this wonderful bill of fare and we took our places with a solemnity befitting the occasion. The first course of the great day lived up to our expectations. Though very thin it was really oatmeal and there was certainly some sweetening in it. This was our first meal without turnip soup. The taste of the sweetened oatmeal lingered in our mouths all morning and brought us to the mess hall for lunch in a high state of expectation.

The sausage was what we were waiting for. Walter himself served it to us. The instant he threw the piece of sausage in front of each man, it was snatched up with the greediness of a starving dog.

I sat there for a moment contemplating the tiny piece of meat. It was as long as the first two joints of my forefinger and not much thicker. It was a mixture of bones, skin, and tendon from some unknown animal of indeterminate age. Even Stupid Bernard, who gobbled down everything he could get into his mouth, had trouble crunching and swallowing this. "What damn beast did this come from?" he asked the table. Somebody suggested bear but Walter from his superior knowledge informed us that it was reindeer.

And for this we had worked three hours overtime every day for two weeks. We consoled ourselves with the thought that the big treat of the day, the cutlet, was still to come.

The weather that May first was beautiful. The warm sun tempted many of the sick men and women to come out and sit on the infirmary steps. Even Maria came out from the death chamber. Her knees were still stiffened in a bent position but she hobbled about in the sunshine with the aid of a short stick. "I have to celebrate too," she said, "and besides I have to walk around or else I'll forget how and have to learn all over again."

There was a definitely holiday atmosphere and the rules against intermingling were relaxed. It was a free day, the Soviet equivalent of Sunday. Theoretically all workers were entitled to one free day a week but as this was conditioned on fulfillment of the quota, none of us ever got it except a handful of skilled mechanics and the usual privileged few.

We were still in the Easter season and I took advantage of the afternoon to hear a few confessions.

One Eye walked around the yard spreading word about the night's entertainment which would be topped off by a big dance in the mess hall. There would first be a "rally" with an open forum for free discussion of the wondrous achievements of the Soviet Union's workers. Then there would be music and dancing.

Because of the dance, supper was an hour early. We marched into the mess hall behind Walter, our limping brigadier. Our memories reached back till we could hear the sizzle and smell the fragrance of a well-done pork chop. I had my doubts, but I kept saying to myself, "A cutlet is a cutlet no matter what they do with it."

Our mouths were quite literally watering by the time it was placed before us.

Never in all that had happened to us had we felt so shockingly cheated. It was white instead of brown and it crumbled. The "cutlet" was a millet pancake carrying a faint smell of the fat in which it had been fried. In the let-down from the big build-up it was gall and wormwood.

Some of us wept, some of us cursed. Alois exploded. "This swindle! This is the reward for the blood and sweat they squeezed out of us. These saviors of humanity! Exploitation of the working class. That's what they always preached against. Now I know what it means."

He was clenching his fists and trembling with rage. I had a job convincing him that he should hold it till we got back to the barracks if he didn't want an extra ten years added to his time.

There was no wild talk that night. The bigmouths were over at the dance. Outraged disappointment had brought the rest of us as low as we had ever been.

I took my rosary ring and went outside to be alone for a while. It was the first day of May, the month of the Blessed Virgin. I prayed to the Woman who had crushed the head of the serpent to intercede with her Son to break the power of the tyrants who promise paradise without God and succeed only in creating a hell on earth.

The sounds of an accordion and thumping feet came from the *stolovaya*, or mess hall. I passed the women's ward and knew there were others who had forgone the dance to remember another kind of May Day. The women were singing the old May hymns. I could hear the German words to the Salve Regina: "Hail, Holy Queen, Mother of Mercy, hail our life, our sweetness, and our hope. To thee do we cry, poor banished children of Eve, mourning and weeping in this valley of tears..."

I sat down on the steps and hummed along with them.

The dance, it turned out, fell flat. Helwig made a windy propaganda speech, the leaders of the work brigades made servile declarations of loyalty, Walter applauded loudly, presumably on our behalf, and then One Eye played the accordion for dancing. The queen of the party was a dark-haired girl named Bobbie, Helwig's mistress. She was still strong enough to dance with everyone. But the atmosphere was strained and artificial. Even the most privileged and conniving prisoners were disappointed because they were given neither vodka nor makhorka. They did not so much as get a crumb to eat. When the guards and officials left the mess hall for a carousal of their own, the prisoners lost heart completely and went back to the barracks.

May second was also a free day. The principal reason for it seemed to be to give the officials a chance to sober up. We were served the routine meals. It was very much a matter of the same old miserable inertia, when Helwig, his lids still heavy and his eyes bloodshot, came into the barracks with a great flurry.

He took a stance in the middle of the floor and bellowed out, "Hitler's dead! It's in the papers. And the Red Army has taken Berlin."

In that roomful of Germans, there was no apparent sign of reaction. The news just did not mean anything. Our prison life had become some deadly separate reality of its own without connection with Hitler or anything else in whatever outside world might still exist. Helwig was left standing there with his big announcement falling on empty air. Some of the men did not even look up. Others just stared at him listlessly.

Talking the announcement over afterward, some of us hoped it might mean the end of the war and the end of the war might mean we would be sent home before it was too late. But we were not optimistic enough to count on anything like that. We felt like the vodka-loosened delousing chief who boldly spoke his mind: "Hitler's *kaputt*, all right. But as long as the other pig is still alive, it doesn't mean a thing." It would have cost him another ten years if someone had denounced him for this somber appraisal of the political situation, certainly not flattering to the "great *vozhd* Stalin." When we were back at our sawing the next day, Alois and I struck a gold mine that meant a lot more to us than either the feast or Hitler's death. While the Bulgarian was unloading his logs his scrawny horse, nosing around the thawing kitchen garbage pile, uncovered what I thought were reindeer bones. I picked some of them up and cracked the joints open with my ax. Then I pushed a wire through them and scraped out some tiny particles of marrow. I was so excited at this discovery that I quickly pushed the bones into my pocket and under my hat so that I could examine them in the privacy of my bunk at night. Several times during the day I sneaked out a bone and probed it again to make sure the wonderful marrow was real. The bones looked as if they had been cooked about five times already, but as long as there was marrow in them they were the makings of a real feast. On my next trip with wood to the kitchen I asked one of the helpers if she would let me know when she was throwing away any more bones.

Alois was as excited as I at the sight and taste of the marrow. He practically raved about our find, "Any bones will make soup if you cook them long enough. There's calcium in them, too, and other minerals we need. We'll let them cook all night on the stove."

During the night we took turns replacing the water as it boiled away in an aluminum pot that was Alois' prize possession. Half an hour before rising time, we divided the fruit of our labor—half a pint each of salty brown soup, real bone soup. There was still a little marrow in the bones so we hid them in a German motorcycle cap under my bunk. No one had noticed what we were cooking as there were always a few pots on the stove containing bread soup or turnip ends.

The next night the kitchen helper gave us some fresh bones. Alois and I went behind the barracks in the darkness and gnawed like dogs at the thin layer of tendon and ligament on the joints. Then we strolled nonchalantly back to our bunks. I retrieved my cap from its hiding place to put the new bones with the rest.

The cap was empty.

THE following evening we got an unexpected food treat that made us think perhaps the war was over and things would get better after all. We were told that we were each entitled to a special ration of American sugar cubes. They should have been giving us half an ounce a day and our accumulated share was now one pound each. We never knew what lay behind this mysterious decision, unless some of the camp bosses had found reason to protect themselves, but we were too happy to care.

The intemperate who sucked away the whole pound that night paid dearly for it in dysentery the next day. I rationed myself to three cubes a day to be eaten only with other food. That, along with the nightly bowl of bone soup made me feel like a new man. The swelling, however, of my face, hands, feet, and legs increased so much that at the next medical examination, the Black Stork's assistant took one look at my feet, told me it was not necessary to undress further and ordered me once more to the infirmary.

My old corner bunk was again available. Its most recent occupant had been taken to the death chamber. So had my former bunkmate, a Masurian boy who had consistently refused to wash or delouse himself. The other patients, with their macabre humor, told me the lice had carried him there. His place was occupied by the gluttonous Stupid Bernard. Pastor Theo was also in the ward and I was pleased to have his company again.

There was always work for me in the death chamber. On my first day back I assisted at the death of an old maidservant. It was pathetic to find that her last thoughts were about her former employers. She kept worrying about how they had managed to get along, helpless and in their old age, after she had been taken away.

It was a struggle to have her turn her thoughts to the obvious fact that she was at that moment dying herself. She did not want to think of it. Only after I had anointed her in her last few minutes of consciousness did she understand and become reconciled. She breathed her last before I had finished the prayers for the dying.

Maria, still in the death chamber, showed me proudly how she could straighten her knees a little more. "Another few weeks, Pastor, and you will see me walking around as good as ever."

The most miserable person in the death chamber was Martha, who had collapsed while cleaning the Black Stork's office. Her features were twisted with pain as she tossed feverishly on the plank and she raved deliriously about her home and her mother. When she quieted down for a moment her spasmodic breathing was loud through the room. I suggested gently that she pray with me. She stared wildly at me and cried out, "Die? No! No! I won't die! No!" and turned away sobbing uncontrollably. I prayed the Our Father by her bunk and was just giving her my blessing when the Black Stork came into the room. He saw me but said nothing.

During the night the Black Stork himself helped One Eye carry Martha's body back to his office for an autopsy.

Her death was such an obvious blow to him that his tender concern for the girl changed him into a new man in our minds. Maria told us how he had waited upon Martha all during her sickness. He had been in and out many times a day doing everything he possibly could for her, even bringing her his own food. One day he had traveled seventy-five miles on a rail car to a black market for potatoes which he fried for her. The day before she died he had walked ten miles to get a small bottle of goat's milk from a railroad official.

When he came to inspect us the day after Martha's death, his whole manner had changed. He carried a tray with bottles of homemade medicine and went from bunk to bunk stirring up some kind of herbal tea for us. His considerate manner in serving it did us more good than the medicine itself.

Then he sat down by the stove and completed the reversal of his old attitude by striking up a casual friendly conversation with us. He asked where we came from and told us in turn that he had spent six years digging canals in various camps before having his sentence changed to a further five years of exile as an official in these northern camps. Had he been a practicing physician before his political imprisonment he would have been getting a salary of five hundred and fifty rubles a month to keep the laborers of a *kolkhoz* or of a *kombinat* in good working condition. He was hoping to be set free at the end of the war.

Martha had been right about him. His six years of hard labor and five years of exile had increased rather than extinguished his sense of pain at being one grinding cog in the merciless collective machinery. His hard shell of bitterness had been cracked by the preserved ability to love one human being as a person and to feel loss and guilt at her death.

Death and the grim business of robbing the dead continued to be features of life in the infirmary. Hans, the hunchback assistant to One Eye, had a tough and shrewd companion racketeer named Roman, a prisoner from Upper Silesia. Though they were amateurs compared to their boss, they constantly schemed to outsmart him, and each other, in getting first to the clothes and belongings of the dead. They were badly fooled one time by Ostrowski, a Masurian peasant who liked to talk to me about his philosophy of life and his individual idea of religion. The old farmer slipped into unconsciousness one evening and Hans moved over close to him, his eye on the dying man's warm sheepskin coat. The man was still breathing steadily, though unconscious, when Hans slipped off his coat. Next he took the suit coat and when the Masurian continued unconscious through the evening, he felt safe in trading the two garments to Crooked Boot for egg powder and a couple of potatoes. The ghoul cooked himself a meal and then went to sleep on it.

In the morning a weak voice called from the Masurian's bunk, "Where are my clothes?" The cold had revived the tough old man. Hans sat up in bed trying to look innocent as a lamb while One Eye towered over him cursing and the old farmer kept crying out for his clothes. Wilhelm, one of Walter's cronies who had toadied to the senior by abusing me at every chance, had come down from his bunk and was reaching over for his shoes when he toppled to the floor and died without a sound. Hans stripped him instantly and handed the still warm clothes over to Ostrowski. This time he was lucky. Wilhelm did not come to life again.

MAX Abromeit had at last lost his energy. Feeling very low, he called Theo and asked him to read from the Bible. Theo went over to him and opened the holy book. Before starting he looked up and asked if he would be allowed to read loudly enough for all to hear. The loudest approval came from the ever righteous One Eye. That settled the matter, so Theo read in his manly voice the Beatitudes from the Sermon on the Mount. Everyone was so attentive that he went on to give an excellent meditation on the passage. For fifteen minutes we had complete peace and silence in the ward. No one protested when Theo repeated this service for the next few days. He even managed to do the same in the women's ward. On Sunday mornings I was also able to read the liturgy of the day in both wards. I was neither sneered at nor interrupted, though we Catholics were a small minority.

Two of the many who died in the ward during that time were old companions from the boxcars. Georg I had liked from our first meeting. We used to take our meals together sitting on the side of my bunk or on the stove ledge. Even here in the infirmary he retained his equanimity, always dignified, making the best of things and well able to handle the circumstances and the people. He always managed to have a bit of salt and saccharine with which he would season his crude prison food in the manner of an epicure.

Death all around made little impression on him. He merely became more careful in balancing his diet and economizing his energies. He professed a sophisticated disinterest in religious matters but occasionally, "to relieve his boredom," he would explain, "not for devotion," he would borrow my missal. He would return it remarking that he had found the scholarly introductions quite interesting.

In spite of his care his feet swelled so badly that I had to boost him up to his tier. Finally he had to resort to a vacant lower bunk. He grew a little worried about his condition but not enough to respond to several attempts I made to have him think of the moment we all had to face. After a last frustrating talk with him, I was standing at the door looking up at the stars when I heard a deep sigh from his corner. I ran back in time to take him in my arms as he breathed his last.

Gregor was a different type and his end was different. He was proud of having been a hard-boiled metalworker during the old fighting union days and he died showing his toughness.

I was coming back to the ward with an armful of firewood when my way was blocked by a skeleton figure clothed only in a short prison shirt. His grinning face was like a death's-head, the eyes rolling wildly and half turned back in his head. He held both arms in the air, a pipe in one hand, a bag of tobacco in the other.

"Gregor," I shouted, "come back to your bunk. You're too sick to be out."

"No! I have to see my old friends one more time." His jaws were already stiffening and the words came through clenched teeth. The man was in his death agony even as he stood there. Somehow he managed to open the door. With a surge of strength he lunged forward and collapsed on the floor as I dumped my armful of wood into the bin. He lay there, a naked skeleton still clutching the pipe and tobacco. He turned his head and screamed into the horrified ward, "Just one more pipe! One more! Then the devil can come and get me. Just one more pipe!"

Kurt, his friend from the union days, and One Eye rushed over and carried him to One Eye's own well-upholstered bunk. One Eye took the pipe and tobacco over to the stove and lit a pipeful. He had difficulty forcing it between Gregor's clenched teeth. Then he had to close the lips over the pipe-stem. But Gregor apparently was not able to take a single puff. Instead, he dredged up enough energy for one last defiant gesture. He pulled the pipe from his rigid jaws and threw it with the tobacco into the middle of the ward, making an indescribably fiendish sound through his teeth and screaming, "Take the filth! Now bring on the devil!" The last word was long and drawn out, and then Gregor slipped over the side of the bunk and crumpled up on the floor like a piece of paper thrown into the fire.

His friends were the first to recover from the horror that froze the room. Kurt picked up the pipe and, hardly even wiping the foam from the mouthpiece, started smoking greedily. One Eye, Roman, and a couple of others dove simultaneously at the tobacco.

MAY ninth was the vigil of the feast of the Ascension. In the Epistle, St. Paul was speaking to the Ephesians, applying to Christ the words of the psalmist: "He led away captives."

Early in the morning Helwig came into the ward and made another solemn announcement: "Germany has surrendered unconditionally to the Allied forces. All of Germany will now be an occupied country."

Our only response was a few questions he couldn't answer:

"Does that mean we'll get some more sugar?"

"An egg powder cake?"

"Will they let me go back to Austria now?"

Theo and I talked it over. We felt that this was good news that gave us our first real hope of getting home. We spoke of the hard days that would lie ahead, of the burden of atonement that all must share for the crimes committed in our country, as well as in all other countries afflicted by the ravages of war, of the need there would be for Christ's spirit of forgiveness.

Wild rumors began to fly round the camp. One from the women's barracks even set a definite date for our return home. The most casual remarks from officials were astonishingly transformed into definite statements about our release. And in the peculiar atmosphere that was created it was as much as your life was worth to dare question the validity of any of them.

But it did not take much thought to realize that, at the very best, we could not be released until autumn. The railroads to and from Germany would be taxed to capacity with the business of reparations, occupation, and demobilization.

We were all called before the board for a new medical examination. I thought I heard myself being put into a category "still transportable" but I did not know what it meant.

One Eye mystified us still further and built up our expectations by posing as our friend and benefactor. He actually began taking care of some of the men in the infirmary. He practically fawned over us. He even offered to brew us some "vitamin beer" from bread remnants, the old Russian *kuass*.

Before long he made a little speech that gave us an idea of what it was all about. The commissar might be coming around one of these days to ask us if we would like good old One Eye to keep on being our infirmarian when we were transferred to the new hospital camp. He was sure we all knew he was our friend.

The important item, that we were being shipped to a "hospital camp," was confirmed when a barber who traveled from camp to camp arrived to give us our first shave. He was a small tubercular man with a racking cough. He spent most of the time after his arrival bartering lard for clothes. But we didn't mind; we were in no hurry to have him shave us. His only claim to being a barber was that he had a straight razor. As before we had to lie down on a plank to be shaved all over our bodies like pigs. His razor was dull and every customer finished up bleeding from a dozen cuts. Our new friend One Eye turned up with a razor he had organized somewhere and proved his helpfulness by shaving a few of the men. When he tired of the novelty he asked me if I was handy with a straight razor and turned the job over to me. Those still waiting tried to get their turn with me instead of with the visiting barber who was nervous and shaking.

Although I did not know it at the time, Pentecost was my last Sunday for reading the Mass texts to my "parishioners" of the infirmary at Column Seven. This beautiful Mass speaks of the birth of the Church, of the Holy Spirit coming down from heaven to dwell with us always, and gives us this Oration: "O God, Who on this day didst instruct the hearts of Thy faithful by the light of the Holy Spirit, grant us, by the same Spirit, to relish what is right and evermore to rejoice in His consolation."

On the evening of May 25 the Black Stork called out the list of those who were to be transferred to the hospital camp. Theo and I were on the list. We had no idea what lay ahead, nor, when we looked over the ninety-six prisoners who made up the shipment, could we make out exactly what criteria had been used to determine who was to go. Most of the infirmary men and women were with us, but not all. We also had One Eye and Walter and a handful of their hangers-on. It might have been the current list of OK's and sick, with the exception of those who were too sick to be transportable and including some, like Gertrud, who had recently been found too sick for the canal.

We did know that One Eye's list of the dead from our group had reached number seventy-one with the death of little Adalbert, who had wanted so badly to go back to Vienna. We had lost seventy-one out of our original two hundred sixty in five weeks at the camp.

Eventually we were lined up outside the main gate to wait for the train. For the first hour it drizzled lightly, then the moon came out and the fence and the watchtowers along the tracks cast long shadows. A locomotive finally appeared pulling a passenger coach and we climbed in. We looked back through the dirty windows at Column Seven. It was much less formidable now beneath the stars and the moon than it had been on that first day when we stumbled like moles out of the darkness of the boxcars into the sunlight and blinding snow.

CHAPTER XII : *Dominion of Death*

THE MORNING FOUND US RIDING ALONG IN NASTY SPRING
weather through slushy swamp and tundra stretching as far as we
could see on either side. Not once on the three-day journey did we
see a settlement of any kind. We were traveling north and east in
directly the opposite direction from the lands from which we had
been taken. Paralleling the tracks was a narrow log road already rotting: a monument to the Russians, Poles, and other prisoners who
had slaved to build the railroad we were riding on.

On the first day of the journey we received regular prison meals
plus a quarter ounce of fat. On the second day the guards told us
the compartment holding our supplies had burned up. The only fire
we saw was in the stove on which the guards fried their pancakes
swimming in fat. We had nothing at all to eat that day.

On the morning of the third day the train stopped and we were
ordered out. A pale and lifeless line of men and women, we peered
through the rain for a sight of our new camp. All we could see was
a wooden water tank standing alone in a wilderness of swamp and
scrub trees. For a hundred yards on either side of the raised roadbed there was nothing but swamp and tree stumps.

We started walking along the tracks, trusting that the guards
who had set us in motion knew where we were going. After the first
mile of marching in the rain our ranks had stretched out into a long
thin line of stragglers spaced at irregular intervals.

Even Theo and I, who settled down to a slow deliberate plod, found ourselves passing others who were having all they could do to keep their feet moving at all. Far ahead was One Eye, eager to arrive first and introduce himself to the doctors as the "big uncle" of our wretched band. He had enlisted a band of stockholders to carry his baggage in return for present and future dividends payable in makhorka. Walter puffed alongside us for a while, hurrying his limp so that he too could get in his bid as a leader. He was wheezing and groaning under two heavy knapsacks plus an extra bundle wrapped in underwear. He looked like one of the old peddlers from Slovakia I used to admire when I was a boy.

"How will I ever make it?" lamented Walter.

"Throw away half of your ballast," answered Theo, "and you'll sail along faster."

"That's all right for you to say," Walter snarled, "but I have three children. I have to make sure I get home."

"I have three of my own," answered Theo, "and my anxiety for them is burden enough for me to carry."

The short exchange was typically Theo. His remarks were always to the point. Just, enduring, and uncompromising, he could suffer anything but dishonesty. He never hesitated to stand up with a straight tongue and fearless conscience against anything wrong.

Alois, Bernard, and Big Max, the teamster, were trudging along behind us. Max was as garrulous as ever. "This is cruelty to animals. Driving us along like cattle without even a drop of schnapps! If I had just one mouthful I could easily make another two miles. My stomach is an empty bag of wrinkles. I think it slipped down to my feet." He lifted one of the feet into the air and showed us the shapeless mass of blubber it had become.

Gertrud and other women brought up the rear of our procession. Stumbling along on swollen legs and with rags wrapped around their heads in an attempt to hide their baldness, they recalled Jeremiah's lamentation, "Woman has lost all her beauty..."

The march was only two miles, but in our physical misery, and our second day with no rations, it seemed endless. We rounded a last curve and saw our new home. It was a replica of Column Seven. But this one was in a valley and completely surrounded by swamp. The wooden fence around it was rotting. Our first view of it in a steady rain made the desolate scene even dirtier and more distressing than it was.

The weathered lettering over the gate said, "Column Five." The yard was swimming in water and we had to balance our way over planks set on bricks to reach the usual delousing station. Among the men watching us from barracks doorways we recognized some old companions from the boxcars and some of the batch of fifty that had left Column Seven a month previously. When we were able to get together with them to compare notes we estimated that half of our shipment of deportees had died in the three months since Heilsberg.

While we were waiting at the delousing station I was given a terrible shock. A woman came up to turn in an armful of clothes. She said to the attendant, "These are from the girl Christa Fittkau who just died."

Christa was the name of my youngest sister.

I asked the woman, "How old was this girl?"

The woman was walking away but she turned around and answered me, "Nineteen or twenty."

Christa was nineteen. I sat there for hours waiting my turn in the delousing station thinking about Christa. A senior in high school, she had been drafted for work in an airplane factory just before graduation. I could do nothing but pray and wait for a chance to question some of the women and find out if that had been our Christa or not.

Ever since we arrived One Eye had been bustling around trying to give the impression he was some kind of official. Around noon he waved in a group of men carrying armloads of firewood and made a point of letting us know he had gone to considerable trouble to save us from freezing. In point of truth, the camp officials had sent the wood over and he had nothing to do with it. A feeble fire was started but the rain outside was changing to snow and it was still much too cold for our nakedness.

Late in the afternoon a man in a doctor's white jacket appeared with the usual sheaf of papers under his arm. One Eye jumped up like a rabbit and offered himself as an interpreter.

The official looked at him coldly and said in understandable German, "You needn't bother, my dear sir. I'll manage without your services. Just you get back in line."

One Eye's face dropped and the rest of us grinned.

The doctor was a small, dark-haired Tartar with piercing intelligent eyes. He was a well-disciplined man of few words who knew his business, and we felt he would treat us fairly. After the usual questions, the looking at the tongue for dysentery and testing the buttock muscles, he put a wooden stethoscope on our hearts—the first time a medical instrument had been used on me. When he noticed that Theo and I had undergone chest operations he made a precise examination of our lung condition, tapping the affected side of our thoraxes and making us take breathing exercises. When he had finished with me he said shortly, "Thick lining, latent process, no immediate danger." We appreciated his professional attitude and the familiar routine examination for tuberculosis.

The results of his examination were entered on the front of a four-page folio headed "Patient's Record." All future records were entered here until at the end my folio was half an inch thick. Such records were of primary importance in this camp. We had been sent here, we learned later, not so much to die or to be healed as to furnish information about malnutrition and the survival of humans under extreme conditions. We were there as human guinea pigs in a research project of the Moscow Institute of Pathology. The real care and personal interest several of the camp personnel took in our recovery did not alter this basic fact.

The doctor, with his poorly made canvas boots and the shabby uniform under his white coat, had impressed us favorably. I agreed with Theo that he was in the best tradition of dedicated medical men. Throughout our stay in the camp we reserved for him alone of all the staff the title "Herr Doktor."

Our first impression of the camp was so good that we momentarily forgot our miseries in the expectation of better things to come. It was not to be so. At the end of our balancing act back across the rickety planks we found ourselves in a dark, narrow barracks much worse than any we had so far seen. The ceiling was so low that the men on the second tier could not sit up, and the mud plaster had fallen from the log walls, making the room as drafty as a corncrib. The wooden floor had rotted away in several places and the holes were filled with water. Dozens of large coal-black rats lived in the stinking floor; there were many more rats than men in the barracks.

Theo and I stepped around the men fighting for good bunks near the door and raced to stake our claim to the top tier in one of the far corners. I took a place next to a large hole in the wall, thinking it a small price to pay for the relative privacy of the corner. But the following days of driving rain and cold taught me that the price was higher than I had thought.

We got our first food the second evening in camp. It was a promising improvement. The bread had some wheat in it and was well baked, the gruel smelled of oats. We began telling ourselves that we might have a chance of sticking it out. Big Max disagreed. "I managed to drag my duffle bag in here," he said mournfully, "but I'll never drag it out." And all of us were sobered whenever we saw One Eye, who had obtained a semiofficial job through favoritism; he carted the dead to their dumping place in the delousing station, and he was making as many as five trips a day.

The place was so much the dominion of death that before the month of June was over twenty of the original twenty-eight in our ward were no longer with us and I had been present at a procession of deaths, both wretched and edifying. Big Max had been right in his premonition. He died one midnight after pouring out an incoherent jumble of words followed by a clear and strong recitation of the Our Father from beginning to end. Alois, the last of our faithful and good staunch friends, suffocated from severe bronchitis after a long and painful agony. To the end he told us how grateful he was for our friendship but refused our attempts to offer religious consolation. He died in complete despair.

Gertrud wasted so rapidly that on the fourteenth day after our arrival her friend Maria came running over to get me. I was jeered by One Eye and a bunch of Walter's friends, and took the risk of their reporting me, to get to her. She could scarcely breathe. Her once full and pink cheeks were sunken. Her wide-open eyes acknowledged my arrival and she could only nod in answer to my questions for her last concession. I prepared her for Extreme Unction loudly enough for everyone to hear and follow the ceremony. Gertrud tried to articulate, "Jesus, for Thee I live..." but the effort sent her back into her last lassitude. I gave her the final blessing for the hour of death.

Gertrud was still staring at me when the *politruk* came in and stood over me. I wondered whether One Eye had informed or if the *politruk* merely happened by. He was a Volga German named Lachmann, but unlike Helwig, his counterpart at Column Seven, he did not seem to relish his job. "It is forbidden for you to come into the women's ward," he told me.

"But I'm a priest helping a dying woman who sent for me," I answered. "You have to leave at once," he said heavily, and I had the feeling as I rose that he was not acting any more freely than I. The last thing I saw was Gertrud's wide-open eyes speaking an apology for having caused me trouble.

My own condition deteriorated so rapidly that I did not feel very far away from the death that surrounded me. The June thaw dried the ground and drained the swamp till we could hear a stream running behind one side of the palisades. But the warm weather also brought insects and mosquitoes, and a skin disease that came very close to being the last of my troubles. Dirt, heat, and the lack of vitamins left us defenseless against the small sores that began to erupt on our bodies. They had started on my hips and abdomen back in Column Seven. Now they spread over my body. First they appeared in the joints, the crooks of the elbows, the inner thigh, the knees, and between the fingers. The sores spread and met until they made one continuous covering over my entire body, like the bark of a tree, only wet with running pus.

When I crawled beneath the blankets for protection against the mosquitoes the heat became intolerable, the air so close I almost suffocated and my wounds smarted from the sweat.

Theo and I were made still more wretched by an upsurge of ridicule and abuse directed at us by the gang who had taken over the barracks. The places left vacant by our dead had been filled mostly by prisoners of war. One Eye and Walter and Roman had found among them a group of foul-mouthed youngsters who joined their clique and vied with each other in making life miserable for Theo and myself and anyone who dared stand up for us.

The work brigade in the camp was under a Comrade Keil who liked to call on the sick to help him raise his quota. Theo and I were inevitably assigned to him no matter what condition we were in, and in spite of having been classified as unfit for labor. A young Hitler youth leader named Harry was Keil's toady and the more bitter and vindictive of the two. They gave us the job of covering a hole in a sagging wall of rotting wood. We had shingles for patching, a clumsy, top-heavy hammer and pieces of wire for nails. My hands were raw and bleeding from open sores. When we did succeed in getting a stretch done, they strutted over, cursed us for being clumsy and tore down the piece of wall we had so laboriously completed.

Worse than the physical abuse was the filthy campaign they built up against us out of our visits to the dying. We were accused of having thought up a racket to get the possessions of the dead by being on the spot at the right time. When we went to the women's barracks, or when women sent for us, the accusations were still more vile.

One thing I noticed throughout my experience in these camps of men and women was that sex was not the pervading problem one might have expected. There were always a number of liaisons. Guards and other officials kept a few chosen girls well fed, the One Eyes and the Walters had mistresses with whom they exchanged stolen extras, but in general, in the camps I knew, human vitality was at such a low ebb that lust found little place. The rougher types vented their penchant for obscenity either in casual conversation or in attempts to shock, ridicule, revile, or abuse people like Pastor Theo and myself.

That was the sort of thing we were exposed to in a distressing degree at this "hospital camp." It reached such lengths that a number of prisoners from other barracks began to believe the repeated calumnies. Some of them would cross to the other side of the compound when they saw us coming. The atmosphere of hate and bitterness that was generated made any other spiritual work than assisting the dying next to impossible. We tried to set an example by suffering in silence and doing whatever was openly and decently possible for our own survival.

Another trial I had during this time was an onset of anxiety about my family. The best information I could get from the women indicated that the Christa Fittkau who died in the camp had not been my sister. But the thought had been planted in my mind and I could not rid myself of unhappy speculations about my father and mother and Irmgard and the rest of the family.

I was in this state of mind when a towel I noticed hanging on a line shocked me to the depths.

I recognized it. It had been embroidered by my mother. Irmgard's initials were worked into it and there was no mistaking my mother's inimitable handiwork or the fine linen she always used. Closer inspection revealed the laundry mark used by Irmgard at the school for social workers.

I rushed to the washerwoman and asked her where she got that towel. She could give only vague answers that left me no peace about my sisters or even about my mother. The good woman did give in to my pleading and let me take the towel. It was a strange feeling to lie back in my bunk with that fine piece of our own good family linen, so mysteriously met in this place, shielding my scabrous face from the mosquitoes. It stimulated me in the daily rosary I prayed for my scattered family and friends. And when that much sustained prayer became too great a drain on my energy, the sight of the towel was enough to lift my thoughts to theirs.

July 1 was the sixth Sunday after Pentecost and once more the Mass of the day held out the key to the Christian meaning, not only of what we were going through, but of life itself. The Epistle brought us St. Paul's letter to the Romans: "Know ye not that all we, who are baptized in Christ Jesus, are baptized in His death? For we are buried together with Him by baptism into death; that as Christ is risen from the dead by the glory of the Father, so we also may walk in newness of life. But if we have died with Christ, we believe that we shall live also together with Christ; for we know that Christ, having risen from the dead, dies now no more, death shall no more have dominion over Him" (Rom. 6:3–9).

As I was meditating on these words I saw to my horror that the opposite page of my missal, where the Gospel and the Offertory and Communion of this Mass should have been, began with the last part of the Gospel for the fourteenth Sunday after Pentecost. Someone had torn out the Masses for the next nine Sundays.

I rose and addressed the whole barracks with as much control as I could muster: "If anyone ever again feels it necessary to get his cigarette paper from my missal, will he please come to me first. I would like him at least to leave until the last the pages I need most."

As I turned away looking sorrowfully at the mutilated book, my eyes fell on the first page after the torn section. The words leaped out at me in reproof: "Seek first the kingdom of God and His justice, and all these things shall be given you besides." So even the missal had been put into my hands by the Church and then taken away that I might learn the one great lesson, to seek and adore His will alone.

In this grim, demoralizing atmosphere rumors flared up that Column Five was going to be raised to the status of a model camp and that the whole place would be renovated. A specialist was coming as assistant to Herr Doktor and everything—food, quarters, conditions, and medical treatment—would be improved.

The specialist did come, but the only improvement in our barracks was the amount of research they did on us. The new doctor was put in charge of the women. Maria told me about him when she brought me a bowl of gruel she had saved. She was full of praise for "the highly educated doctor with a Polish name." He really took a personal interest in the welfare of the sick and had even given some of them injections and ordered new bunks to be made.

The next day I got my first sight of him, a tall man in a worn summer uniform walking with great strides across the yard, holding himself stiffly erect. He held an empty amber cigarette holder between the fingers of his right hand. In the weeks that followed I never saw him without that holder. It meant something to him. It was a symbol, a reminder of better days. The new man was so obviously an educated person that we all took to referring to him as the Professor. We learned that one of his specialties was the study of advanced cases of skin disease.

One Eye did his little bit to make me an object of the specialist's attention. He had been put in charge of the prisoners' water supply and was exploiting his power over us to the hilt. Only as a special favor would he give a man his daily pitcher of washing water and then only if the man begged for it. Between that and a closing down of the delousing station for repairs, I was soon in an even sorrier state than before, and getting worse from day to day. The parts of my body that came into contact with the bunk were masses of moist sores that broke out afresh at every move. The color of my body had changed from angry red to sickly chocolate. Each hair root had become a small reservoir of pus. I was finally ordered to the specialist and Theo took me over.

The small office was clean and equipped with a few medical instruments. Three large posters on the walls had pictures of fruits and vegetables with tables of their nutritive values. The Professor sat behind a desk toying with his amber cigarette holder. He welcomed us in German with friendly courtesy.

After a very thorough examination he told me I had an advanced case of pellagra resulting from lack of vitamins and a too exclusive maize diet.

"The only cure for you," he said, "is to eat greens as much as possible and all the fruit you can get."

He smiled in understanding when I gave him a puzzled look and offered us a few drops of milk in a cup saying, "I'm sorry I can't give you any more. But this is all I get myself for the week. Even if it is only a mouthful for each of you, it may help as a homeopathic medicine. I promise you that I shall do everything I can to improve the food here."

As I thanked him, I noticed his own pale complexion, heavy asthmatic breathing and pain-wracked face so I added, "If you don't mind my saying so, doctor, you look as if you could use a little special treatment yourself."

"Yes," he said, "I don't suppose I'm a very healthy specimen. But I have a big job to do and I would like to get it finished."

He pulled over two large albums resting on his desk, flipped them open and showed them to us. They were filled with delicately colored drawings showing various stages of pellagra, the mutations, corruptions, and destruction of various organs affected by the disease. Some of the drawings had been made from living (or dying) persons and others from corpses after dissection. They had obviously been drawn by an expert and painted with great exactitude. The legends accompanying the illustrations were executed in the neat, sharp hand of an engraver or draftsman. They gave lengthy details of each case history.

I remember there were three pages with nine drawings depicting the tongue at various stages of the disease, but most of the illustrations were concerned with the disintegration of the intestinal tract and of the corruption of the outer layer of skin.

He talked to us frankly about his training and his ambition to do something worthwhile in pellagra research. He had studied at the Academy of Arts in Leningrad and was now attached to the Institute of Pathology in Moscow. Our conversation was carried on in the two languages he had taken up for research: German and English. He showed us his Russian-German and German-English grammars as well as three thin expurgated German versions of Andersen's *Fairy Tales* and *Till Eulenspiegel*, issued by the Soviet State Publishing Company.

He was intelligent and charming, but, as he told us himself, there was not much he could offer us except his interest and friendship. After asking me if I would mind returning sometime to pose and allow him to add some of my more interesting manifestations of the advanced state of the disease to his collection, he was at pains to make sure we would forgive him if he passed us in the yard without talking. "You understand, I know, that we are forbidden to fraternize with the prisoners. It will be better for you if I do not recognize you in public."

He seemed as genuinely pleased as we were to meet someone with whom he could talk of learning and human understanding.

One Eye had been promoted to a job he loved—dissecting corpses with the doctors. His equipment was a butcher knife, a pair of large shears and a pail. Such an important position made him independent of the pickings in the barracks, and he bothered us less and less. Walter, however, took over and demonstrated what an able boss he was by making his victims squirm more than ever. There was, however, a strange, though brief, interlude when he let up on us.

A night doctor started bringing him watches to repair. The black market was apparently flooded with watches broken by the Soviet *kultur soldaten*, who did not know how to wind them without breaking the springs. Using his good left hand and the thumb and little finger of his crippled right hand, Walter did remarkably well and got quite a few of them running again. He achieved such fame that a visiting political commissar from Moscow stopped by one day to admire his skill.

This taste of public recognition led our barracks boss to think about the possibilities of a political career. One evening, to my great surprise, he took me aside and asked me in a humble tone if I would please help him with advice on a difficult problem. I was a little suspicious at being singled out for this distinction, but I told him I would help if I could.

His story was that Lachmann, the political commissar, had suggested that he, Walter, someday could qualify as liaison officer between the party and the people in Germany. In preparation for the post Lachmann had invited him to study the doctrines of Marx, Engels, and Lenin and the Communist Manifesto. What did I think he should do?

The whole thing smelled of dead fish, so I kept a serious face and gave him an answer that stopped any more questions: "Your own conscience could best answer that, Walter. But apart from your conscience it might be that you should say 'No' just as a matter of saving your own skin. If you get mixed up with the party's business they'll be sticking their nose deeper into your record. It might not take them long to find out something they don't know about yet, your old job as an SS sergeant in a concentration camp. That could make the price of becoming a Communist official a long term in a disciplinary camp for war criminals. But it's entirely up to you to figure out if it's worth the risk."

He went away looking a little deflated. A few days later, however, he was around handing out Soviet booklets. One "proved" the Germans guilty of the Katyn massacre, another described the war crimes trials of German officers in Kharkov, a third was a speech by Molotov on the wonderful democratic federalist principle of the great Soviet Union, and the fourth was a speech by Stalin on the Red Army.

These dull, dry leaflets were the only reading matter ever provided us in the camps. I would probably have read every last word of them, but I succeeded in getting through only the Molotov talk and the Katyn fabrication before the whole windfall of paper had either been burned up in cigarettes or put to an even more practical use. The Molotov speech was sheer boredom. The Katyn booklet drew on such feeble and far-fetched arguments to prove Hitler guilty of the wanton mass slaying of several thousand Polish officers that it left me completely convinced that for once the Nazis had spoken the truth when they said the Reds had committed the massacre.

Theo, ever the man for positive action, thought he might capitalize on the *politruk*'s evident desire to get some Russian reading into our hands. "Let's do away with the middleman," he suggested, "and go directly to Lachmann." Our subsequent interview with the *politruk* was a revelation of how little background such men have. In reply to our questions he could only parrot the familiar Communist clichés. He offered us a copy of *Pravda*, which was very good of him since paper was so valuable. When I asked if he could get us some good Russian literature, Tolstoy, for example, or Dostoevsky, he scratched his head for a moment and answered that he might be able to get us the poems of the Soviet writer Alexei Tolstoy. But, rack his brains as much as he could, he could not think of any author named Dostoevsky.

Walter's "friendly attitude" lasted no longer than his falsetto plea for advice. He turned his gang of tormentors loose on us again and things were as bad as they could get. Our rations were frequently stolen, we were driven out to carry water and make plaster with hands covered with pus and blood and men from other barracks called us corpse looters every time we crossed the yard. Day by day we became more rundown, nervous, and weak. Herr Doktor did not help matters any when he came in one day and classified us among the eight extreme cases who were to get a little extra ration. As he was leaving he called Theo "Mister Goebel." He was no sooner out of the door when Walter gleefully announced that the English word "Mister" was a title of nobility. This brought on a salvo of rude jeers and shouts that the days of the "Misters and the Dukes" were over. After that they believed themselves completely justified in increasing their efforts to see that we got the worst of everything.

We were more and more alone and more and more hated. It was Theo who picked up his Bible and reminded both of us that we should not be surprised at this. He read 2 Cor. 6:8f.: "By honor and dishonor, by evil report and good report; as deceivers and yet true; as unknown and yet known; as dying and behold we live; as chastised and not killed; as sorrowful yet always rejoicing; as needy yet enriching many; as having nothing and possessing all things…in all things let us exhibit ourselves as the ministers of God…"

We escaped the intolerable atmosphere as often as we could by hiding behind the barracks. Sitting in the shade of a piece of camouflage canvas, we took turns reading to each other from Theo's Bible, my missal, and the Professor's Moscow edition of Andersen's *Fairy Tales*. Occasionally we were visited there by Maria and a friend of hers, Mrs. Skierat, who worked in the bakery. They would sit in on our reading and then ask us to talk about the scripture texts.

Mrs. Skierat was a warm-hearted religious woman who had been separated by war and the deportations from her husband and four children. Her job in the bakery enabled her to help us survive at a time when rations had fallen so low that two pounds of groats were being cooked in water to make soup for two hundred people. We bartered the nourishment we needed so badly. My feet were so swollen and covered with sores that I had given up hope of ever needing shoes again, so I polished up my old boots with saliva and Mrs. Skierat traded them to her boss for two-thirds of a pound of used fat.

Theo and I made a pact to watch over each other, so that neither would eat too much of this wonderful acquisition at one time. By restraining ourselves to half a teaspoonful taken morning and evening with our bread, we made the fat last for a whole month.

Another break in the diet, and a lift in our lives, came through the Professor. He identified a vitamin-laden herb growing wild around the camp and ordered that twenty-five pounds of it should be collected each day and fed to the prisoners. The plant was called the Willow Rose because it had leaves shaped like those on a willow tree and wore a crown of purple flowers when in bloom. The entire plant was utilized. The stems and roots were boiled, making a purplish liquid served as "vitamin tea," and the leaves dried and used for tobacco. Our own name for this universal herb was "Ivan Tschai (tea)."

The herb gathering meant more than food to Theo and me. The Professor always included us in the small group of prisoners he was allowed to take out to collect it. Even though we could hardly drag our legs, we were grateful for the double blessing of getting out of the camp and enjoying his company. He liked to talk to us, improving his German and English and throwing in some Russian words when he was stuck. His trained botanist's eye noted each new plant or flower, and he would stop to point out its features and tell us its Russian name. This one was called the Mother-in-law because its leaves were polished smooth on the upper side and covered with a layer of rough hairs underneath.

We lived in a different world for those hours, a normal world where the mind ran free and human reactions were natural and spontaneous. But our conversations had to be intermittent to avoid raising the suspicions of the rifle-carrying guard who accompanied us.

Once by the bank of the stream we came upon some patches of sauerampfer, a plant my mother used to gather and cook as the first vegetable soup of spring. While we picked it, paying for every leaf with a mosquito bite, the Professor told us something of his story. He was a Russian of Polish descent and had already spent nine years in exile. He would not tell us the reason for his sentence. He still looked forward to seeing his family again, though he assumed that they too had been exiled. He liked best to speak of his studies, his research and of once attending a medical congress in England by special invitation.

Near the end of the day's herb gathering we asked him about the rumors that some of us might be sent home soon. His answer was not encouraging: "Since Churchill's last speech to the British Parliament, tension is increasing between Russia and the other Allied powers. Peace is far away. Far away."

On the way back to camp he broke a period of silence to give us a cryptic and cautious but urgently voiced warning: "Be careful what you say in the barracks. Keep silent. Keep quiet. There are men around you who would like to get you into trouble."

In the long dull days back in the barracks I could feel myself sinking into an almost lifeless lethargy. I had the impression that my body was feeding on its very nerve cells and brain fibers. There were days when I simply vegetated, no longer able to resist the progressive dissolution of body, mind, and personality. The effort of a coherent prayer was beyond me. I could not even get through an Our Father from beginning to end.

Theo was not much better off, but in spite of pellagra he was able to hold a book and read to me from his Bible and my missal.

It was those readings, this communion of minds in mutual under-standing, that kept us from complete inner collapse and despair. Close as our relationship was, however, it did not fail to add its own dash of wormwood to those bitter days.

With all the good will in the world, he could not understand my attachment to the life of the visible Church. He could not under-stand that the sacramental presence of Christ among men meant more to me than any other consolation, that I united myself with Him wherever He was hidden in Russia, perhaps in the next camp.

When I tried to share with Theo my joy in this deep underlying meaning of my vocation as a priest, I could not reach him. From the same source, the truth and beauty and justice of God as presented by the Church each day in the missal, we could both draw grati-tude for a gift we were privileged to share. It would pain me to have to disagree as he urged his own conclusions upon me: "Can't you see it, Gerhard? Here we are on this Petchora camp bunk entirely united at last as Christians should be; the way St. Paul spoke of, 'Our life is hidden with Christ in God.' What do all the visible signs and crutches mean here? All that is needed, all that is left, all that saves us here is *faith alone*, faith in the Word of God. We are living now in what our theologians call 'the eschatologic existence.' We are living in the extreme distress preceding doomsday described in Matthew 24."

His powerful conviction, his accurate appraisal of our present situation, almost overwhelmed me. I was too weak both mentally and physically to do more than hint at the other reality I had to fall back on to explain to him that the sacramental character of my priesthood was reaffirmed both in the challenge to follow Christ in His kenosis and by the consoling fact of sacramental union with Christ in His visible Mystical Body.

Whenever able to do so, I would go over to the Professor's office and "pose" for his drawings. The good man had made a principle of never asking me to do this unless he could reward me with a piece of bread or some other food, usually taken from his own ration.

One evening he sent for both Theo and me. We had to support each other across the yard and before we had completed the short journey I was convinced it would be my last. But we received another one of those little psychological lifts that make the blood pulse again with hope.

The Professor introduced us to a woman of thirty-five or forty dressed in a neat and clean nurse's uniform. On the desk before her record sheets lay alongside a wooden rack of tiny test tubes for taking blood samples. To us old hospital habitués, the scene was as familiar and professional as it was unexpected up here in the wilderness.

Using a regular trigger-release hypo with connecting rubber hose to draw the blood into a small tube, she took samples from my fingertip and left arm with the skill of the best nurses I had known in Swiss or German hospitals. When we told her we appreciated her deftness, she said she had had a lot of practice.

Herr Doktor stopped by and left her a piece of freshly caught fish. We could hardly believe our ears when, at the end of the examination, she invited us to stay and share the fish with her. The Professor then came back bringing her a full bowl of gruel and fresh berries, and she divided that up with us too.

We began to feel alive again and the four of us were soon in lively conversation. The nurse spoke French, we spoke German and all of us understood each other.

She was the wife of a Soviet diplomat whose reward for several years of service outside Russia had been banishment to Siberia in the great purge of the thirties. Under the notorious Article 58 of the Soviet constitution, which condemns to the labor camps the relatives of convicted "counter revolutionaries," she had been declared a "*shena*" (wife of an enemy of the state) and was sent to the camps and worked her way up to her present position. She had not seen her husband or their child for nine years.

The simple fact of being in her presence was a pleasure. She had an intelligent and amiable face. Her hair was combed straight back, her hands were comely, white, and clean. She was the first Russian we had seen whose fingernails were pared rather than torn or bitten off. Even the fastidious Professor kept his nails under control by biting them. We had become so used to our own dirt that just looking at her clean hands was a great relief.

"I know you are both Christians," she said. "I am one too. I am Orthodox."

So we sat there and talked, the Orthodox Christian, the Protestant minister, and the Catholic priest shaping in a forlorn spot on the Arctic tundra a fragmentary symbol of some "ecumenical community" yet to come.

"If our Churches hadn't separated," said Theo, "we would never have come to the situation we are in now. Look at us! Three of us representing a divided Christendom and the Professor an agnostic, not able to find any meaning to the things that are happening."

"It does no good now," I put in, "to sit around blaming the separation we inherited. What we have to do is dig down to the root evil that caused the separation—the weakening of faith within the Church. If the sufferings we are going through now will tear that root out of our hearts and let our faith grow mature and strong, then maybe these same sufferings will be the instrument of uniting us all again in Christ. Only in Christ and through Christ can the lost unity be restored."

Our little congress was independently getting at the very heart of the "Ecumenical Movement" which at that same time was taking a new lease of life in Christian countries. But Theo, like most Protestant leaders, could not yet bring himself to accept the Catholic premise that, though the ostensible unity of Christianity had been broken, the historical unity of the visible Mystical Body of Christ had never been lost and *can* never be lost.

The three of us prayed together and then the nurse excused herself, "I had better go before I get us all into trouble." She hesitated a moment at the door, then said softly, "I'm sorry to have to say this, but I don't think either of you will leave this camp alive." But she added impulsively, as though to soften her unhappy prognosis, "But God just might know better than I." She remained in the camp for thirteen days but we didn't get an opportunity to talk to her again.

What proved to be our last trip into the fields brought out the Professor's despairing equivalent of a profession of faith. The walking was torture for Theo and me but the day was beautiful and we luxuriated in it. There were no fences hemming us in; all around us the easy, fresh freedom of nature was mirroring God. We could have stretched out on the soft layer of moss with the dwarf-size multicolored wildflowers waving gently around us, and stayed there, forgetting about everything. But hunger and the mosquitoes drove us on to a task that was particularly painful for me. We were gathering moss berries, but my ulcers made it impossible for me to bend at the waist. Therefore, I would plop down on my knees with my upper body erect and pick the berries gropingly from that position.

Toward evening the Professor gestured us over to a little hilltop. He was looking down on a clearing that held three rows of sandy mounds. Lying on some of them were crosses made of moss. I wondered if Alois, who had been on the burial detail before he died, had made that gesture toward his comrades before joining them. I raised my hand in blessing of the mass graves. There were twenty or thirty of them, ten corpses to each.

The Professor had been watching me with thoughtful eyes as I gave the blessing. When he motioned it was time to get back to camp, I said to him, "Even this lost place will be remembered at the Resurrection. God will not forget anyone."

He shook his head and said bitterly, "I refuse to believe there's a God who knows all that's happening here and lets it go on."

The effort of walking and talking at the same time was a bit too much for me, but I had to make the attempt to pour something into this fine man's loneliness.

"Couldn't you turn that around and see all this as an example of how miserable man is without God? Of his nothingness without God? Someday, I know, you will see it in the one way that gives it meaning. You will come to understand that God wants man to realize *that* He is and *Who* He is; wants him to see and acknowledge that he, man, exists only because of Him and for Him. With that you will see that our whole physical, intellectual, and moral universe is ordered with respect to God, not to man. Then things will make sense. Then you will have hope and faith. You and all men who make the same acknowledgement will have charity and these things will not be possible."

He listened patiently but gave no response. Thoroughly exhausted, I fell so far behind the others that the guard had to stand quite a while at the gate waiting for me to straggle up with my sixteen berries in the bottom of a cup.

Our barracks began to fall apart so badly in the early part of August that they moved us in with the working brigade headed by Comrade Keil. The move tore the last shred of privacy from our lives. Theo and I were assigned to share a bunk made for two with Walter and a sergeant from the Luftwaffe. My place was between Walter and the sergeant. Theo, the tallest of the four, was cramped into the shortest length of the odd-shaped berth. They had great fun tormenting us out of whatever rest we might have been able to snatch.

Walter bragged that he had read fifty books in his lifetime and delighted in giving us mock instructions from his vast knowledge. The sergeant's specialty was obscene verse and epigrams, with perversions of Scripture his prize specimens. They would concoct nonsensical double-talk about anthroposophy and astrology and feed it to us as religious discussion. We tried at first to turn their thrusts aside with light remarks, but this was futile. Then we ignored them and waited for them to get tired or run out of things to say.

When the goading tactics failed they turned back to abuse. Walter would shout, "Look at these scurvy pigs we have to bunk with."

He spread a report around that my pellagra was really syphilis and I wasn't fit to live in the barracks.

Walter himself was rotting with that disease. One night the pain of it sent him into such a fit of depression that he even turned to me for comfort. He admitted he had been unfair to me and asked if there was anything he could do to make it up. I suggested two things. For ourselves, all we asked was to be let alone; and would he mind stopping the practice of lending his pipe to the young boys. He understood that the last had to do with exposing others to his disease and he agreed to follow both suggestions. We shook hands.

Our peaceful relationship lasted one whole day. Then it exploded into the worst official trouble of my camp experience. In keeping with our resolution to do everything legitimate to stay alive, I had bartered a good shirt I still had left in my bag for a pound and a half of dry millet. Mrs. Skierat had been the middleman and a girl in the kitchen was cooking it for us.

The first intimation of trouble came during roll call out in the yard. *Politruk* Lachmann made one of the solemn pronouncements that went with his job: "There has been bartering of stolen goods in this camp. The offenders are going to be punished."

Nobody took this too seriously and there was a cackle of laughter from the ranks. It would be a fantastic job to trace the goods that had been stolen and restolen and bartered for other stolen goods. And it would have to end with the guards punishing themselves.

But things came a little closer to us that evening. Mrs. Skierat came sneaking over while Theo was reading to me in our canvas covered refuge. She was trembling with fear. "We're done for!" she said. "I knew it! Yesterday I saw a big black pig in the sky and that always means something awful is going to happen. They came and took away the millet. They're going to call us up before the guard and sentence us. Oh, what's going to happen to me?"

We calmed her down and tried to soothe her fears of black pigs in the sky. But when we got back to the barracks one look at Walter's face was enough to tell us trouble was in the air. His expression of triumph was the meanest he had ever shown. He made a great to-do of calling the men together, rolled his eyes to the ceiling in mock horror and announced that the pious pair, Herr Fittkau and Herr Goebel had been ordered to report to the office of the guard on criminal charges.

It is an old Gestapo-MVD principle that terror strikes more effectively in the deep of night, and we were kept waiting till near midnight before being taken in to the guardhouse inner sanctum. The fat chief guard sat behind his desk in the light of a fitful oil lamp. In front of him was a long, printed form waiting to be filled in. He did not look in the least angry and his voice was friendly as he asked us to sit down.

But Comrade Keil, the work brigade boss, played the role of prosecutor and his manner was hostile from the beginning.

"Did you or did you not barter a shirt for millet?" he barked.

"I did."

"Did you not know that this is forbidden? Do you know that it will add three years to your sentence?"

Since I had never received any sentence that I knew of, this perplexed me. But it was hardly the moment to bring the matter up. I remained silent.

"Why did you do this when you knew it was forbidden?"

"The doctor told us millet gruel would help us recover from pellagra. The Soviet government told us we had been sent to this hospital camp to get better. I thought if I could get the millet to make us well I would be giving my shirt to help the government's plan."

Comrade Keil was not impressed. "It's forbidden and you knew it."

"I know it is forbidden to barter government property or stolen goods. This was neither. It was my own shirt. I brought it with me from home."

"That is not true."

"It is, and I can prove it. On the left hand pocket there is a tiny monogram stitched by my mother."

The chief guard asked me if I could describe the monogram. Then he had me make a drawing of it on the charge sheet.

But Comrade Keil had no intention of letting up on us.

"We've known the truth all along, Herr Fittkau; we have information. We know that you are both SS men! We've caught you now and I'm going to see to it that you are sent to a correction camp."

The chief guard was listening carefully, so I decided I had better nail that statement at once. "Everyone in the camp knows we are pastors. And that includes yourself, Comrade Keil. Last time you inspected the barracks you picked up my missal and had a great time having one of your men stand in front of me going through the motions of an altar boy swinging incense."

The hearing came to an end. We were told we would be informed of the decision. The chief guard's manner was as friendly when he dismissed us as it had been when we entered. Every man in the room knew that everyone present had at some time engaged in bartering. We had the impression that they were not going to be too hard on us, but for some reason or other they had been compelled to make an issue of this case.

Walter and his friends gave us such a rough welcome back to the barracks that it would have been better for us had we been sent to solitary confinement. Theo passed an extremely painful night and his illness went into a crisis. In the morning his face was flushed with fever. I induced a medic to order him removed to a whitewashed room with eight benches reserved for the mortally ill. The ward overseer who came to take his temperature was our old friend Hans, the hunchback assistant of One Eye at Column Seven. He removed his thermometer from under Theo's armpit, inspected it and announced airily, "You're all right. It's only a little over 103."

For the next few days Theo lay with his long legs hanging over a bench barely five feet long, tossing feverishly in near delirium. On the fifth day a doctor came and ordered him an extra daily ration of a few spoonfuls of milky farina soup. He could get this down and the relief it brought was obvious. I brought the soup to him each day, and distributed what he was unable to swallow among the others in the ward.

His neighbor was Ostrowski, the Masurian who had recovered after his clothes were stolen. The testy old fellow had become quite peaceful and amenable. In a surprising show of gratitude for the extra soup he offered to darn the holes in my socks, which I had been unable to mend because of the condition of my hands. And he brought me an even greater surprise than that.

Lying on his bench were a few unbound printed pages inside a black cover. "What have you got there?" I asked him.

"Oh, it's just a part of some kind of prayer book. I don't understand all of it, but there are bits of the Bible in it."

I was almost frightened when I saw what it was. It was a section from the Schott missal, a different edition from my own. But this folio, torn at random from a volume of twelve hundred pages, contained the masses from the third to the twenty-fourth Sundays after Pentecost—exactly the section that had been torn from my missal with perhaps a dozen pages more!

I was half silly with delight at the discovery and carried it gleefully over to Theo. His eyes lit up at the news and he looked at me for a long moment in wordless appreciation of the marvelous return of our great loss. "Let's thank God for His kindness," he said.

We prayed a Te Deum together and followed it with a heartfelt repetition of Theo's favorite Psalm 23: "The Lord is my shepherd and nothing is wanting to me..."

For three weeks I had not been able to get any rest at night for the pain of my body touching the rough planks. My forehead was the only part of my body with whole skin and I had devised a way to use this to get some sleep. I would sit on the edge of the bunk near a post in such a way that as little of my body as possible touched the wood. Then I would place my missal against the post and lay my forehead on it to take the weight of my upper body. In this position I could sometimes doze off.

I had gone to sleep like this after leaving Theo when I was awakened by the voice of the *politruk* droning out some information to the prisoners. The first words I made out were "humanely transferred." Gradually my mind cleared and I gathered he was explaining the Potsdam Agreement. He seemed to be putting together confused scraps of information that concerned our homeland in Eastern Germany. It was to be divided up between the Russians and the Poles and the German residents were to be "humanely transferred" out of it across the former Polish Corridor into the German mainland.

Clear thought and analysis were beyond me at this stage, but I had a sickening realization of what this might mean. What would happen to twelve or fifteen million people uprooted from centuries of tradition-soaked living and dumped where there was neither room for them nor place for their way of life? How could this be done "humanely"? The thought passed my mind that the spirit of Hitler had triumphed after his death. He had attained his wish that if he fell he would pull all Germany down with him. The communities of my own Ermland had survived and kept their continuity through a dozen invasions by Poles, Lithuanians, Hussites, Russians, Swedes, and French. They had seen Gustavus Adolphus and Napoleon fight great battles over their land long before Hitler and Stalin. Now they would cease to be. I saw the tremendous work among distressed people that would lie ahead if I managed to survive to take part in it.

Walter did not share our concern. "It's a very good thing," he gloated. "The Poles and the Russians will give the common people a fair deal. They'll just kick out the priests and the bosses. Then there'll be plenty of land for everybody."

The only consolation we could draw from Russia's having won the lion's share at Potsdam was that the victory might lead to some concessions about the treatment of prisoners and possibly to our quick release. That hope increased a few days later when a commission arrived to reclassify the prisoner-patients.

Out of the tangle of rumors we winnowed a few things that seemed to be facts: prisoners of war would be separated from noncombatants; there would be trials for war criminals; the innocent would be sent from the penal camps to rehabilitation work in destroyed cities, factories, or collective farms in the Soviet Union. Our own best hope lay in the report that those too sick to work would be released.

While the mysterious investigations were going on, Lachmann, the *politruk*, called me to his office. They were going to ask the religious affiliations of all the prisoners and he wanted me to give him a breakdown of the religious groupings in Germany. I was very cautious in my answer. If I gave them a specific list of churches and sects they might either use it to trip up the prisoners in the questioning or to arbitrarily condemn one group or other. So I contented myself with a general description of Catholics and Protestants.

While he had me in his office Lachmann made an unconvincing attempt to discredit the priesthood. He gave a long rambling account of a Siberian Orthodox priest during the tsarist regime who had betrayed his people and caused many of them to be executed. The moral seemed to be that priests were evil and untrustworthy people.

In return I gave him a brief sketch of how the Ermland priests had suffered with their people in the present situation and how they had stood up against Hitler. I used Theo as an example of the same devotion among the Protestant clergy. Then I asked him if it did not bother him at all that the Communists had banished to Siberia so many hundreds of thousands of their own citizens, including his own Volga countrymen of German descent. He did not have anything to say.

We were lined up the next day for the religious questioning. Most of the men claimed to be Christian. But the man directly in front of me was Roman, the bullying friend of Hans and Walter, and he put on quite an act. I knew he was a German from Upper Silesia, a Catholic and quite proud of having been a sergeant in the German army. He claimed that he was a Pole, had no religion, had been forced to work for the German army and had deserted as soon as he got a chance. The *politruk* looked at him blandly and yawned as Roman went through this dramatic little piece. Since Lachmann already knew all about me, my questioning went quickly.

It was now the middle of August and one morning my name was on the list to report for reclassification. A young officer sat at the *politruk*'s desk rolling a cigarette in a piece of *Pravda*. He paged casually through my thick dossier and asked me one single question:

"Can you explain how you got to be a parish priest at such a young age?"

"I was in my thirty-third year. I had been ordained eight years. Besides it was a small, unimportant parish and a lot of our priests who should have been pastors were drafted into the army, jailed, or exiled."

That was all. No comment. No decision.

The same afternoon I got word that the Professor wanted me to report to him in my capacity as research specimen. He had come from the autopsies of two girls, one just fifteen, and he was weary and depressed when he joined me in his office. They had died of starvation accentuated by the fact that they had been raped before deportation and were six months pregnant. He had sat up with them two whole nights and fought desperately to save them.

"I don't really want to make any drawings today," he said. "I have no bread left to offer. What I wanted to ask you is if you were in the group questioned this morning by the man from Moscow."

When I told him I had been, he was quiet for a moment and then said, "Now, please don't take anything for granted. I don't want to raise false hopes, but you've seen those trainloads of new prisoners going past on their way north?"

I nodded.

"Well, it just might be that not all of those trains will go back empty."

I swallowed hard and felt my heart beating heavily in my breast.

It wasn't definite, I told myself. I shouldn't let myself think of it. But I knew the man too well to believe he would have spoken if he did not have good reason to believe it were true.

I was going home.

CHAPTER XIII : *"Arise and Go"*

I GOT BACK TO MY BUNK IN A MENTAL AND EMOTIONAL fog. Walter and his boys were in one of their moods for making a party by outdoing each other in thinking up abuse. But I scarcely heard them. Now that the moment seemed to be suddenly at hand, I just couldn't make any sense out of the prospect of being free. The feeling of joy I wanted so much just would not come. Instead I sank back on my bunk and fell into a fit of exhaustion and near despair that I would even stay alive much longer.

It was impossible to rest or even sleep so I turned for consolation to the Mass for the coming Sunday, the thirteenth after Pentecost: "Still, Lord, my trust in Thee is not shaken; still I cry, Thou art my God, my fate is in Thy hand... Look, O Lord, and be mindful of Your promises. And do not forsake Your poor ones forever. Arise, Lord, and decide Your own cause. And do not forget the voices of those who are seeking You. Remember the shame of Your servant."

I was so stirred at the appositeness of the words that I took them over to Theo and we prayed together the Oration from the same Mass: "Almighty eternal God, increase our faith, hope, and love, that we may become worthy to receive what You have promised us: make us love what You command."

The following Monday, August 20, was Theo's birthday. It was also the day the camp began to stir with the first results from the reclassification. A detachment from the work brigade and a few women, including Mrs. Skierat, were ordered to prepare themselves for transfer back to Column Seven. As a parting gift Mrs. Skierat brought me a bowl of thick millet gruel and some berries. We arranged the berries on the gruel in crude imitation of a birthday cake and brought the dish to Theo. All he got out of it was surprise and pleasure. He couldn't eat. But we did persuade him to keep it by him for the two days before the food would go sour.

I spent my free time that day reading to him and staggering back and forth from the stove with the hot brick Herr Doktor had ordered used to bring Theo's boils to a head.

Back in the barracks that evening I was mulling over the hope in Christ's words of the last Sunday Gospel to the one leper who returned to give thanks: "Arise and go, your faith has saved you," when Herr Doktor appeared in the doorway with a list in his hand and called out, "Mr. Fittkau, do you want to go home?"

He added the names of two others who had been classified too sick to work but still "transportable" and ordered us to be at the guardhouse in ten minutes.

I panicked with excitement, grabbed everything I could off my bunk, threw the old fur coat over my shoulder and made a beeline for the door.

Outside the whole camp was in an uproar. The women's barracks had got the notice first and the word "release" had spread like a flash fire. People were running back and forth calling excitedly to each other to find out who was going.

I made straight for Theo in the infirmary. When he saw me come in the door with my bundle under my arm and excitement written all over my face, he said, "Thank God! It's true. You're among them."

No word of the disappointment that his "combatant" status as a draftee meant staying on indefinitely longer in this misery.

There was time for no more than a hurried, awkward embrace, a whispered promise to pray for each other and his parting message,

"The Lord be with you and if you really make it back, bring my love to my wife and children."

At the guardhouse I waited in an agony of apprehension as the full list was read out till at last I heard "Fittkau" and knew it was true. My name was really there.

In single file we marched in the pale Arctic dusk through the gate. It was a trembling sensation to walk past the high fence and the watchtowers and know that we would not be marched back in again under rifles a few hours later. Our way lay past one of the corner towers. In its shadow a fire blazed in a metal barrel silhouetting a figure poking the flames. It was Maria, heating gypsum for the wall plaster. I slowed down as I passed and called over, "May God bless you, Maria. Thank you for everything. Do what you can for Pastor Goebel."

She looked over, swallowed hard and answered, "May God stay always with you, Father." Turning around not to show her emotion, she went on poking the fire.

We reached the tracks and sat down on our baggage to wait for the train. The prospect of freedom did not stir up the joy one might expect. We were too exhausted and too suspicious of what was ahead of us to react simply and wholeheartedly. Some of the guards made little fires so we could warm ourselves against the night air while we waited. Comrade Keil, the work boss, was a transformed man. He ran among us literally jumping with happiness at our fortune. He rushed from one to the other, pumping hands vigorously and shouting, "You're going home, fellow! Do you know it? You're going home! Really going home!"

He had been warmed by a little vodka but there was no doubt that he was genuinely happy for us. All the sternness, the sternness that had not stopped at cruelty, was gone. "You're all going to get well," he promised. "You won't be sick again. We slaughtered a calf for you. Tomorrow on the train you'll get a piece of it as big as your fist. And bread—you'll get bread with berries in it, just like cake."

The Professor walked about more calmly, reassuring us. There was no trick in this, he told us. There would be no disappointment, we really were going home. He gave particular attention to those lying on stretchers, talking with them, doling out the last of his tobacco.

Dawn brought a locomotive with one car. It was not a boxcar but an old passenger car from tsarist times with windows and three tiers of bunks on either side of a narrow passageway. There were two compartments, one for prisoners, the other for guards. I was put in the second tier near the center of the compartment with women in most of the bunks around me. In the place beneath me the Professor put a young Catholic girl, taking great care to make her as comfortable as possible. His care turned out to be in vain. She did not live through the first night of the journey home.

The night doctor from the barracks came in with a big tray and served us a ration of bread and a piece of genuine veal. It was big as a fist, as Comrade Keil had promised. We were too weak to cheer but sighs of gratitude and delight could be heard as we turned the meat over and over in our hands, pressing it gently with our fingers. It was real and freshly cooked. And the bread did have berries baked into it, just like raisin bread. Then there was a third course, a dollop of margarine out of an American container. We had had no such nourishing food for months. It changed our vexed excitement into calm joy and rational hope that we would survive the long journey that lay ahead.

But the initial feast was a false promise. The girl's death on the first night recalled us poignantly to our true condition and reminded us we were not home yet. The next day's rations were more like what we had become used to.

For two days it rained incessantly as we rolled and jerked along, and on the third day the train stopped. We pushed against the grimy windows to see where we were. We were standing outside the gate of Column Seven. Some of the women started screaming and men groaned helplessly. We were frightened at the prospect of being put back to work in our old camp. But only two women and two army prisoners of war, all from the work brigade, were ordered off. As the train pulled slowly over the great wooden bridge spanning the Izhma, I looked down on the well-remembered scene…the canal, now deeper and longer, the four watchtowers and the wooden fence with the barracks roofs peeping over it, the arch with its Column Seven inscription more weather-beaten than before, some unrecognizable prisoners dragging themselves across the bare yard.

Beside the tracks two teams of three women each set down the wheelbarrows they had just hauled up from the canal and peered up to see who was looking out at them from the murky windows. They were all clothed in the same ragged gray pants and jackets but some of them had their hair back again. A woman behind me in the car started pointing, banging on the window and calling out, "Lena! Lena! Look, that's Lena!" I looked in the direction she was pointing and recognized the sun-browned features and disheveled blond hair. Her pants and sleeves were rolled up revealing bare brown feet and arms. While she was staring up trying to puzzle out who was calling her name, a guard came over and punched her in the ribs. She bent over passively and wearily put her weight against the sand-filled wheelbarrow. The train moved on and I thought how much it would have pained Gertrud to have seen this.

There was another stop farther along the Izhma. The night doctor and the guards from Column Five got off, taking with them a few of our blankets and some of our rations for souvenirs. But before it started up again we had a pleasant surprise. The Professor had followed the train on a motorized handcar for a last check on his patients. He went from bunk to bunk with a quick look and a word for everyone. He grabbed me gently but warmly by the wrist as I tried to express my thanks for all he and Herr Doktor had done for us. There was more for me to say than I could hope to get out in the brief moment he could stop. I was convinced that if I should survive I would owe it most of all, under God's providence, to this Sovietized Polish gentleman. "There is no way I can show my thanks," I told him, "except by praying for your release. Please keep taking care of Pastor Goebel."

"Forget about it. Just you take care of yourself and get well."

Another day and another night of jolting along found us falling back into dull monotony and the old habits of barracks bickering. Our energies were so low that every little crest of normal enthusiasm, like welcoming that first meal or greeting the Professor, was paid for by a plunge into a trough of weakness and discouragement that seemed as black and everlasting as a bottomless pit.

Before dawn the next morning—we had stopped asking why things always had to happen in the night—the train stopped and we were ordered out. Trying to obey, like willing children, the automatic "Hurry up!" chant of the guards, the prisoners ahead of me got jammed up in a knot and started shouting and pushing at each other. I gathered there was some obstruction in the narrow doorway and when I got there I saw what it was.

Lying across the exit, still breathing hard and groaning but obviously dying, was my old bunk neighbor Stupid Bernard. I tried to talk to him, to make him recognize me, but the pattern the camps had stamped on him made the only words he could struggle out a repetition of his constant cry, "I'm hungry. Have you anything to eat?" I persuaded a couple of men to help me lift him down the steps and lay him on the ground away from the tracks. The guards chased us on and we had to leave him there to die.

We were taken down a path toward another prison camp, larger and much better looking than the one we had left. There was a well cultivated vegetable garden in the yard with flourishing radish, potato, and cabbage beds. The barracks were whitewashed and in good condition, the muddy ground had planks laid over its worst spots.

They halted us in front of a small shed which we soon recognized as the "Kultur Institute," the delousing station. We sat down on our bundles and nodded as we waited our turns to go inside. When my turn came the men behind me protested. "Stay out, you scabby pig," they shouted, "till the rest of us have finished. We don't want to catch that from you." I was well aware of my filthy scabrous appearance and I had become used to such remarks in Column Five. I sat down again on my bundle, put my head in my hands and prayed to St. Raphael, patron of travelers, to help me complete this journey.

I was still in this position, half-awake from fitful dozing, when I noticed someone standing before me wearing women's shoes and black stockings. I was too far gone even to look up. A voice penetrated my dulled senses and I caught one phrase, "Father Fittkau." At the sound of my name I tried to get to my feet. A gentle hand helped me up and I found myself looking into a clean, good, smiling face under a nurse's cap. It was Sister Imelda.

"Good God, Sister," I said, "how did you get here?"

"I'm here, Father, but how did you ever get to be such a mess as this?"

"It looks bad enough, Sister, but it feels worse. My clothes are sticking to me like adhesive plaster. If I do get a bath all it does is open the sores."

She told me to go in and wash anyhow while she hunted up some disinfectant, salve, and bandages. I followed the last of the others into the delousing plant, but I was no sooner inside than a Russian nurse came and chased me out. Sister Imelda led me to my barracks, introducing me on the way to a couple of old Ermland farmers, one of whom was a brother of Father Podlech from Reichenberg. Then she had to rush off, leaving my new friends to tell me about this camp.

Their news was good. This place was serving as a regrouping center for people who were being shipped home. A transport was supposed to be put together within two days to ship several hundred prisoners back to Germany. The new groups who kept arriving in the place all through the day were cheerful and excited at the prospect. But the inevitable sword of suspense was still hanging over us. There was to be a medical examination the next day to determine who could be rated as "transportable."

Sister Imelda came in the evening and brought me to her ward for treatment. In one of the hundred bunks in the clean orderly room I found an old friend, Mr. Schlegel, who had been with Father Kolfenbach and myself in the prison at Insterburg. Though beyond hope of recovery, he recognized me and was grateful to have a priest prepare him for death.

Compared to what we had known this camp was a model of care and consideration. I learned from Sister Imelda that in the six months since I had seen her the good work she had been doing had been recognized by appointment here as chief nurse. She had nothing but high praise for the Soviet woman doctor in charge of this hospital camp. Sister Imelda's immediate staff consisted of two other Catholic nuns, a Protestant deaconess, and a former Red Cross nurse from an East Prussian hospital. The five women had each been assigned a small room at the end of the ward.

Sister Imelda had even been provided with a special small cabin, where the sisters could meet for prayers and recreation. They had transformed a small brick stove into an altar with a cross of evergreens fixed to the chimney over it.

While the good sister cleaned my sores and soothed them with ointment, she told me how she had "nosed out" a priest among a shipment of German prisoners of war, a Bavarian Benedictine. The chief doctor had not only allowed them to adopt Father Folger as "chaplain" but had helped them get wine from a distant black market and bake rolls that could be used as hosts for Mass. The sisters, however, in keeping with some ineradicable tradition, looked after their chaplain too well. He was found well fed at the next medical examination, transported for harder work to one of the tougher labor camps and never heard from again.

Although Sister Imelda did her best to live up to the good traditions of the nuns in taking care of their chaplain, there was no danger that I would prosper too quickly and share Father Folger's misfortune. My fear was that I might be held in the camp or shipped back to Column Five.

Among the new arrivals next day was a second batch from our old hospital camp. They told me that Theo was still alive, that Herr Doktor had lanced his boils successfully and started him back on the road to recovery.

Sister Imelda came back from a visit with the commandant's wife, a fine woman who worked closely with the chief doctor in doing all she could for the welfare of the prisoners, with the news that the names of those to be shipped homeward might be called out at any moment.

About a thousand of us gathered in the yard for the all-important roll call. All of us fixed our eyes on a group of officials standing on a little knoll, each of us hoping and praying fervently that his name would be on the list. The slow process of reading names, consulting papers, then reading more names, stretched out for hours. The crowd gradually thinned as the lucky ones picked up their baggage and filed through the gate.

There was still a small group of disappointed prisoners left to be marched back to their bunks when I heard the music of my own name in the last section of the list. I gathered up my bundles, muttering "Thanks be to God," and stumbled blindly, as fast as I could make myself move, before anybody could decide that it was a mistake and I wasn't well enough for shipment after all. I made it through the gate and then stopped, too exhausted to continue. The crowd waiting for further orders was only fifty yards away, but I couldn't force myself to walk the short distance. A young blond lad helped me to join the group in time to rest and march with them when the guards moved us on.

That march, which lasted for hours along a narrow sandy road at the edge of woods of thin pine, required as great an effort of will as I have ever made. I concentrated doggedly on the long legs of the boy ahead, forcing my own legs to follow their motion step by step, not daring to let myself collapse so near the goal.

When we finally came upon the train, the sight was a vision of hope. It was the usual string of boxcars, but they looked different now. It was not at all like that time we had first seen the boxcars behind a wheezing Russian locomotive at Insterburg, or like that black rainy night they had taken us north from Column Seven. These boxcars were even being painted bright by nature. It was a warm autumn evening and the sun, low on the horizon, bathed the scene in colors that made the train as inviting to our eyes as it was to our hearts.

The bare old cars had been improved by the addition of raised platforms that increased the floor space. Instead of locking us up in the airless dark, the guards left the big side doors open. We could breathe, we could feel that we were part of the outside world, we could watch the scenery slipping past, we could even get out and walk around when the train stopped.

Relations among the prisoners were also changed for the better. The senior of our car, a sixty-year-old man from eastern Poland, was by far the best senior we had ever had. He did his job quietly and considerately throughout the journey.

Our stops were usually at junctions where spur lines brought in prisoners from other slave labor areas like tributaries joining a big river. More and more cars and eventually another locomotive were added to our train.

The first stop brought an old friend, August, the town crier of Frauenburg, into the place beneath me. I reached down, put my wrist into his big broad hand and asked, "How's your sore throat, August?"

"That honey you gave me six years ago cured it, Father," he said, coughing as he spoke, "and I haven't had any trouble since."

The journey out had taken twenty-one days and we had no reason to believe that the trip back would be any faster. As we settled down to the long days ahead and got to know each other better, the exhilaration of "going home" faded into the fretful pessimism of men whose recent experiences had deadened their capacity for sustained hope. One or two optimists kept insisting that we were being sent straight home, but their words had the sound of whistling in the dark. The pessimists had decided we were headed for a different kind of prison labor, either in the Moscow area or in southern Russia. I shared the majority feeling that we would be used somewhere in the part of our own East Prussia now controlled by the Soviets. My hope was that I would then be able to make contact with any of my fellow priests who had survived. None of us guessed right about where we were actually being taken. Meals were prepared in a special car down the line and the person in charge of that car turned out to be none other than Sister Imelda! We were making the full cycle together, from the first troubled days in Suessenberg out to the Arctic camps and now back. I was grateful for the dispensation of providence that had lent me the strength of this wonderful nun at moments when I needed support badly. Twice a day we had the same unvaried but satisfying menu: a generous helping of millet gruel with margarine, corn soup and bread plus pieces of sugar. The food was served whenever it was convenient for the train to stop.

The long journey home might have been a time of meditation and evaluation of our experience, but we were still too sick and too uncertain for any sustained analysis or for any feeling of being away from something unpleasant that was over and done with. A rough board plank on a springless boxcar is not the ideal place for convalescence. For myself, it was still a matter of fighting to survive rather than of trying to get well. The ointment on my wounds dried up, the bandages lost their cleanliness and began to fall off, my sores festered again. I neither looked like a whole man nor felt like one and a lot of my time was spent in the grim half-world of the very sick.

The first city we saw was Kotlas on the Dvina, a river that empties into the White Sea near Archangel. Looking at buildings, even the grimy slums that usually line railroad yards, made us feel that we were in touch with civilization. Then the land flattened out and we passed enormous collective farms of rye, wheat, and potatoes. The barns of these factories-in-the-field did not generate the feeling of quiet comfort one normally gets from farm buildings standing bravely alone in empty stretches of green. They were drab buildings hundreds of feet long, somber and somehow threatening.

After about eight days we crossed a long high bridge over a wide but shallow valley. Ahead of us, on the far bank of a broad river, we saw the tall sooty stacks of a large industrial center. We passed through dirty suburbs and then took an hour to crawl through the yards of a huge plant. At the end of the yards a few hundred identical log cabins were clustered beneath the familiar watchtowers of a labor camp. We stood in silence with sober faces looking at it as we passed.

The river had been the Volga and this was Gorki, the former Nizhni Novgorod. This had been one of the cradles of the old Russian state. Founded by Scandinavians, it had been developed by the old Russian princes into a seat of government, trade, and industry. Now it was a major center of heavy industry, fed with coal, oil, and ores from the Petchora valley. Its place in the Soviet scheme was to keep heavy industry producing on supplies from the north brought over the Petchora railway system in the event of German invasion cutting off the Volga route from the south.

The prisoners who joined our train here were soldiers from the Gorki-system labor camps. They had spent two to three years in coal and metal mines around Molotov, Sverdlovsk, or ChelYabinsk in or beyond the Ural mountains. They told us they had come across large camps of civilian deportees, many from East Prussia.

Most of the civilians they had met were women who had worked alongside them in the mines, in the forest and in the brick factories at Chel Yabinsk where there was a work camp of twelve thousand civilian internees.

The soldiers were in rags and their physical condition was no better than ours. They told us we had been lucky if our death rate had not gone over eighty percent. Their eyes were dull and their voices listless as they gave us this information. None of them showed any emotion about anything. The only spark of interest came from the men who walked around asking if anyone could give them a bit of tobacco.

From Gorki the train went straight west to Moscow across a long stretch of fertile farmland, past areas of light industry and through the suburbs. Here we were halted long enough to have gangs of street boys gather around the cars pointing out every miserable feature of our appearance and yelling gleefully, "Fritzky, Fritzky, look at the Fritzkies!" In Moscow itself we were halted for the day alongside of an apparently endless row of huge cable drums bearing American trademarks. When we finally moved on we caught a glimpse of a fast-moving suburban train with a swarm of passengers clinging to the ends of the cars and standing on the running boards of each carriage. On a road paralleling the tracks the only traffic we saw was two or three motorcycles.

For another week we kept going southwest through European Russia and regions that bore the marks of war.

During a long halt in Orsha, we saw sidings jammed with burned-out locomotives and ruined freight cars. Every stopping place provided Russian civilians with an impromptu marketplace. They were especially eager for clothes and blankets. One old blanket would bring fifty to eighty rubles. I traded my old work gloves and a pillowcase for a small cupful of fresh blueberries and a cucumber. I ate the cucumber, bitter rind and all, with more relish than I had ever found in the most delicate fruit.

About halfway between Moscow and the Polish border we were stopped for two days at a deserted station. A familiar face, framed now by a fur cap and a black beard, poked itself into our car and asked, "Are there any Ermlanders here?" It was Alphonse, a priest friend from my seminary days. Sister Imelda had sent him to me after she had made him baptize a child just born in a boxcar. They could not find so much as a handful of straw to ease the bare boards that were the woman's bed. But Sister Imelda and the doctor had collected from the other women some strips of linen to wrap the newborn child.

In Minsk, the capital of White Russia, we were unloaded for one more delousing. I was glad my turn did not come till twilight had screened from other eyes the disgusting condition I had again fallen into. August, the town crier of Frauenburg, had to help me peel off my rotted, filth-caked shirt. It was good only to throw away. The exertion was almost too much for me. When we started back across the tracks my heart was thumping so wildly that I had to fall out of line and sit on the ground, hoping the heartbeat would get back to normal in time for me to get up and catch the train before it moved on. I had another moment of thinking this was the end, that I had survived the camps only to die by a railroad track.

While I was slumped there motionless, Sister Imelda came running along, grabbed me by the wrist and pulled me to my feet. She had come to fetch me to the side of a dying fourteen-year-old girl. The girl's bunk was on the second tier and it took several of her companions to push and lift me up to her side. She was in great anguish and breathing very hard. I administered the last rites and watched her grow quiet. Shortly afterward she died.

From Minsk to Brest-Litovsk our way lay through territory annexed from Poland by the Soviet Union. At frequent intervals we were treated to railside pictures of misery that etched out the Russian interpretation of the Potsdam phrase, "humanely transferred." Bewildered and wretched looking groups huddled on their bundles around cooking fires, apparently waiting for trains to take them to unknown places. We saw thousands of these people.

Brest-Litovsk brought us one reason for cheerfulness and one for worry. We were changed to a train with the narrower wheel gauge of the railroads of Europe. That made us confident that wherever we were going it was not back into the deep Russia we were leaving. But if they were really taking us home as they had said, why were we in Brest-Litovsk? Why were we not following the route we had taken out through Vilna, Kaunas, and Insterburg?

Too weak to think, let alone help with the work of moving, I sat on the edge of a bomb crater and watched a procession of the weakest and sickest women being led to the first ready places in the new train. Their unfeminine appearance, their wretched physical condition, their dispirited manner, was something worse than any words of material description could re-create. When August and Alphonse joined me, I repeated some verses from the lamentations of Jeremiah: "Weeping she hath wept in the night, and her tears are on her cheeks...her children are led into captivity: before the face of the oppressor...her filthiness is on her feet... O, all ye that pass by the way, attend, and see if there be any sorrow like to my sorrow... their face is now made blacker than coals, and they are not known in the streets; their skin hath stuck to their bones, it is withered and is become like wood."

The early autumn weather continued warm and sunny as our train headed south and southwest through eastern Poland. Across the dark green meadows we could occasionally see men and women seated contentedly at the windows of their farmhouses. For some it was still possible to have a world of life and peace.

We stopped for three days between Lublin and Krakow. The tracks around us were lined with long trains of locked boxcars with the familiar lavatory chutes sticking out from the sides. That was what we had looked like on our trip into Russia. We knew what was locked inside those wired doors; we knew what they would go through on the way north and what would befall them when they got there. It was hard to find any joy or pride in our own survival.

Some women and children, apparently waiting to be assigned to cars, sat in little groups around fires between the tracks. One woman wearing a black babushka stuck her head into our car and asked where we had come from. We answered, "Petchora," and she cried out, "I knew it! That's where we'll be going. I knew it!"

They had been on the move for five years. First Hitler had sold their land to Stalin for oil and moved them to West Prussia. When the Red Army came they fled to Bavaria. Then the Americans had put them into a camp near Nuremberg and had just handed them over to the Russians. Now the Russians were taking them away and they knew better than to hope that they were being taken anywhere but to forced labor.

The journey began to seem literally endless. My sores got worse, my energy seeped away until I reached the stage of thinking there would never more be anything else to life but lying painfully on bare boards in a freight train that would just jolt and jolt onward day after day without ever getting anywhere.

Eventually the guards told us we were in "Gorzow," and I recognized the church tower and skyline of Landsberg an der Warthe, a town less than a hundred miles east of Berlin. It seemed to be a city of the dead. We knew we were on the main line between Königsberg and Berlin, but when our train turned west instead of east and north we also knew that our last hope of being taken directly home to East Prussia was gone. Under the circumstances, the familiar sights failed to rouse me from my lethargy.

Some of the men with a little energy left got a whiff of familiar air and decided to set out on their own. The guards made no attempt to stop them.

At another stop, an elderly refugee couple climbed into our train and we were filled with wonder at having someone with us who was not a prisoner. They told us we were not far from Berlin and were headed in the direction of Frankfurt an der Oder. They had got out of Berlin by hitching a ride since there was no transportation for German civilians. They told us of a Berlin buried in debris, money with no buying power, a bread ration of three slices a day. Their drawn faces were filled with distrust and anxiety and they would speak no word of their personal experience.

At Frankfurt I was still miserable and helpless. We waited, the only train in the half-repaired station, for about six hours. August and Father Alphonse helped me out of the car and over to meet Sister Imelda so we could talk over our situation.

We sat on our bundles and talked of making for Berlin, where we should be able to get help. Suddenly my heart started pumping vigorously again in my veins. I had caught sight of a priest walking along a platform just two tracks away. He was a real-life priest, dressed as a priest! He was walking freely along in the robes of his order, healthy, vigorous, and chatting with animation to the well-dressed man alongside him. I was so excited and thrilled that I started off at once in a straight line to where the two were walking. When I stumbled and fell across the tracks I could not get to my feet again, but crawled on my hands and knees across the rails. I did not mind that the gravel tore at me, I did not even notice that my sores were ripping open. Though my heart pounded with the effort of pulling myself up and over the first platform and sliding down again to the next track, I had room only for joy. I was back with my own again. I was going over to meet another priest, to claim again the great, warm, all-conquering, fellowship of the priesthood.

I got across the second track, reached my fingers up to the platform and clung to it waiting for him to pass.

When he drew near I called out excitedly in Latin, beginning with the traditional greeting, "*Laudetur Jesus Christus! Sacerdos sum....* I'm a Catholic priest. Just back with this transport from nine months at the Petchora. Bless me, Padre."

He heard me, but he did not even stop. Without breaking stride, he turned his head slightly and said in very good German. "I am not a German. I am a Pole. There is nothing I can do for you." Then he turned away and resumed his conversation with his well-dressed companion.

It took some moments to accept the shocking truth, that this brother and son of the Seraphic Saint had no intention of acknowledging any kinship with me. My fingers slipped from the platform. Numb and half blinded I stumbled and scrambled back across the tracks and the other platform.

The people standing around our train had watched the whole sorry spectacle. They had seen my excited rush toward the priest, witnessed my eager greeting and watched my humiliation. Some were laughing loudly, others were silent and grim-faced.

I made my way blindly to the boxcar, crawled into a dark corner and did something I had never done in Russia. I wept. I wept at the black meaning of the thing that had just happened more than at my own frustration. This was how deep the hatreds engendered by the past years had penetrated! This was the price that would have to be paid for the crimes of all our nations. This was the most intimate and most painful wound of war that would first have to be suffered and then slowly healed. I was so saddened that I thought it would have been better if I had died and not come back. Cast down by this completely unexpected blow, I did not have the strength to realize that at that very moment I was being called to atone for this outgrowth of hatred which had entered like a cancer even into the living body of the world-wide community of the Church.

CHAPTER XIV : *In Germany, But Not Home*

I WAS STILL IN THE CAR, DESOLATE AND DOUBLY WEAK, when I heard the shouts of the guards, "Everyone out! Everyone out!" August gave me a hand and we joined the others, who were being made to line up four abreast. Our destination was the old Eichhorn Army Barracks in the town of Frankfurt an der Oder, three miles away. After twenty-eight days on the train we were in poor shape for walking, and the group was soon spread out beyond any semblance of a line of march. The guards announced that those who did not feel they could make it should fall out and they would be carried to the nearest hospital.

We had had enough of Soviet hospitals. Alphonse joined us and said, "Let's try to make it. If we fold up, then they can take us to their hospital."

Along the way we had abundant proof that though we were again in Germany we were still under Soviet rule. Immense pictures of Stalin, Lenin, and Molotov were posted on every large building that had not been completely ruined. Some of them had wreaths of colored bulbs which were burning in full daylight, as though to claim worship as saviors risen out of a grave.

Disorderly bands of Russian soldiers roamed the streets as they had done during those first days of Suessenberg. The guards directed us and we walked dumbly where we were told as we had done for months. Hunger and pain and weakness were the only sensations we had room for. There was no feeling of being free, of being home.

After several stops to let the thumping of my heart slow down I found myself looking at four brand-new watchtowers sticking up from the corners of the old barracks. The wooden arch over the main gate was ornamented with a symbol of the bright new Soviet dawn. An architect's drawing showed a cluster of bright modern homes illuminated by the rays of a rising sun. Crowning the promise of better things to come were portraits of Stalin and Lenin.

We waited again like uncomplaining cattle till the last stragglers had caught up. Then we were counted for the uncountable hundredth time before the gate of promise opened to let us in and closed again behind us.

A German army sergeant bellowed through a megaphone to assemble us in a sandy square. The man enjoyed his work and he was putting so much gusto into it that it was obvious a little matter like changing masters did not mean anything to him. Winnowing the orders from the military cursing, we learned that the men and the women were to be separated. This sent one woman into hysterics. She was sure it meant reshipment to another camp.

Then the sergeant gave us a short speech with the rough accents and the glibness of a circus barker. He must have made it so often that it came out automatically: "You are now in the new liberated Germany. Tomorrow you will be completely free to do as you want. You will be supplied with food for two days. You can go anywhere in Germany you want."

This sounded as though they did intend to turn us loose. But what did that mean? Was Soviet rule any different here from the other places we had seen it? Where would we go? How would we get there? The sergeant continued to yell through his megaphone, and at least part of our unspoken questioning was answered: "Anywhere in Germany means anywhere in the new Germany. It is forbidden to go to places that are now part of Poland, the Soviet Union, or Czechoslovakia."

Then his voice went into its drone again and started reeling off names like a railroad announcer calling off the stops for a departing train: "It is forbidden to go to the provinces of East Prussia, West Prussia, Pomerania, Brandenburg-east-of-the-Oder, Posen, Upper Silesia, Lower Silesia...." The list included the places that practically all of us present called home. Where would we go?

The sergeant helped us to answer that too. "All the people from those forbidden provinces will line up in the other courtyard and stand under the letter corresponding to their names. You will be asked where you want to go in Germany. If you don't know where to go, you will be told where to go. You will go to a resettlement camp and be shipped out from there."

Many of us knew no one in central or west Germany. We had to think up places we might possibly meet someone who would help us. Anything was better than another camp. August gave Rotenburg as his destination and I said Fulda. I had no idea where my family was or where the bishop was, or even if they had survived.

I knew some friends who used to live in Fulda but it seemed a whole world away and I had no idea how I would get there. Suppose I were picked up wandering loose in this Soviet Zone and shipped off again? How could I travel anyhow, even if I were not picked up? I sat down on my knapsack and dropped my head to my knees in the only position that gave me a little rest. I don't know what I would have done had it not been for another minor miracle.

Just as in a similar moment I had heard my name called and looked up to see Sister Imelda standing before me, I again raised my head at a voice saying, "Gerhard," and saw a familiar face that made all the difference between giving up and carrying on. It was Stefan, who had been the closest friend of my brother Hans in the seminary. He had been ordained during a sick leave and was now serving as a medic at this barracks.

He took me to his room, got me some food, and then had to return to duty. He was kept busy with the sick all day and into the night. But he managed to slip away three times and bring me at each visit a dish of gruel and boiled potatoes. I ate them all greedily, but was in that stage of exhaustion that is past sleep.

When Stefan returned in the middle of the night he calmed me down for a while, heard my confession and then produced a small wooden box with the ℟ monogram carved on the lid. He placed the pyx on the table. It had been nine months since I could kneel before Our Lord in the Blessed Sacrament. We gave each other Holy Communion: "May the Body of Our Lord Jesus Christ preserve thy soul to life everlasting."

Within a few blessed moments all the anguish of doom and death vanished into the freedom of the new life which the Risen Lord gives those whom He has deigned to share His agony.

We made our thanksgiving together, and then Stefan bandaged my feet, hands, and back. While he worked he told me that there was so much danger of being shipped to Russia from this barracks that he had been planning to escape from it as soon as he could get a suit of civilian clothes. I gave him Mr. Werr's old fur coat. It had served me well and it just fitted him.

It came time for me to report for roll call and dismissal into freedom. Stefan had to go on duty but he gave me one urgent warning: "Don't get on any train near this camp or you'll end up in Siberia. They have prisoner quotas to fill. They are always short and they pick up anyone they can."

First we had to line up for our two-day ration. Then we were called one by one to get certificates of dismissal. When my turn came around noon I was handed a scrap of paper with a big Red Army stamp over a mimeographed Russian text that was practically unreadable. My name, date of birth, and destination had been crudely written on the blanks provided in the text.

We were again lined up and the sergeant gave us one more

blustering speech to which nobody paid any attention. All eyes were on the gate ahead of us. Stefan came up and gave me a little hand wagon he had made for his escape. With this for my baggage, I would have a much better chance of making the fifty miles I must walk to the first safe railroad.

I started for the gate in the rear of the slow-moving mob. I had only gone five steps when a wheel fell off the wagon and the whole thing tipped over.

I tried to lift my baggage, but it might as well have been nailed down for all I could budge it. While the rest were moving out the gate, I just stood there staring stupidly at the ground. And I was not alone. Five or six men and boys had overexerted themselves in their eagerness to get outside and collapsed. Their faces showed the terrible strain of not being able to make their legs move when freedom was just across the courtyard. And the gate was closing.

Stefan came rushing over to my rescue. "We can still make it," he said. "Come on!" He threw the stuff on his shoulder, grabbed me by the arm and rushed me round the side of a building where a horse-drawn wagon with high sides was just about to start moving. He said a few words to the surprised driver, then heaved me in the back of the wagon and my baggage after me. "The driver is a Russian," he whispered, "but don't worry. He's the one who smuggles hosts and wine in to me. He'll take you to the Catholic rectory."

I was just beginning to notice where I was when Stefan broke away with some parting advice. "Keep down in that wagon till it stops. Don't let yourself into any Russian hospital!" The wagon rolled out the gate and past the guards while I kept as low and as still as I could. I was almost as still as the other occupants of the wagon—thirteen dead and dying.

Within a matter of fifteen minutes I was being ushered into a rectory by a housekeeper who asked no questions but told me to help myself to what was on the table. By the time the pastor arrived his two slices of bread and small jar of marmalade were gone. But the friendly face beaming out from under snow white hair assured me no apology was necessary.

This was more like home. The kindly priest told me that Bishop Kaller still lived, probably in a hospital in Berlin. It would be best for me to make for there at the first opportunity. But it did not take him long to recognize that I was in no condition to even talk about the things that meant most to me. He sent his sacristan over to the Gray Sisters to ask their advice and the man brought back a heart-warming message.

Sister Imelda was there! She told him to put me in his hand-wagon and take me to the old folks' home at once. The good nuns fed me a boiled potato and three carrots from the first rations they had received since the Russian invasion. Then they took me to a bedroom and I climbed into a feather bed.

A hot meal, a feather bed, and a room of my own! Surely this was the height of comfort and the end of hardship.

But it was neither. The warmth of the feather bed made my body itch so violently that I couldn't stand the torment. I had to get out and lie on top of the blankets. Before daylight, Sister Imelda came with the word that we had to keep moving if we were not to risk being sent back. She had just spent the night in jail after being picked up on someone's denunciation. She had been treated fairly and released after questioning, but she was most anxious to get on to Berlin.

We sneaked through the city streets before daybreak and made our way to the railroad tracks west of the city. There we found a line of hopper cars packed with released prisoners and civilians. Although mindful of Stefan's warning about trains leaving this place, I accepted the westerly direction and the assurance of the others that these cars were headed for Berlin.

They did go to Berlin and we got there with them. We found St. Gertraud's Hospital still standing and I really believed for the first time that my prison camp days were over.

I probably gave the first sign of this when Sister Superior greeted me at the hospital by the title German custom gives to a curate: "Good God, Herr Kaplan, what a sight you are?"

"Kaplan?" I answered. "I would have you know, my dear Sister, that I'm a pastor."

She laughed heartily and came back at me, "You'll make it all right, Father. There's life in there yet for us to patch up."

Through the open door I could see a table set for breakfast with two rolls on it. Sister Superior noticed the direction of my glance and said, "What's it going to be first, wash up or eat?"

"Eat."

After a visit to the chapel and two delicious dry wheat rolls, I turned myself over to the care of a strapping Lithuanian Jesuit lay brother. He soaked me in a tub, scrubbed me almost raw, drenched me in some very soothing concoction, swathed me in bandages like a baby and carried me to a cool bed. I was feeling like a king when the hospital chaplain, Father Wehner, who had formerly been provincial of the Jesuits, came in and deflated me a bit. He told me I looked like Job sitting on the dung heap scraping his sores with a potsherd.

It was only later I had a chance to look at my missal and find the last of the comforts the liturgy of the Church had brought me through the experiences that had lasted almost exactly one liturgical year: I had been brought to the hospital on September 24, the Feast of Our Lady, Ransom of Captives.

FOR a month I lived in a sort of twilight world of convalescence. Each morning Father Wehner would bring me Holy Communion. Every Sunday I was wheeled into the chapel for High Mass. At the Mass for the first Sunday in October, the Feast of the Holy Rosary, I reminded Our Lady about one of the fifteen mysteries of the rosary, the finding of Our Lord in the Temple and of her joy at seeing the Holy Family reunited after it had become separated during a pilgrimage to Jerusalem. I asked her to share that joy by letting me hear something of my own separated family and my scattered flock.

The nurses wheeled me back to my room and lifted me into bed. I was drifting off into the haze of exhaustion any effort still brought when a tall smiling priest came through the door and stretched out his hand, "Welcome back, Gerhard! The bishop says it's about time you got back to work!" It was Father Wolski, a priest from my own diocese. There was joy in the greeting I gave him, but there were also tears in my eyes.

He handed me a large brown envelope from under the small stump that was left of his right arm and asked, "Do you recognize the handwriting?"

It was my mother's. Inside the envelope was a twenty-two-page letter written three months previously. There was also a letter from Bishop Kaller.

Father Wolski was the first of many victims who had to sit and listen to sections from that long family letter. Irmgard had got back home safely, my father had returned from the Volkssturm in time to join them and my pregnant sister Birgitta in flight from home during the snowy February night before Russian troops arrived in the village. On their way to the Baltic coast and down to the German mainland they had gone through all the dangers, sufferings, and horrors known to all refugees fleeing blindly in the dead of winter.

At the time the letter was written my mother knew that five of her eight children were alive, one son was killed and two, including myself, were missing. They now had a small attic room near Osnabrueck, in the British Zone, and my father had hopes of finding a teaching job.

The bishop's letter was a message of welcome. He suggested that when the hospital could release me I should go to my parents and try to build up my strength before returning to work with him.

Those letters were better than any medicine. Two weeks after I got them, there were definite signs that the disease was being pushed back. The blood circulation was improving, parts of my skin were beginning to heal, and I was even growing some hair.

Although my hands were still bandaged, I was able to sing my first High Mass on November 1, the Feast of all Saints. The hospital chapel was filled with returned prisoners and expellees for whom the Gospel, from the Sermon on the Mount, might have been specially written: "Jesus seeing the crowds...taught them, saying, 'Blessed are the poor in spirit for theirs is the kingdom of heaven. Blessed are the meek for they shall possess the earth. Blessed are they who mourn for they shall be comforted. Blessed are they who suffer persecution for justice's sake for theirs is the kingdom of heaven. Blessed are you when men reproach you, and persecute you, and speaking falsely, say all manner of evil against you, for My sake. Rejoice and exult, because your reward is great in heaven.'"

By the end of November I was well enough to leave the hospital and continue my convalescence near Osnabrueck, where my parents had found refuge.

EPILOGUE : *The Aftermath*

FOUR DAYS ON A BRITISH COAL TRAIN OPEN TO THE SKIES brought me to Osnabrueck where I eventually learned that my father was teaching school in a nearby village.

It was a great reunion. Hans had arrived safely from a British prison camp in Norway. Christa had joined the family to tell her own story of crossing a stretch of the frozen Baltic alone. We all bore the marks of our experiences. I hardly recognized my mother and father. They had aged twenty years in one year.

A three-mile walk to church was no pleasure at first and meant spending half the day recovering from it. But it gave me back the use of my legs and helped me to build up strength.

In a few months I was able to take an appointment as chaplain to a Catholic action center in a former woman's labor camp. I preached to pilgrimages of refugees at the Shrine of Our Lady of Sorrows near an old Cistercian church. I wrote articles for the diocesan paper. And all the time I tried to get in touch with my old parishioners of Suessenberg.

We were cut off altogether from our homeland. Königsberg was now part of the Soviet Union. Suessenberg was under Polish administration. Both were forbidden territory to the people whose fathers had lived there for centuries upon centuries.

The first news of what had happened to my parish after I left came in a letter from Father Teschner. A long list of the dead included Uncle Franz, Aunt Elizabeth, and Aunt Anna. They had been taken to the cellars at Heilsberg and the first two had died soon afterward. Aunt Anna had survived the others by almost a year. She had gone to my rectory, tried to put it in order, and died there.

The story was the same all over Ermland. Now the entire surviving German population was to be driven out by the Polish government and all their possessions confiscated.

In July 1946 Bishop Kaller called me to take over my old job as his secretary. The bishop himself now had a "diocese" that crossed all boundaries and did not even stop at any of the occupation zones. Pope Pius XII had appointed him special apostolic delegate for the more than twelve million German expellees. He was "bishop of the homeless." He was penniless like his subjects. We had one room for both of us to sleep, eat, and work in.

The job meant looking after the spiritual welfare of five and a half million Catholics living without homes and, for the most part, without churches or priests. The bishop was a man of vision as well as courage. He saw the Church in Germany entering into a new phase of its history, becoming "the wandering Church," sharing the condition of its people who were without homes, security, or material support.

Bishop Kaller consumed his remaining strength at his extraordinary task. He died in my arms at Frankfurt am Main in 1947.

In our work of trying to reunite broken families I was able to get in touch with a number of my old parishioners and invite them to a reunion at St. Gertraud's Hospital in Berlin on the Feast of the Ascension, in 1948.

About eighty of them came. They straggled in all morning from the different sections of the Russian Zone to which they had been delivered in boxcars. Among them they had brought enough potatoes for the sisters to fix a meal for all of us.

At first it was like a meeting of any group of old friends who had not seen each other for a long time—meeting in a place far from home. But there is much more than simple nostalgia in the revived memories of a place that once was the only home ever known and which now does not exist anymore.

God knows there was enough tragedy in the room to make a book of horrors. But it was kept buried under present worries, present cares, and even under present laughter. Old Grandpa Grimm could joke about his beard having grown in again without dwelling on how it had been plucked out by Soviet soldiers. One of our young mothers was tending her baby and worrying about its future, in case her husband should still return. For this surviving child had a Russian father, while the two children of her husband had perished.

The children and their future were at the heart of the most deeply felt grief. No schools, no churches, no sacraments, no Catholic teaching, such as they had always depended on as the center of their living. At best hurried visits from the few available priests who said Mass as many as four times a day in movie halls or taverns rented for an hour. They, the old, could still hold to the firmly rooted faith. But what of the young? What would happen to them?

As I listened to them bring up the very questions I had been helping Bishop Kaller to answer, I felt keenly again my own position as pastor to a new kind of wandering Church.

These were the people I had come so quietly and proudly to serve in a fixed place, by time-honored methods long determined by immemorial customs. I saw with the bishop that they were still my people, they were still my parish, and I still had to be their priest. It was my function to explain in terms of eternity the meaning of their lives, the meaning of all that happened to them, the meaning of what was happening to them now. "In humble repentant prayer," the bishop had written his people, "we will accept whatever God wills. Through prayerful participation in the divine sacrifice of Our Lord, we will always find again the strength to crucify our heart with its unruly passions, its greed and envy, its vengefulness and its hatred.

"Our sacrifice must be joined to our prayer. For us, this consists in the patient, faithful endurance of the injustices which we have suffered. That is how we can follow our Savior and carry with Him the terrible accumulation of guilt in this world. Only in this way do we break the power of evil."

This was the message I had to give to my people of Suessenberg that day in the hospital in Berlin. At High Mass, with the nuns singing the old Ermland hymns, there was an emotional moment of return to the little church that had been so much a center of their lives. It was repeated in the afternoon when we gathered again in the chapel for Vespers, which they had sung for generations in their own tongue, without fully realizing its meaning.

Before the closing prayer of the Magnificat I turned and read the Epistle for this Feast of the Ascension:

"They therefore who were come together asked Him, saying: Lord, wilt Thou at this time restore again the kingdom of Israel? But He said to them: It is not for you to know the times or moments which the Father hath put in His own power: but you shall receive the power of the Holy Ghost coming upon you, and you shall be witnesses unto Me in Jerusalem, and in all Judea and Samaria, and even to the uttermost part of the earth."

I asked my people if they were not feeling as the apostles had felt, remembering as they had remembered the ignominy of Christ's death and of their own expulsion and scattering, asking in their hearts the questions the apostles had asked. And did they not feel rather disappointed, as the apostles did, to be told, "It is not for you to know the hour...?"

As gently as I could I put it to them that if they were thinking only of returning to Suessenberg they had not yet learned the lesson Christ spent three years teaching the apostles: we have not here a lasting dwelling place but must seek a home yet to come. I asked them if perhaps we did not all need the comment made by the Evangelist about the failure of the apostles to understand Gethsemane: "They understood none of these things..."

I offered them the comfort of the promise Christ had given in that day's Epistle, and I could feel the satisfaction of it bringing ease to their hearts and understanding to their minds as it did to mine: "You shall be witnesses unto Me...even to the uttermost part of the earth."

It seemed that the drawn faces relaxed a little and the wrinkles of sorrow smoothed out as they thought of their own experience in terms of the Christian mystery of triumph through the Cross. They began to understand that their fidelity had defeated their oppressors, even if they never went back to Suessenberg.

CLUNY MEDIA

Designed by Fiona Cecile Clarke, the CLUNY MEDIA *logo
depicts a monk at work in the scriptorium,
with a cat sitting at his feet.*

*The monk represents our mission to emulate
the invaluable contributions of the monks
of Cluny in preserving the libraries of the West,
our strivings to know and love the truth.*

*The cat at the monk's feet is Pangur Bán, from the
eponymous Irish poem of the 9th century.
The anonymous poet compares his scholarly
pursuit of truth with the cat's happy hunting of mice.
The depiction of Pangur Bán is an homage to the work
of the monks of Irish monasteries and a sign
of the joy we at Cluny take in our trade.*

"Messe ocus Pangur Bán,
cechtar nathar fria saindan:
bíth a menmasam fri seilgg,
mu memna céin im saincheirdd."

Made in the USA
Middletown, DE
04 June 2023

31728090R00159